Business Law
in Canada
Casebook

D'ANNE DAVIS
British Columbia Institute of Technology

Prentice Hall Canada Inc.
Scarborough, Ontario

Canadian Cataloguing in Publication Data

Davis, D'Anne
Business law in Canada casebook

ISBN: 0-13-295106-1

1. Commercial law–Canada–Cases. I. Title.
KE918.5.D3 1995 346.71'07 C94-931296-7
KF888.D3 1995

Prentice-Hall, Inc., Englewood Cliffs, New Jersey
Prentice-Hall International (UK) Limited, London
Prentice-Hall of Australia, Pty. Limited, Sydney
Prentice-Hall Hispanoamericana, S.A., Mexico City
Prentice-Hall of India Private Limited, New Delhi
Prentice-Hall of Japan, Inc., Tokyo
Simon & Schuster Asia Private Limited, Singapore
Editora Prentice-Hall do Brasil, Ltda., Rio de Janeiro

ISBN 0-13-295106-1

Acquisitions Editor: Jacqueline Wood
Developmental Editor: Maurice Esses
Production Editor: Kelly Dickson
Production Coordinator: Sharon Houston
Cover and Interior Design: Olena Serbyn
Page Layout: Stephen Lewis

1 2 3 4 5 RRD 99 98 97 96 95

Printed and bound in the USA

DEDICATION

To the memory of
Dorothy F. Drach Joyce and George E. Drach

PREFACE

Enjoy. The study of law is the study of our collective effort, over time, to establish rules to curb some human behaviour. The law is wise—it knows us in all our variety, complexity and perversity. The law is, or aims to be, good—it attempts to balance competing interests, to do justice. With instantaneous communications, rapid technological changes and human inventiveness, however, the law lags behind. The difficulties come first; the rules to govern later. Therefore, we have to depend on you to create rules for new situations. For example, how do we deal with defamatory statements made on Internet? Should we create legislation for rating video games for violence? Should we set up rules for surrogate motherhood, genetic engineering, assisted suicides? The study of the law prepares you for the task.

In choosing these cases and accounts, my primary concern has been to provide you with judgments that contain a clear articulation of the legal principles being discussed in your course. My second concern has been to give you memorable cases—memorable either because the cases set significant precedents, involve known people, relate directly to student concerns, or contain somewhat bizarre facts. Lastly, I have favoured inclusion of cases and accounts that deal with contemporary events and issues. These characteristics work not only to give you the information you need about the legal system, the established legal principles and judicial reasoning, but also to encourage you to participate in the discussion of current legal matters.

In this casebook, I have three types of entries:

1) Extracts from the law reports. These cases are designed to acquaint you with judicial reasoning, to reinforce your knowledge and appreciation of legal principles, and to show application of legal theory to human reality
2) Case summaries
3) "Fillers" or "snippets"

This collection of cases is not intended to be covered in its entirety. Your instructor will choose, or allow you to choose, the cases most appropriate to your studies or inclinations. It is my hope that the material in the casebook will be sufficiently illuminating and entertaining that your mastery of the legal system, the law and judicial reasoning will develop with ease and prepare you for a good argument on what course we should take to solve our contemporary ills.

Readers of *Business Law in Canada, Fourth Edition* (Richard A. Yates, ISBN 0-13-293119-2), will notice large and small icons in the margins of that book which refer the reader to corresponding sections in this casebook. The large icon alerts the reader to actual extracts of relevant cases from laws, while the smaller icon refers to summaries of cases from other, secondary literature.

I wish to thank my beloved first-string support team, Craig, Lauren and Ethan—masters of the mysteries of computers, stalwart typists and researchers, and patient trouble-shooters; Marjorie and Carole for their unique forms of assistance. Thanks also to the reviewers of this text: Paul Atkinson, Sir Sanford Fleming College; Julia Dotson, Confederation College; Barry D. Gaetz, Camosun College; Katherine Krug, Conestoga College; and John R. O'Donnell, Confederation College. I also wish to express my gratitude to Richard Yates for his encouragement, Anna Holeton for hands-on library help, Dave Thomson, Matt Baxter, Frank Williams and Chris Clark for computer counselling, Bill Hooker for good works, Margaret Briscall and Mary Hamm for robust camaraderie and to my other colleagues at B.C.I.T. who make my work more like play.

D'Anne Davis

TABLE OF CONTENTS

TABLE OF CASES

The italicized cases, below, are cases in their entirety or extracts from cases. The cases not italicized have been summarized. For example, see *Ramsden v. Peterborough (City)* on page 5. The cases followed by an asterisk (*) are decisions of the Supreme Court of Canada (S.C.C.), those upheld by the S.C.C., or those the S.C.C. refused permission to appeal.

A

B

C

D

E

F

G

H

I

K

L

M

LIST OF ABBREVIATIONS

A.C.	Appeal Cases (British)
A.P.R.	Atlantic Provinces Reports
B.C.L.R.	British Columbia Law Reports
C.C.C.	Canadian Criminal Cases
C.C.L.I.	Canadian Cases on the Law of Insurance
C.C.L.T.	Canadian Cases on the Law of Torts
C.E.L.R. (N.S.)	Canadian Environmental Law Reports (New Series)
C.P.R.	Canadian Patent Reporter
D.L.R.	Dominion Law Reports
E.R.	English Reports
K.B.	King's Bench (British)
Man. R.	Manitoba Reports
Nfld. and P.E.I.R.	Newfoundland and Prince Edward Island Reports
O.A.C.	Ontario Appeal Cases
O.R.	Ontario Reports
R.P.R.	Real Property Reports
S.C.R.	Supreme Court Reports
Sask. R.	Saskatchewan Reports
W.W.R.	Western Weekly Reports

I

THE LEGAL SYSTEM

A. Philosophical Basis of the Law

In essence, natural law is a broad philosophical tradition which holds that there are certain principles of right and wrong which human beings, through the diligent use of reason, can discover and apply in the creation of a just society. Some natural-law exponents are religious thinkers who ground their philosophy in a divine creator; others are secular philosophers who regard certain moral principles and rights as beyond doubt or compromise. Applied to jurisprudence, natural-law precepts have acted as a check on those in power—medieval popes no less than democratic majorities. Historically, campaigns of civil disobedience against unjust but validly enacted laws have been mounted on the supposition that universal moral principles do exist.[1]

Newsweek *September 23, 1991, p. 20 in an article giving the background necessary for an understanding of the intense questioning of Judge Clarence Thomas by some members of the U.S. Senate. Judge Thomas, nominated by President Bush to serve on the Supreme Court of the U.S. was being questioned to determine if his professed belief in natural law would diminish his respect for the rule of law and precedent.*

B. Constitutional Matters:

Questions

When does a case involve a "constitutional issue"?
How does a constitutional issue get before the courts?

Allocation of Power/Charter of Rights and Freedoms

The Ontario Environmental Protection Act survived a challenge when the Ontario Court of Appeal found the Act was not *ultra vires* the provincial legislature. *R. v. Canadian Pacific Ltd.* (unreported)[2]

The *Tobacco Products Control Act*, a federal statute, came into force on January 1, 1989 purportedly to address a national public health problem. The Act, among other things, banned advertisement of tobacco products. Cigarette manufacturers challenged the statute, alleging that the statute was unconstitutional. Judge Chabot of the Quebec Superior Court agreed; he struck it down by holding that it was *ultra vires* the federal government.

The judge held that the effect of the law was to eliminate advertising and that such commercial activities were within the jurisdiction of the provinces—covered by *The Constitution Act* s. 92(13) [property and civil rights] or 92(16) [matters of a local or private nature]. He rejected the argument of the lawyers for the Attorney General that the federal government had the right to create the statute under its residual power to pass laws for the "peace, order, and good government of Canada." Furthermore, the judge held that, even if the purpose of the legislation was to protect the public health, such matters came within the jurisdiction of the provinces. The judge also found the legislation offended against the *Charter of Rights and Freedoms* because it violated s. 2(b), the freedom of expression. Nor could it be saved by s.1, as an infringement that could be justified in a free and democratic society.

Imperial Tobacco Ltd. v. Le Procureur General du Canada
Summarized from The Lawyers Weekly *August 23, 1991 p. 9*

This decision was reversed by an appellate court, the Cour d'appel du Québec, District of Montreal. The Supreme Court of Canada has given the tobacco companies leave to appeal.

Maclean's *October 25, 1993 p. 11*

The Alberta Court of Appeal was asked by the lieutenant governor in council of Alberta for an opinion as to the validity and effect of the federal statute creating the Goods and Services Tax, the GST. The questions included the following: was the act *ultra vires* the Parliament of Canada. The court held that the GST Act was not *ultra vires* Parliament. (Reference Bill C-62).[3]

All the appellants, Askov, Hussey, Melo and Gugliatta, were charged with conspiracy to commit extortion. As well, Askov, Hussey and Melo were jointly charged with the offences of possession of a prohibited weapon, possession of a weapon for a purpose dangerous to the public peace, pointing a firearm and assault with a weapon. Hussey was also charged with criminal negligence in the operation of a motor vehicle. All were arrested between November 5 and 30, 1983. The trial was finally set for September 2, 1986. When the trial began, counsel for the accused moved to stay the proceedings on the grounds that the trial had been unreasonably delayed, contrary to the constitutional rights of the accused. The stay was granted by order of the judge. The Crown appealed the order to the Court of Appeal, which set aside the stay and directed that the trial proceed. The matter was then heard by the Supreme Court of Canada.

In his reasons Judge Cory of the Supreme Court of Canada first set out the issue for the court: "Section 11(b) of the *Canadian Charter of Rights and Freedoms* provides that any person charged with an offence has the right to be tried within a reasonable time. What constitutes an unreasonable delay of a trial must be determined on this appeal. In order to reach a conclusion it will be necessary to consider and apply criteria or factors which should be used to ascertain if a delay is unreasonable and in particular, to consider the consequences of so-called institutional delays."

Judge Cory gave a detailed factual account of what transpired after the arrest, reviewed the lower court decisions, the principle of providing a trial within a reasonable time and the purpose of s. 11 (b) of the *Charter*. He applied the principles to the facts of the case, and concluded that "in a situation such as this where the delay is extensive and beyond justification there is no alternative but to direct a stay of proceedings. In the result, the appeal is allowed and a stay of proceedings is directed." The other judges concurred with his conclusion.

R. v. Askov
74 D.L.R. (4th) 385
S.C.C.
October 18, 1990

Note: ***The Lawyers Weekly*** **(August 2, 1991 p. 2; September. 6, 1991 p.1) reported that from the time of this judgment in October, 1990, 43,000 criminal charges had been stayed (held in abeyance) or withdrawn in Ontario alone on the basis of the Askov decision. Serious case backlog due to shortages of courtrooms, prosecutors, or judges and other systemic delays are now seen to violate the right of the accused to have a trial within a reasonable time.**

The frequent use of the Askov decision has resulted in the coining of new words, as in: "The 'Askovites' who have this tremendous desire to get rid of the backlog are driving us nuts." (*The Lawyers Weekly* Sept 6, 1991, p. 9); and "The shortage of judges had led to ... fears that some criminal cases might have to be 'Askoved'." (*The Lawyers Weekly* November 22, 1991, p. 3.)

Unfortunately Elijah Askov is back in the news; he was "charged with a break-in and with the possession of burglary tools last month in Niagara-on-the-Lake, Ont." (*The Lawyers Weekly* October 15, 1993 p. 4.)

R. v. T.L.

THE DISTRICT COURT OF ONTARIO
FILE NO: YOA 2/89 COBURG, ONTARIO
MAY 9, 1990

Summary of the facts: A Crime Stoppers tip led to the search of a teenager, who was found to have a vial of hash oil and a stolen wallet. He was arrested, read his *Charter* rights and charged with possession of stolen property. He was found guilty by the trial court. The conviction was appealed on the grounds that the police, by acting on a Crime Stoppers tip, had breached his rights under s. 8 of the *Charter* to be free from unreasonable search and seizure.

Kerr, D.C.J.:

... It appears that the trial judge took the view that the police have the right, solely on the basis of an anonymous tip, to conduct a search of the accused. While I am sure that anonymous tips are useful tools in enabling police to initiate criminal investigations, I do not accept the proposition that they are entitled to conduct warrantless searches on members of the public without anything further. Constable Dunn at the time of conducting the search of the accused had nothing but a suspicion based on the anonymous call to his fellow officer. There was no evidence of the caller's identity, reputation or motivation. No subsequent investigation by Constable Dunn was conducted which would provide him with reasonable and probable grounds for suspecting the commission of an offence and under these circumstances he could not, in my view, have obtained a search warrant. If such warrantless searches by the police were condoned by the courts the right sought to be protected by Section 8 of the Charter would be meaningless. I conclude that there was a breach of the accused's Charter Rights under these circumstances.

In fact, on the argument of this appeal it was conceded by the Crown that the police had breached Section 8 in searching the accused, but the Crown submitted that the evidence being "real" evidence ought to be admitted notwithstanding the breach and that I ought not to apply Section 24(2) of the Charter to exclude the evidence obtained on the search. He relies on Collins vs. R. (1987) 33 C.C.C. 3rd, 1 (S.C.C.). However I am of the view that the appellant has met the onus upon him to establish on the balance of probabilities that the admission of this evidence would bring the administration of justice into disrepute when one considers the long term consequences of the regular admission of such evidence on the repute of the administration of justice. If the evidence obtained by Officer Dunn under the circumstances of this particular case were extended into a general policy to admit such evidence it would become readily apparent that the right of a private citizen to be secure from an unreasonable search and seizure would evaporate whenever real evidence was found. It is my view that Section 8 of the Charter has been in place for a sufficiently long period of time so that any competent and conscientious officer should realize that he does not have the right to conduct such a search without something more than a mere suspicion. A malicious or mischievous informant protected by anonymity could well create havoc with the rights and reputation of a well-respected, honest, average citizen. It was to protect the security of such citizens against a search of this type that Section 8 was enacted. Accordingly, the appeal succeeds on that ground...

The police had acted on the basis of a drug-courier profile, a list of suspicious characteristics of the typical drug runner, and stopped a suspect. Andrew Sokolow, nervous, wearing a black jump suit and gold jewelry, paid cash for two round trip tickets from Honolulu to Miami. He returned within three days without luggage. Stopped for identification, he had none. A dog indicated he was carrying drugs. He was arrested and a search revealed 1,000 grams of cocaine. The issue before the U.S. Supreme Court is whether or not the suspect's right to freedom from unreasonable search and seizure under the Fourth Amendment was violated when he was stopped merely because he fit the drug-courier profile.[4]

A more detailed account is given in *Newsweek* Oct. 10, 1988 p. 79.
The U.S. Supreme Court upheld the conviction for possession thereby supporting the character profiling used by the Drug Enforcement Administration.

Kenneth Ramsden, a member of a band, was convicted of putting an advertising poster on a hydro pole, contrary to a city by-law. His appeal was dismissed. He was given permission to appeal to the Ontario Court of Appeal, before which he argued that the by-law was unconstitutional because it restricted freedom of expression guaranteed by s. 2(b) of the *Canadian Charter of Rights and Freedoms.* The majority of the court agreed; furthermore, they held that the by-law was not saved by s. 1 of the *Charter*, that is, it is not a limit which can be demonstrably justified in a free and democratic society.

The amended by-law under which Ramsden was convicted prohibted putting posters on "any public property" and the court felt that the absolute nature of the prohibition created the problem. With regard to one argument made by the City, Justice Krever wrote:

> As between a total restriction of this important right and some litter, surely some litter must be tolerated. It would be a very different matter if the by-law purported to regulate where "postering" was permitted and where it was forbidden. ...The severe nature of the infringment of the right of freedom of expression outweighs the by-law's objectives

Because the by-law was held to be unconstitutional and therefore invalid, the convictions were set aside and Ramsden was acquitted.

Ramsden v. Peterborough (City)
85 D.L.R. (4th) 76
Ontario Court of Appeal
October 22, 1991

This judgment was upheld by the Supreme Court of Canada in a 9 to 0 decision.

The Lawyers Weekly *September 24, 1993*

Note: The cities will now be forced to draft by-laws to avoid constitutional challenges.

R. v. Thompson

30 C.C.C. (3D) 125
BRITISH COLUMBIA COURT OF APPEAL
SEPTEMBER 29, 1986

The judgment of the court was delivered orally by NEMETZ C.J.B.C.:

...On February 25, 1985, Thompson received a ticket under s. 217(4) of the *Motor Vehicle Act*, R.S.B.C. 1979, c. 288, for failing to wear a seat-belt. On May 3, 1985, he appeared before a judge of the Provincial Court and applied to quash the charge on the basis of s. 24(1) of the *Canadian Charter of Rights and Freedoms*. The basis of his submission was that the law conflicted with his religious freedom as guaranteed by s. 2(a) of the *Charter*.

In evidence accepted by the Provincial Court judge, Thompson stated that he believes in free will and is of the conviction that he "creates his own reality." His submission, therefore, was that the *Motor Vehicle Act* provision infringes his religious freedom because it suggests that (quoting from his own material) "the universe is unsafe to him personally," a proposition which he does not accept.

The Crown's submission was that Thompson had failed to establish an infringement of his freedom of religion and that, in any event, the impugned provision was a reasonable limit under s. 1 of the *Charter*.

Following the Crown's submission, without specifically giving Thompson a reply, the Provincial Court judge dismissed his application. Following the dismissal of this challenge, Thompson was found guilty of failing to wear a seat-belt.

Thompson appealed to the County Court on two grounds: first, that the trial judge erred in denying him the right to reply and, secondly, that the trial judge erred in interpreting the relevant provisions of the *Charter*.

Citing the case of *R.* v. *Big M Drug Mart Ltd.* (1985), 18 C.C.C. (3d) 385, 18 D.L.R. (4th) 321, [1985] 1 S.C.R. 295, a decision of the Supreme Court of Canada, the Honourable Judge van der Hoop held that the seat-belt law was valid on the basis that it is a limitation of a concept of freedom necessary "to protect public safety, order, health or morals or the fundamental rights and freedoms of others." The fact that the legislation infringed the appellant's religious beliefs did not, in his opinion, render the legislation invalid.

An appeal from this decision came before this court and it was pointed out to Mr. Thompson, who apparently is determined to take this litigation by himself, and without a lawyer, that he had first to obtain leave to appeal. This was done before our brother Anderson, in chambers, and leave was refused.

During the hearing of the leave to appeal Mr. Justice Anderson referred to the arguments which had been raised in the two previous courts and had this to say [28 C.C.C. (3d) 575 at p. 576]:

> I have reached the following conclusions. While I doubt that the philosophy of the applicant can in any sense be considered as a religion within the meaning of s. 2 of the *Charter*, I am of the opinion that even if the philosophy of the applicant could be so considered, the "freedom of religion" espoused by the applicant is subject to the laws of the province relating to public safety. I take judicial notice of the fact that the seat-belt laws of this province are based on the reasonable legislative premise that such laws were necessary in the public interest to protect drivers and passengers from injury.

He went on to say: "I would also hold that the alleged infringement is so insubstantial so as not to be considered as a breach of s. 2 of the *Charter*."

I am in full agreement with what he said. Assuming that we have jurisdiction (I say this without deciding that question) I would dismiss the appeal on the grounds set forth by our brother Anderson.

MACDONALD J.A.:—I agree.
CHEFFINS J.A.:—I agree.
NEMETZ C.J.B.C.:—The appeal is dismissed.

Haig v. Canada

[RE HAIG ET AL. AND THE QUEEN IN RIGHT OF CANADA ET AL.]
86 D.L.R. (4TH) 617
ONTARIO COURT (GENERAL DIVISION)

McDonald J: ... The facts surrounding Mr. Birch's complaint are briefly as follows. The applicant Joshua Birch was a member of the Canadian Armed Forces from February, 1985 to April, 1990. Upon informing his commanding officer that he was a homosexual, Captain Birch was informed that the policy directive regarding homosexuals in the Armed Forces would apply to him and that effective immediately Captain Birch would no longer qualify for promotions, postings, or further military career training.

With no career opportunity left to him, Captain Birch was released from the Armed Forces on medical grounds and seeking some kind of redress he turned to the *Canadian Human Rights Act*, S.C, 1976-77, c. 33, only to find that his situation, namely discrimination based solely on his sexual orientation, was not covered in the Act.

Section 3(1) of the *Canadian Human Rights Act* reads as follows:

> 3(1) For all purposes of this Act, race, national or ethnic origin, colour, religion, age, sex, marital status, family status, disability and conviction for which a pardon has been granted are prohibited grounds of discrimination.

Clearly the Act does not cover discrimination based on sexual orientation.

The applicant then turns his attention to s. 15(1) of the *Canadian Charter of Rights and Freedoms* which states that every individual is equal before and under the law and has the right to equal protection and equal benefit of the law without discrimination and in particular without discrimination based on race, national or ethnic origin, colour, religion, sex, age or mental or physical disability.

He then looks to s. 24(1) of the *Charter* which states that anyone whose rights or freedoms, as guaranteed by this *Charter*, have been infringed or denied may apply to a court of competent jurisdiction to obtain such remedy as the court considers appropriate and just in the circumstances. ...

The applicant's case is based on the proposition that if lesbians and gays are not in the classes of persons set out in s. 3(1) then they as individuals or groups are not afforded the equal benefit of the law as set out in s. 15(1) of the *Charter*.

Captain Birch, as I understand his application, is not asking this court to decide whether or not he has been the victim of sexual discrimination. He is seeking however the right to put his case before an appropriate tribunal convened under the *Canadian Human Rights Act*.

To put the case in its simplest terms: "Should any Canadian who perceives discrimination on sexual grounds not have some recourse to a legislative tribunal?" If the Charter purports to give him such a right then is s. 3(1) of the *Canadian Human Rights Act* not underinclusive and therefore discriminatory as being contrary to the guarantee of equal benefit of the law set out in s. 15 of the *Charter*?

I have concluded in the affirmative and I am therefore declaring that the absence of sexual orientation from the list of proscribed grounds of discrimination in s. 3 of the *Canadian Human Rights Act* is discriminatory as being contrary to the guarantee of equal benefit of the law set out in s. 15 of the *Charter*.

So far as I am able I also declare that this decision shall be stayed for a period of six months from the date or until an appeal has been heard within which time period the existing legislation shall remain in full force and effect.

Application allowed in part

Note: This judgment of Justice MacDonald declaring the *Canadian Human Rights Act* (CHRA) discriminatory was appealed by the Attorney General of Canada; Graham Haig and Joshua Birch cross-appealed asking the judgment be varied to include (1) a declaration that homosexuals are entitled to equal benefit and equal protection of the CHRA, and (2) a declaration that homosexuals are entitled to seek and obtain redress against discrimination on the ground of

sexual orientation from the Canadian Human Rights Commission. The Court of Appeal of Ontario dismissed the appeal and allowed the cross appeal. Following a recent Supreme Court of Canada case (Schachter v. Canada (1992) 10 C.R.R. (2d) 1), the court, instead of striking down the CHRA as invalid, chose to "read in" so that the order of Justice McDonald was varied by a declaration that the CHRA "be interpreted, applied and administered as though it contained 'sexual orientation' as a prohibited ground of discrimination in s 3 of that Act".

Haig v. Canada 9 O.R. (3d) 495 Court of Appeal for Ontario

Question

When should the beliefs of an individual yield to the interests of society as we perceive those interests?

Mennes v. The A.G. of Canada, The A.G. of British Columbia, and the Law Society of British Columbia

SUPREME COURT OF BRITISH COLUMBIA
VANCOUVER REGISTRY NO. A913595
OCTOBER 4, 1991

Master Patterson (in Chambers) The plaintiff brings this ex parte application pursuant to Schedule 1 of Appendix C of the Rules of Court for a declaration that he is indigent. The rule is as follows:

> Notwithstanding anything in this schedule, no fee is payable to the Crown by a person to commence, defend or continue a proceeding if the court, on summary application before or after the commencement of the proceeding, finds that the person is indigent unless the court considers that the claim or defence
>
> (a) discloses no reasonable claim or defence as the case may be,
>
> (b) is scandalous, frivolous or vexatious, or
>
> (c) is otherwise an abuse of the process of the court.

The effect of such a ruling on indigency status is that the plaintiff, if successful, will not have to pay fees to the Crown in this case.

The plaintiff has commenced fourteen actions since May of 1990, and in each of those actions has made an application for indigent status. In some of those actions, the order was made but in others, the order has been denied. ...

The basis of the plaintiff's complaint, and this action, is that the plaintiff made a complaint to The Law Society which was referred to the Society's Complaints Review Committee. The members of the committee at the time in question were two Benchers of the Law Society, both women, and one other member who was a man. The plaintiff attended at the offices of The Law Society on the day set for the hearing, September 17, 1991, but refused to appear before the committee because women were members of it. As a result, the committee dealt with the plaintiff's complaints in his absence.

The plaintiff alleges that the makeup of the committee violated his fundamental freedoms contained in *The Charter of Rights,* particularly his freedom of conscience and religion. In his material, the plaintiff alleges that amongst the tenets of his religious beliefs, there is one that forbids women to have authority over men. He further alleges that The Law Society, by having a committee so constituted rather than an all-male committee, failed " to preserve and protect (his) fundamental freedom of conscience and religion as to women."

The plaintiff further alleges that, by having a committee with women as members, "(his) right to security of the person against rule by women or any woman at all" was violated.

Since the hearing, I have ascertained that Master Doolan refused the plaintiff indigent status in a similar application in Vancouver Registry No. A912622. That action, as I understand it, also related to the composition of the Complaints Review Committee and the fact that there were women members.

I have no doubt that the plaintiff is indigent, but in my view, the proposed action and the claims made in it by the plaintiff disclose no reasonable claim, are scandalous, frivolous and vexatious, and are an abuse of the process of the Court. In my view, not only are the claims made scandalous, frivolous and vexatious, but they are also extremely offensive, and particularly offensive to women.

As a result, the plaintiff's application is dismissed, he is not entitled to indigent status with respect to this action, he is, of course, entitled to continue the action on the usual basis and pay the proper fees to the Crown as required.

Dated at Vancouver, British Columbia, this 9th day of October, 1991.

C. Civil Litigation

Question

Who must prove what to win a civil action?

In his reasons for judgment, Judge Bouck began as follows: " On the afternoon of 7 July 1985 Richard Robert Krusel suffered a tragic accident and became a quadriplegic. He alleges he came down a swimming pool slide head first into the water and struck his head on the bottom of the pool. He says the slide was improperly placed at the side of the pool since it was too close to the shallow end. He also contends the slide lacked adequate warning labels." After reviewing the evidence of sixty-five witnesses who gave testimony over a thirty-five-day trial, the judge concluded that "the plaintiff did not prove the slide theory on a balance of probabilities. There are any number of reasons as to how the plaintiff suffered this tragic injury. First, he could have been pushed in. Second, while standing near the slide and close to the edge of the pool, he could have lost his balance and started to fall into the pool. Instead of just letting himself collapse into the water on his back or stomach, he may have unthinkingly converted the fall into a dive at the shallow end of the pool. Third, the same manoeuvre could have occurred if, as he argues, he was at the bottom of the slide at one time splashing water up onto the dry slide. Fourth, inadvertently, he could have just dived into the shallow end and struck his head on the bottom of the pool. Etc. ... Over all, the proof offered by the plaintiff does not reach that degree of certainty where I can find he proved negligence on the part of any defendant on a balance of probabilities.

"Evidence on the issue of damages illustrated the enormous loss suffered by the plaintiff as a result of this accident. On the morning of 7 July 1985, a bright future lay ahead of him. He was engaged to be married. He just purchased a new house. His employers spoke glowingly of his work skills. He was upgrading his qualifications as an electrician by taking a course at B.C.I.T. The accident took all of that promising future away from him. A catastrophe is the only word that comes close to his situation.

"But, he is not a person who gives up easily. Since the accident he has acquired computer skills. He is optimistic by nature. He is not a quitter. He lives in a group home with 2 or 3 other people with similar kinds of handicaps. Government and community assistance make his life as comfortable as possible.

This judgment will undoubtedly cause him great anguish and disappointment. The law is sometimes a blunt instrument. Often, a judge is left with two unpalatable choices. Both are before me in stark contrast. Based upon the evidence, the law compels me to dismiss the action as not proven.

The action is dismissed as against all defendants."

Krusel v. Firth, et al.
Supreme Court of British Columbia
Vancouver Registry No. C862311
August 23, 1993

D. Enforcement of Judgments

Questions

What can you do if someone owes you money but won't pay?
Do you have to have judgment against the person before you take such steps?

1. Garnishment

Income Tax legislation which came into effect on February 25, 1992 allows Revenue Canada to garnishee refunds for outstanding delinquent student loans and unemployment insurance overpayments.[5]

In Canada, in an effort to collect almost $30 million in child and spouse support, the federal justice department seized $437,000 in income tax refunds and unemployment insurance payments from men in arrears. The departments paying out funds to these men had received more than 4,000 garnishment summonses over a period of about 8 months.[6]

An amendment to the Ontario *Support Custody Orders Enforcement Act* which provides for automatic payroll deduction from payors' employment cheques began on March 1, 1992.[7]

Under Ontario's Family Support Plan, the wages of parents not making support payments are garnisheed. In its first year of operation it assisted in collecting $166 million.[8]

2. Execution

In a California court Mr. Kroll sued the Soviet Union and *Izvestia* for libel. *Izvestia* had called him a spy, which allegation caused him to lose his business license after 15 years of selling medical supplies from a Moscow office. The plaintiff was awarded $413,000. In his effort to collect the award of damages, the plaintiff's lawyer seized a manual Russian-language typewriter used by an *Izvestia* correspondent in Washington.

The article quotes the lawyer for the plaintiff as saying "The typewriter is just the start.... We had a writ to seize everything in the apartment that belongs to *Izvestia*.... There are also three desks, three metal filing cabinets, some bookshelves and a big color television set. I'm going back for all that tomorrow with a truck."[9]

Mortil v. International Phasor Telecom Ltd.

23 B.C.L.R. (2D) 354
British Columbia County Court
Judgment: February 16, 1988

Wong, C.C.J.

Secrets are easier heard than kept: Jewish Proverb

This is an application by the defendant judgment debtor, International Phasor Telecom Ltd., for a declaration that its rights in the Phasor Code 1000 Computer Software and instruction manual for same are not liable under s. 49 of the *Court Order Enforcement Act*, R.S.B.C. 1979, C. 75, to seizure and sale under a writ of execution.

At issue is whether a computer software program incorporating a trade secret is exigible for execution purposes.

On 4th May 1987 the plaintiff judgment creditor, Mortil, obtained default judgment against the defendant, inclusive of interest and costs, in the amount of $6,946.11. On 4th December 1987, pursuant to a writ of seizure and sale, one copy of the defendant's two copies of Phasor Code 1000 Computer Software System and one instruction manual were seized by the sheriff.

The defendant's business is now defunct but it is the registered owner under the federal *Trade Marks Act* of the trade mark "Phasor Code" used in connection with the distribution of Phasor Code 1000 Computer Software products and owns the copyright protecting the form in which the idea for the Phasor Code 1000 Computer Software System is expressed.

Basically, Phasor Code is a system of cryptography to encode and decode classified information put into computers.

The defendant distributed its Phasor Code 1000 Computer Software products to purchasers only under licence agreements containing non-disclosure provisions. In addition, copyright notices were affixed on all Phasor Code 1000 Computer Software products. The following elaborate security measures were also in place:

(1) The defendant limited access to the information relating to the software system to key employees;

(2) The defendant required the author of the Phasor Code 1000 Computer Software System to sign a confidentiality agreement;

(3) The defendant established work rules affecting access.

However, in January 1987 the master software copy, from which copies are made for subsequent sale, was stolen and never recovered.

There is a concern by the defendant that if the copy seized by the sheriff is sold, under writ of seizure and sale, the secret nature of the Phasor Code 1000 Computer Software System will be lost.

I think it is established law as outlined by Professor Dunlop in his book, *Creditor-Debtor Law in Canada* (1981), at pp. 152-53, that s. 49 of the *Court Order Enforcement Act* and analogous sections of execution statutes in other provinces have been restrictively interpreted by the court to disallow writs of fi. fa. to reach trademarks, patents or industrial design rights because under common law incorporeal or intangible property was not subject to seizure and sale. Section 52 of the same Act, however, extended the common law somewhat by permitting seizure of specified categories of intangible property—which does not include intellectual property rights.

Counsel for the plaintiff submitted that what was seized by the sheriff was only the physical computer software—clearly tangible property and therefore "goods and chattels"—which are expressly exigible assets under s. 49 of the *Court Order Enforcement Act.* Provided the purchaser of the seized computer software does not infringe the trademark or copyright of the defendant, the purchased software is no different than the purchase of any brandname product. She also submitted that if Phasor Code 1000 System was indeed a trade secret, it was no longer such when the master copy was stolen and never recovered.

There is no reported Canadian judicial decision as to whether a tangible asset with a non-divulged trade secret is exigible to a writ of seizure and sale.

After consideration, I have concluded that this tangible property, like any other corporeal asset, is exigible under s. 49 of the *Court Order Enforcement Act.* However, to safeguard the secret process of the Phasor Code, I direct that its sale be subject to terms. The terms of sale will be a requirement that the purchaser enter into a trust agreement with the defendant concerning non-disclosure and prohibition of unauthorized use of the Phasor Code System, similar to the terms of the licence agreement required by the defendant in its ordinary sale to others.

If counsel cannot agree on the wording of the terms of sale, they may apply for directions.

If the potential purchase is to include the defendant's intellectual property rights, that is a matter not within the concern of this application but a matter for negotiation between the purchaser and the defendant.

As this was a novel point of argument with divided success, there will be no order as to costs.

Order accordingly

ENDNOTES

1. From *Newsweek*, September 23, 1991. © 1991, Newsweek, Inc. All rights reserved. Reprinted by permission.
2. *The Lawyers Weekly*, July 2, 1993, p. 28
3. *The Lawyers Weekly*, November 22, 1991, p. 23
4. A more detailed account is given in *Newsweek*, April 17, 1989
5. Summarized from *The Globe and Mail*, March 10, 1992, p. A8
6. *National*, January, 1989
7. *The Lawyers Weekly*, November 15, 1991, p. 5
8. *The Lawyers Weekly*, February 19, 1993, p. 10
9. A more detailed account is given in the *Vancouver Sun*, November 14, 1986

II

THE LAW OF TORT

A. Distinction Between Criminal and Civil Actions

Questions

What is the difference between a criminal and a civil action?
Can the same incident attract both types of action?

Note: The facts below illustrate behaviour that did or could lead to both a criminal and a civil action.

A beer fight at Koo Koo Bananas in Whitby, Ontario resulted in charges of common assault being laid against Eric Lindros, a hockey player with the Philadelphia Flyers. The judge, finding the Crown had failed to prove its case beyond a reasonable doubt, dismissed the charge after a four-day trial.[1]

In Halifax, Mr. Rent repeatedly rammed his house with his tractor after a matrimonial dispute.[2]

Several women, sexually abused as children, have taken civil actions against their abusers although appropriate criminal actions were taken.[3]

In Penticton B.C., a snowplow went off the road and crashed into the living room of Ms. Alaric.[4]

In Spokane, Washington a naked Mr. Brown injured a policeman and a Mr. Jones by hitting them with a bowling ball.[5]

Ms. Boteler, alleging Chuck Berry, rock musician, hit her causing a cut requiring five stitches, sued him in a civil action for $5 million. He faced criminal charges for the same incident.[6]

A funeral director in Halifax had bodies transferred from the chosen expensive caskets into cheap pressboard boxes before cremation.[7]

B. Intentional Torts

Questions

When will the loss suffered by the plaintiff be shifted to the defendant?
When is the defendant at fault in law?
Should we ever make the defendant pay when he is not at fault?

1. Battery

...when a fist-fight broke out Monday between two surgeons performing an operation in a northern English hospital, a junior doctor stepped in to finish the operation.[8]

Mr. Umpierrez, a 26-year old Uruguayan man, bit several passengers aboard a jetliner on its flight from Costa Rica to Rio de Janeiro. The crew members reported that his teeth had been filed down to sharp points.[9]

Mr. Rollins, the accused, was led into the courtroom for the closing arguments of counsel. He jumped his lawyer, repeatedly punched him while screaming "You sell me out...and I will kill you." The accused had 64 previous convictions, including one for murder. The judge denied the lawyer's request to withdraw from the case.[10]

A customer in Bloomingdale's New York City store was sprayed with perfume by a salesperson. The customer suffered a severe allergic reaction which resulted in her being hospitalized for eleven days. The store settled out of court for $75,000.[11]

Malette v. Shulman

37 O.A.C. 281
Ontario Court of Appeal
March 30, 1990.

Summary of the facts: Mrs. Malette, seriously injured in an automobile accident, arrived at the emergency ward unconscious. The doctor gave her a blood transfusion even after it was brought to his attention that she was carrying a card indicating her unwillingness to have such treatment. She sued. The only defendant (of many) found liable at the trial level was the doctor; liable for the tort of battery. The plaintiff was awarded $20,000. The following is an excerpt from the decision of the court hearing his appeal.

Excerpts from the Ontario Court of Appeal:
Robins, J.A.:...

[12] I should perhaps underscore the fact that Dr. Shulman was not found liable for any negligence in his treatment of Mrs. Malette. The judge held that he had acted "promptly, professionally and was well-motivated throughout" and that his management of the case had been "carried out in a confident, careful and conscientious manner" in accordance with the requisite standard of care. His decision to administer blood in the circumstances confronting him was found to be an honest exercise of his professional judgment which did not delay Mrs. Malette's recovery, endanger her life or cause her any bodily harm. Indeed, the judge concluded that the doctor`s treatment of Mrs. Malette "may well have been responsible for saving her life."

[13] Liability was imposed in this case on the basis that the doctor tortiously violated his patient's rights over her own body by acting contrary to the Jehovah's Witness card and administering blood transfusions that were not authorized. His honest and even justifiable belief that the treatment was medically essential did not serve to relieve him from liability for the battery resulting from his intentional and unpermitted conduct. ...

[22] On the facts of the present case, Dr. Shulman was clearly faced with an emergency. He had an unconscious, critically-ill patient on his hands who, in his opinion, needed blood transfusions to save her life or preserve her health. If there were no Jehovah's Witness card, he undoubtedly would have been entitled to administer blood transfusions as part of the emergency treatment and could not have been held liable for so doing. In those circumstances he would have had no indication that the transfusions would have been refused had the patient then been able to make her wishes known and, accordingly, no reason to expect that, as a reasonable person, she would not consent to the transfusions.

[23] However, to change the facts, if Mrs. Malette, before passing into unconsciousness, had expressly instructed Dr. Shulman, in terms comparable to those set forth on the card, that her religious convictions as a Jehovah's Witness were such that she was not to be given a blood transfusion under any circumstances and that she fully realized the implications of this position, the doctor would have been confronted with an obviously different situation. Here, the patient, anticipating an emergency in which she might be unable to make decisions about her health care contemporaneous with the emergency, has given explicit instructions that blood transfusions constitute an unacceptable medical intervention and are not to be administered to her. Once the emergency arises, is the doctor nonetheless entitled to administer transfusions on the basis of his honest belief that they are needed to save his patient's life?

[24] The answer, in my opinion, is clearly no. A doctor is not free to disregard a patient's advance instructions any more than he would be free to disregard instructions given at the time of the emergency. The law does not prohibit a patient from withholding consent to emergency medical treatment, nor does the law prohibit a doctor from following his patient's instructions. While the law may disregard the absence of consent in limited emergency circumstances, it otherwise supports the right of competent adults to make decisions concerning their own health care by imposing civil liability on those who perform medical treatment without consent. ...

[26] The distinguishing feature of the present case — and the one that makes this a case of first impression — is, of course, the Jehovah's Witness card

on the person of the unconscious patient. What then is the effect of the Jehovah's Witness card?

[27] In the appellant's submission, the card is of no effect and, as a consequence, can play no role in determining the doctor's duty toward his patient in the emergency situation existing in this case. ...

[29]... He argues that it could properly be doubted whether the card constituted a valid statement of Mrs. Malette's wishes in this emergency because it was unknown, for instance, whether she knew the card was still in her purse; whether she was still a Jehovah's Witness or how devout a Jehovah's Witness she was; what information she had about the risks associated with the refusal of blood transfusions when she signed the card; or whether, if she were conscious, she would refuse blood transfusions after the doctor had an opportunity to advise her of the risks associated with the refusal.

[30] With deference to Mr. Royce's exceedingly able argument on behalf of the appellant, I am unable to accept the conclusions advocated by him. I do not agree, as his argument would have it, that the Jehovah's Witness card can be no more than a meaningless piece of paper. I share the trial judge's view that, in the circumstances of this case, the instructions in the Jehovah's Witness card imposed a valid restriction on the emergency treatment that could be provided to Mrs. Malette and precluded blood transfusions. ...

[36]... The doctor is bound in law by the patient's choice even though that choice may be contrary to the mandates of his own conscience and professional judgment. If patient choice were subservient to conscientious medical judgment, the right of the patient to determine her own treatment, and the doctrine of informed consent, would be rendered meaningless. ...

[37] In sum, it is my view that the principal interest asserted by Mrs. Malette in this case — the interest is the freedom to reject, or refuse to consent to, intrusions of her bodily integrity — outweighs the interest of the state in the preservation of life and health and the protection of the integrity of the medical profession. While the right to decline medical treatment is not absolute or unqualified, those state interests are not in themselves sufficiently compelling to justify forcing a patient to submit to nonconsensual invasions of her person. ...

[41] At issue here is the freedom of the patient as an individual to exercise her right to refuse treatment and accept the consequences of her own decision. Competent adults, as I have sought to demonstrate, are generally at liberty to refuse medical treatment even at the risk of death. The right to determine what shall be done with one's body is a fundamental right in our society. The concepts inherent in this right are the bedrock upon which the principles of self-determination and individual autonomy are based. Free individual choice in matters affecting this right should, in my opinion, be accorded very high priority. I view the issues in this case from that perspective. ...

Appeal dismissed.

The plaintiff was a security guard hired to accompany truck drivers delivering produce to retail stores during a strike. The defendants were union members. One defendant had sprayed a substance from an aerosol can into the air intake of the truck; others had harassed her verbally and, among other things, prevented her from leaving the cab of the truck.

The plaintiff suffered laryngitis and chest irritation and was unable to work for nearly a year. The court found the defendants liable for the torts of assault and battery and awarded the plaintiff general, special and punitive damages.

Swanson v. Ballow
Sask. Q.B. June 24, 1991
Summarized from The Lawyers Weekly
September 6, 1991 p. 15

After the Chicago Bears lost to the San Francisco 49ers 41-0, an unidentified woman among a crowd taunting the Bears coach Mike Ditka alleged that Ditka tossed a wad of gum at her and hit her on the head. "Police officer Richard Galliani said the gum 'was found and booked as evidence. What we have is just a basic assault or battery.'"[12]

In Bridgeport, Conn. Ms. Diorios hired Mr. Fuller, also known as Tickles the Clown, to throw a pie in the face of a school dean who had disciplined her daughter, "who went AWOL during a class trip to New York," by suspending her from school. At the girl's eighth grade graduation ceremony, Tickles the Clown gave the dean some balloons, a song and a pie in the face. After his arrest, he alleged that Ms. Diorios, wife of a lawyer, offered him $10,000 to keep her identity a secret. Mr. and Ms. Diorios were charged with tampering with a witness and Mr. Diorios was charged with conspiracy to bribe. (*The Lawyers Weekly* Oct. 12, 1984 p.2) Apparently, a civil action for battery was not taken.

A year later it was reported that in criminal court Ms. Diorios was found guilty of breach of peace. She was not found guilty of bribery or tampering with a witness.[13]

In Hamilton Ontario Mr. Calligan cut about 30 centimetres of Ms. Staracivic's hair and on another occasion about 20 centimetres of Ms. Brown's ponytail.

In a scuffle, one man bit off the end of the other's nose.[14]

2. Abuse of Process

The plaintiff law firm brought an action to recover legal fees of approximately $20,000. The defendant, Mr. Kirsch, filed a statement of defence and a counterclaim in which he alleged that the services rendered were not performed professionally. The plaintiff amended his statement of claim to seek damages for the tort of abuse of process.

Judge Campbell reviewed the material, including the decision of the Registrar before whom the lawyer's bill was taxed (examined), and stated the law: "The authorities indicate that the main elements of the tort of abuse of process are a misuse of the court's process for an ulterior or extraneous purpose other than that for which the process was designed to serve, and some damage flowing therefrom." He then concluded "that the evidence is so overwhelmingly against the defendant, that the only possible inference is that he knew his allegations of unprofessional conduct were false and that he made them to delay judgment and injure the plaintiff's reputation." In holding for the plaintiff, the judge applied the reasoning in Glazer v. Kirsch [1986] B.C.W.L.D. 159 in which it was found that the defendant was liable for abuse of process by attempting to forestall judgment and blacken the reputation of a creditor suing him on a promissory note. In that case Kirsch, the defendant, had alleged that the plaintiff creditor had threatened to kill or maim him or his family. The defendant in the case cited was the same Mr. Kirsch! Manson, the plaintiff in this action, was his lawyer who had prepared the unsuccessful defence in the 1986 case.

Norton Stewart et al. v. Kirsch
16 B.C.L.R. (2d) 221
August 19, 1987

3. Conversion (Trespass to Chattels)

In London, Ontario, Mr. McMahon testified that he had warned his sister's pet budgie that if it did not quit biting his hand he would bite its head off. The budgie paid no heed and continued to bite; Mr. M "followed through with the threat."[15]

4. False Imprisonment

In Falls Church, Va, Betsy Nelson was detained outside a sporting goods store and accused of shoplifting. Those that detained her demanded she disrobe. The bulge was caused by advanced pregnancy; a baby boy was born the day after the detention and after she had met with her lawyer. She asked for $100,000 compensatory damages and $500,000 in punitive damages.[16]

When two Brinks security guards, replenishing funds at an automatic teller machine, inadvertently signalled to the alarm company that all was *not* well, that it was a hold-up situation, the alarm company notified the police, who apprehended them and took them to the police station where they were detained until identified. The guard who did not trip the alarm sued for false imprisonment. At trial he was successful, but an appeal was allowed. The B.C. Court of Appeal held that the police had reasonable grounds for taking them to the police station and detaining them until their authority to be at the bank was verified.

Freeman v. West Vancouver (District)
71 B.C.L.R. (2d) 387
October 14, 1992

5. Malicious Prosecution

Susan Nelles was charged with four counts of first degree murder in the deaths of four infants at the Hospital for Sick Children in Toronto. After a lengthy preliminary inquiry to determine if there was sufficient evidence to put the plaintiff on trial, the judge concluded there was not and discharged her on all four counts. Ms. Nelles commenced an action in the Supreme Court of Ontario against the Crown in right of Ontario, the Attorney General for Ontario, and several police officers, alleging that the Attorney General and his agents, the Crown Attorneys, counselled, encouraged, aided and abetted the defendant police officers in initiating and conducting the prosecution of her, and that the Attorney-General and the Crown Attorneys were actuated by malice. Her Statement of Claim set out the particulars on which she rested her claims for malicious prosecution, negligence, false imprisonment, and the infringement of her *Charter* rights. The defence requested her action be dismissed on the grounds that it showed no reasonable cause of action and it raised a point of law to be determined before a trial, namely whether or not the Crown and the Attorney General and their agents were absolutely immune from all liability for suits for malicious prosecution.

The Supreme Court of Ontario dismissed her action for inter alia malicious prosecution. The Ontario Court of Appeal upheld the judgment and ruled that at common law, an action of malicious prosecution cannot be brought against the Attorney-General for Ontario, or its agents, the Crown Attorneys, for their conduct in initiating and conducting a criminal prosecution. The absolute immunity is justified as it allows the public to trust that the Crown will vigorously bring and conduct criminal prosecutions without fear of law suit.

On further appeal, the Supreme Court of Canada dismissed the appeal against the Crown, but allowed the appeal against the Attorney General. That is, the Crown is immune from a suit of malicious prosecution, but the Attorney General is not. The matter was returned to the Supreme Court of Ontario for trial of the claim against the Attorney General.

J. Lamar, reviewing the law, wrote as follows:

2. The Tort of Malicious Prosecution

There are four necessary elements which must be proved for a plaintiff to succeed in an action for malicious prosecution:

a) the proceedings must have been initiated by the defendant;
b) the proceedings must have terminated in favour of the plaintiff;
c) the absence of reasonable and probable cause;
d) malice, or a primary purpose other than that of carrying the law into effect.
(See J.G. Fleming, *The Law of Torts* (5th ed. 1977), at p. 598.)

The first two elements are straightforward and largely speak for themselves. The latter two elements require explicit discussion. Reasonable and probable cause has been defined as "an honest belief in the guilt of the accused based upon a full conviction, founded on reasonable grounds, of the existence of a state of circumstances, which, assuming them to be true, would reasonably lead any ordinarily prudent and cautious man, placed in the position of the accuser, to the conclusion that the person charged was probably guilty of the crime imputed." (*Hicks v. Faulkner* (1878), 8 Q.B.D. 167, at p. 171, Hawkins J.)

This test contains both a subjective and objective element. There must be both actual belief on the part of the prosecutor and that belief must be reasonable in the circumstances. The existence of reasonable and probable cause is a matter for the judge to decide as opposed to the jury.

The required element of malice is for all intents, the equivalent of "improper purpose." It has, according to Fleming, a "wider meaning than spite, ill-will or a spirit of vengeance, and includes any other improper purpose, such as to gain a private collateral advantage" (Fleming, op. cit., at p. 609). To succeed in an action for malicious prosecution against the Attorney General or Crown Attorney, the plaintiff would have to prove both the absence of reasonable and probable cause in commencing the prosecution, and malice in the form of a deliberate and improper use of the office of the Attorney General or Crown Attorney, a use inconsistent with the status of "minister of justice." In my view this burden on the plaintiff amounts to a requirement that the Attorney General or Crown Attorney perpetrated a fraud on the process of criminal justice and in doing so has perverted or abused his office and the process of criminal justice. In fact, in some cases this would seem to amount to criminal conduct. (See for example breach of trust, s. 122, conspiracy re: false prosecution s. 465(1)(b), obstructing justice s. 139(2) and (3) of the *Criminal Code*, R.S.C., 1985, c. C-46.)

Further, it should be noted that in many, if not all cases of malicious prosecution by an Attorney General or Crown Attorney, there will have been an infringement of an accused's rights as guaranteed by ss. 7 and 11 of the *Canadian Charter of Rights and Freedoms.*

By way of summary then, a plaintiff bringing a claim for malicious prosecution has no easy task. Not only does the plaintiff have the notoriously difficult task of establishing a negative, that is the absence of reasonable and probable cause, but he is held to a very high standard of proof to avoid a non-suit or directed verdict (see Fleming, op. cit., at p. 606, and *Mitchell v. John Heine and Son Ltd.* (1938), 38 S.R. (N.S.W.) 466, at pp. 469-71). Professor Fleming has gone so far as to conclude that there are built-in devices particular to the tort of malicious prosecution to dissuade civil suits (at p. 606):

> The disfavour with which the law has traditionally viewed the action for malicious prosecution is most clearly revealed by the hedging devices with which it has been surrounded in order to deter this kind of litigation and protect private citizens who discharge their public duty of prosecuting those reasonably suspected of crime.

Nelles v. Ontario

60 D.L.R. 4th 609 (O.C.A.)

[1989] 2 S.C.R. 170 (S.C.C.)

6. Deceit

In an effort to win a $100 million contract with the Social Security Administration, Paradyne Corp used phony equipment, an "empty box with blinking lights," to pass as an encryptor and put its name on another manufacturer's gear.[17]

Care Management Inc. (CMI) sued Burroughs Corp., alleging that the company's sales personnel engaged in "deception, fraud, false promises and misrepresentations." CMI alleged it suffered severe financial losses when the system it purchased failed to operate as promised. They sued for $1 million.

Within a three or four year period about 150 lawsuits were filed against Burroughs, usually for deceit or breach of contract.[18]

Hertz Corp. entered a guilty plea for defrauding 110,000 customers and insurance companies, between January 1, 1978 through mid-1985, by billing them for inflated or fake collision repair costs. Hertz agreed to pay a fine of $6.85 million and to refund $13.7 million to those affected from Jan. 1, 1978 through mid-1985.[19]

Ms. Burns, claiming she had both a Ph.D in Medical Sciences and an M.D., when she had neither, worked in the field for thirteen years.[20]

Note: *Although these last two cases resulted in criminal actions against Hertz and Burns, the persons wronged could have sued in a civil action to recover the losses they suffered because of the deceit.*

7. Defamation

Vander Zalm v. Times Publisher

109 D.L.R. (3d) 531
British Columbia Court of Appeal
February 15, 1980

Nemetz, C.J.B.C.:—On June 22, 1978, there appeared on the editorial page of the *Victoria Times,* one of the City of Victoria's leading daily newspapers, a cartoon depicting the plaintiff, William N. Vander Zalm, a Cabinet Minister then holding the office of Minister of Human Resources in the Government of British Columbia. It was drawn by the defendant Robert Bierman, a freelance political cartoonist who had contributed cartoons to the newspaper for many years. Alongside the cartoon there appeared an actual photograph of the Minister, as part of a reprinted editorial criticizing Mr. Vander Zalm's statements and policies. It is apparent that the cartoon exaggerated the facial features of the plaintiff. It depicted Mr. Vander Zalm smiling seated at a table, and engaged in plucking the wings from a fly. Other flies, without wings, were shown moving on the table. On the plaintiff's lapel were inscribed the words "HUMAN RESOURCES."

The Minister sued for damages, claiming that the cartoon libelled him. He pleaded that the newspaper, its editor, its publisher and Mr. Bierman alleged by the cartoon that he was

> ...a person of cruel and sadistic nature who enjoys inflicting suffering and torture on helpless beings who cannot protect themselves.

The action was heard by Munroe, J., sitting without a jury. The defendants pleaded that the cartoon was not defamatory, and that in any event it was fair comment. The learned trial Judge rejected these contentions and found for the plaintiff, awarding damages of $3,500 against the defendants. This is an appeal from that judgment [96 D.L.R. (3d) 172, [1979] 2 W.W.R. 673, 8 C.C.L.T. 144].

Before addressing myself to the issues, I should like to make some prefatory observations as to political cartoons in general. Counsel were agreed that there was a paucity of decided cases concerning libel arising from political caricatures or cartoons — despite the fact that such cartoons have had a long history of publication in Canada as well as in most of the western world. As a result, as noted by the learned editors of Gatley on *Libel and Slander*, 7th ed. (1974), p. 15, footnote 23: "The limits of what is permissible in the way of cartoons... are undefined." I have examined definitions of the word "cartoon" in its modern use (coined, it is suggested, by the editors of *Punch*) and would adopt the one set out by the scholar Winslow Ames in the *Encyclopaedia Britannica* (1961):

> ...a pictorial parody which by devices of caricature. analogy and ludicrous juxtaposition sharpens the public view of a contemporary event, folkway, or political or social trend. It is normally humorous but may be positively savage.

Now the well-known test for whether a statement or allegation is defamatory is set out in *Salmond on Torts*, 17th ed. (1977), pp. 139-40, from which I quote as follows:

> A defamatory statement is one which has a tendency to injure the reputation of the person to whom it refers: which tends, that is to say, to lower him in the estimation of right-thinking members of society generally and in particular to cause him to be regarded with feelings of hatred, contempt, ridicule, fear, dislike or disesteem.

I have placed these two quotations in juxtaposition because it becomes obvious that most political cartoons have, inherent in their satire, a tendency to lower their subject in the estimation of the public. Nevertheless, it has been said that persons accepting public office can expect attack and criticism on the ground that "the public interest requires that a man's public conduct shall be open to the most searching criticism": *per* Bain, J., in *Martin v. Manitoba Free Press Co.* (1982), 8 Man. R. 50 at p. 72. However, the question of what constitutes valid "searching criticism" and what constitutes libel must be examined in the context of all the surrounding circumstances.

I turn now to the consideration of the cartoon. The defendants denied that the cartoon defamed the plaintiff and pleaded that in any event the cartoon was fair comment on a matter of public interest and that, accordingly, there was no libel. I have had the privilege of reading the reasons for judgment prepared by each of my brothers Seaton, Hinkson and Craig, JJ.A., and agree with them that even if the cartoon was *prima facie* defamatory, the defence of fair comment was available in the circumstances. However, I should like to advance my own view of why that defence was available here.

The three elements of the defence of fair comment are well known. First, the matter must be recognizable to the ordinary reasonable man as a comment upon true facts, and not as a bare statement of fact. Secondly, the matter commented upon must be one of public interest. There must, in short, be a public nexus between the matter and the person caricatured. In a case such as this, the cartoonist may not intrude upon the private life of a public man, no matter how interesting such an intrusion may be to the public, nor may he expose a private person to unsought publicity. Finally, as explained by Diplock, J. (as he then was), in *Silkin v. Beaverbrook Newspapers Ltd. et al.* [1958] 1 W.L.R. 743 at p. 747, and by the Supreme Court of Canada in *Cherneskey v. Armadale Publishers Ltd. et al.* (1978), 90 D.L.R. (3d) 321, [1979] 1 S.C.R. 1067, [1978] 6 W.W.R. 618, the comment must be "fair" in that it must, to quote Martland, J., in *Cherneskey* at p. 325 D.L.R., p. 1073 S.C.R., "represent an honest expression of this real view of the person making the comment." ...

Sixteen instances of controversial statements and acts attributed to the minister were pleaded by the defendants as particulars of facts upon which the cartoon was said to comment. Each of them had received considerable publicity. I note that only one, para. (h), was categorically denied by the plaintiff. All of the other 15 were either entirely acknowledged or substantially conceded after qualification.

...[Judge Nemetz then reviewed seven of the statements or acts.]

In my view, these statements and actions of the

Minister including the statement concerning Indians which was publicized only a few days before the publication of the cartoon, provided the necessary substratum of sufficiently publicized facts to enable the ordinary reader to recognize the nexus of the cartoon and the statements. Ordinary and reasonable persons in this country are well acquainted with the allegorical nature of political cartoons and, in my opinion, would have little difficulty in recognizing this cartoon as a comment upon such facts; a comment, indeed, of the very sort which Mr. Bierman testified he intended to make. Nor can it be doubted that the facts commented upon were matters of considerable public interest and concerned the Minister in his public rather than his personal capacity.

The next question that arises is whether the comment was "fair." In charging the jury in the *Silkin* case, *supra*, Lord Diplock explained the test in this was [p. 747]:...

> The basis of our public life is that the crank, the enthusiast, may say what he honestly thinks just as much as the reasonable man or woman who sits on a jury, and it would be a sad day for freedom of speech in this country if a jury were to apply the test of whether it agrees with the comment instead of applying the true test: was this an opinion, however exaggerated, obstinate or prejudiced, which was honestly held by the writer? ...

I conclude from the whole of Mr. Bierman's testimony that indeed represents an honest expression of his real view. No question arises as to credibility since it is obvious that the learned trial Judge did not disbelieve the cartoonist, and no issue arose in this regard. Having these factors before us, is the defence of fair comment available? I think it is. As, in the circumstances of this case, it is my respectful view that the cartoon represents fair comment on a matter of public interest, I would, therefore, allow the appeal and dismiss the action.

Appeal allowed

Mitch Mitchell, the former drummer with the Jimi Hendrix rock band, sued David Henderson, the biographer of Hendrix, for libel. Mitchell alleged that the writer depicted him as a racist bigot. The British jury found that Mitchell had not been defamed.[21]

General Motors Corp. announced it would sue NBC for defamation for its rigged explosion in a purportedly documentary segment on the safety of GM trucks. On *Dateline*, the debate on the safety of the trucks with gas tanks fitted outside the trucks' interior frame was followed by scenes of GM trucks being hit broadside. One burst into flames. On investigation, GM learned that the explosion had been staged; the network had incendiary devises taped under the truck.[22]

On the grounds that an action for defamation must be "of and concerning individuals," Justice Montgomery dismissed a claim purporting to represent approximately 25,000 Canadian veterans of World War II. In a class action suit, the airmen alleged in the statement of claim that they had been defamed by the book and the episode "Death by Moonlight" of the T.V. series *The Valour and the Horror*.[23]

A bank in England mistakenly bounced a cheque drawn by one of its corporate customers, even though there were sufficient funds in the company's account. The company sued successfully for libel.[24]

8. Injurious Falsehood (Trade Libel)

The Canadian Cold Buster Bar, a candy bar developed by Dr. Larry Wang to fend off hypothermia, was pulled from store shelves across Canada after an animal rights group claimed it had injected oven-cleaning solvent into some of the bars. The group claimed that Dr. Wang had "slaughtered thousands of rats" developing the candy bar. Workers were temporarily laid off at the production plant and 250,000 bars were pulled off the shelf.[25] Ten days after the threat new bars were being placed back in the stores.[26]

Tropical Fantasy, a soft drink made by the Brooklyn Bottling Corporation, was becoming the best selling drink in the small grocery stores, when leaflets were distributed in the neighbourhood claiming the drink was manufactured by the Ku Klux Klan and contained ingredients aimed to sterilize men. Delivery trucks were pelted by angry customers and some stores stopped buying the drink. The US Food and Drug Administration and the New York City Council were investigating the matter.[27]

9. Privacy/Misappropriation

Note: In some provinces this tort may be codified; for example, see *The Privacy Act*, R.S.B.C. Sec. 3.

A Christian Dior advertisement showed several celebrities agog over an outfit created by the designer. Among the celebrities was a Jacqueline Kennedy Onassis "look alike." Ms. Onassis began an action charging that the advertisement violated her privacy and commercially exploited her image.[28]

10. Trespass

Mr. Hetu, angry when his lady friend locked him out of the house because he was drunk, razed the house in a twenty-minute attack with a bulldozer.[29]

C. Negligence

Questions

What must the plaintiff prove in order to win an action for negligence?

If the plaintiff proves that the defendant owed the plaintiff a duty of care, fell below the standard of care owed and caused the plaintiff foreseeable damage, does the defendant have any other arguments that may result in the court dismissing the claim, or forcing the plaintiff to absorb some of his or her loss?

negligence

1. DUTY OF CARE

manuf. owes a duty of care to the ultimate consumer.

M'Alister (or Donoghue) v. Stevenson

[1932] A.C. 562
HOUSE OF LORDS

By action brought in the Court of Session the appellant, who was a shop assistant, sought to recover damages from the respondent, who was a manufacturer of aerated waters, for injuries she suffered as a result of consuming part of the contents of a bottle of ginger-beer which had been manufactured by the respondent, and which contained the decomposed remains of a snail. The appellant by her condescendence [pleadings] averred [stated as a fact] that the bottle of ginger-beer was purchased for the appellant by a friend in a cafe at Paisley, which was occupied by one Minchella; that the bottle was made of dark opaque glass and that the appellant had no reason to suspect that it contained anything but pure ginger-beer; that the said Minchella poured some of the ginger-beer out into a tumbler, and that the appellant drank some of the contents of the tumbler; that her friend was then proceeding to pour the remainder of the contents of the bottle into the tumbler when a snail, which was in a state of decomposition, floated out of the bottle; that as a result of the nauseating sight of the snail in such circumstances, and in consequence of the impurities in the ginger-beer which she had already consumed, the appellant suffered from shock and severe gastro-enteritis. The appellant further averred that the ginger-beer was manufactured by the respondent to be sold as a drink to the public (including the appellant); that it was bottled by the respondent and labelled by him with a label bearing his name; and that the bottles were thereafter sealed with a metal cap by the respondent. She further averred that it was the duty of the respondent to provide a system of working his business which would not allow snails to get into his ginger-beer bottles, and that it was also his duty to provide an efficient system of inspection of the bottles before the ginger-beer was filled into them, and that he had failed in both these duties and had so caused the accident.

The respondent objected that these averments were irrelevant and insufficient to support the conclusions of the summons.

Lord Atkin. My Lords, the sole question for determination in this case is legal: Do the averments made by the pursuer [plaintiff] in her pleading, if true, disclose a cause of action? I need not restate the particular facts. The question is whether the manufacturer of an article of drink sold by him to a distributor, in circumstances which prevent the distributor or the ultimate purchaser or consumer from discovering by inspection any defect, is under any legal duty to the ultimate purchaser or consumer to take reasonable care that the article is free from defect likely to cause injury to health. I do not think a more important problem has occupied your Lordships in your judicial capacity. ... The law of both countries [Scotland and England] appears to be that in order to support an action for damages for negligence the complainant has to show that he has been injured by the breach of a duty owed to him in the circumstances by the defendant to take reasonable care to avoid such injury. In the present case we are not concerned with the breach of the duty; if a duty exists, that would be a question of fact which is sufficiently averred and for present purposes must be assumed. We are solely concerned with the question whether, as a matter of law in the circumstances alleged, the defender owed any duty to the pursuer to take care.

At present I content myself with pointing out that in English law there must be, and is, some general conception of relations giving rise to a duty of care, of which the particular cases found in the books are but instances. The liability for negligence, whether you style it such or treat it as in other systems as a species of "culpa," is no doubt based upon a general public sentiment of moral wrongdoing for which the offender must pay. But acts or omissions which any moral code would censure cannot in a practical world be treated so as to give a right to every person injured by them to demand relief. In this way rules of law arise which limit the range of complainants and the extent of their remedy. The rule that you are to love your neighbour becomes in law, you must not injure your neighbour; and the lawyer's question, Who is my neighbour? receives a restricted reply. You must take reasonable care to avoid acts or omissions which you can reasonably foresee would be likely to injure your neighbour. Who, then, in law is my neighbour? The answer seems to be—persons who are so closely and directly affected by my act that I ought reasonably to have them in contemplation as being so affected when I am directing my mind to the acts or omissions which are called in question. This appears to me to be the doctrine of *Heaven v. Pender* (1), as laid down by Lord Esher (then Brett M.R.) when it is limited by the notion of proximity introduced by Lord Esher himself and A.L. Smith L.J. in *Le Lievre v. Gould.* (1) Lord Esher says: "That case established that, under certain circumstances, one man may owe a duty to another, even though there is no contract between them. So A.L. Smith L.J.: "The decision of *Heaven v. Pender* (2) was founded upon the principle, that a duty to take due care did arise when the person or property of one was in such proximity to the person or property of another that, if due care was not taken, damage might be done by the one to the other." I think that this sufficiently states the truth if proximity be not confined to mere physical proximity, but be used, as I think it was intended, to extend to such close and direct relations that the act complained of directly affects a person whom the person alleged to be bound to take care would know would be directly affected by his careless act.

There will no doubt arise cases where it will be difficult to determine whether the contemplated relationship is so close that the duty arises. But in the class of case now before the court I cannot conceive any difficulty to arise. A manufacturer puts up an article of food in a container which he knows will be opened by the actual consumer. There can be no inspection by any purchaser and no reasonable preliminary inspection by the consumer. Negligently, in the course of preparation, he allows the contents to be mixed with poison. It is said that the law of England and Scotland is that the poisoned consumer has no remedy against the negligent manufacturer. If this were the result of the authorities, I should consider the result a grave defect in the law, and so contrary to principle that I should hesitate long before following any decision to that effect which had not the authority of this House. I would point out that, in the assumed state of the authorities, not only would the consumer have no remedy against the manufacturer, he would have none against any one else, for in the circumstances alleged there would be no evidence of negligence against any one other than the manufacturer; and, except in the case of a consumer who was also a purchaser, no contract and no warranty of fitness, and in the case of the purchase of a specific article under its patent or trade name, which might well be the case in the purchase of some articles of food or drink, no warranty protecting even the purchaser-consumer. There are other instances than of articles of food and drink where goods are sold intended to be used immediately by the consumer, such as many forms of goods sold for cleaning purposes, where the same liability must exist. The doctrine supported by the decision below would not only deny a remedy to the consumer who was injured by consuming bottled beer or chocolates poisoned by the negligence of the manufacturer, but also to the user of what should be a harmless proprietary medicine, an ointment, a soap, a cleaning fluid or cleaning powder. I confine myself to articles of common household use, where every one, including the manufacturer, knows that the articles will be used by other persons than the actual ultimate purchaser—namely, by members of his family and his servants, and in some cases his guests. I do not think so ill of our jurisprudence as to suppose that its principles are so remote from the ordinary needs of civilized society and the ordinary claims it makes upon its members as to deny a legal remedy where there is so obviously a social wrong.

In my opinion several decided cases support the view that in such a case as the present the manufacturer owes a duty to the consumer to be careful. ...

It is always a satisfaction to an English lawyer to be able to test his application of fundamental principles of the common law by the development of the same doctrines by the lawyers of the Courts of the United States. In that country I find that the law appears to be well established in the sense in which I have indicated. The mouse had emerged from the ginger-beer bottle in the United States before it appeared in Scotland, but there it brought a liability upon the manufacturer. I must not in this long judgment do more than refer to the illuminating judgment of Cardozo J. in *MacPherson v. Buick Motor Co.* in the New York Court of Appeals (2), in which he states the principles of the law as I should desire to state them, and reviews the authorities in other States than his own.

My Lords, if your Lordships accept the view that this pleading discloses a relevant cause of action you will be affirming the proposition that by Scots and English law alike a manufacturer of products, which he sells in such a form as to show that he intends them to reach the ultimate consumer in the form in which they left him with no reasonable possibility of intermediate examination, and with the knowledge that the absence of reasonable care in the preparation or putting up of the products will result in an injury to the consumer's life or property, owes a duty to the consumer to take that reasonable care.

It is a proposition which I venture to say no one in Scotland or England who was not a lawyer would for one moment doubt. It will be an advantage to make it clear that the law in this matter, as in most others, is in accordance with sound common sense. I think that this appeal should be allowed.

2. Standard of Care

Question

If a person owes another a duty to be careful, how careful does he have to be?

At the Kingston General Hospital, a food tube, filled with pureed food, was accidentally attached to an intravenous line and the food passed directly into a patient's veins, blocked an artery bringing blood from his lungs to his heart, and killed the patient by causing cardiac and pulmonary arrest.

Ms. Hohman sued the heavy metal group Motley Crüe for its failure to provide earplugs or to warn about the decibel level of the sound at their concert. She alleged her right eardrum was shattered and the left ear damaged by the volume.[30]

During a concert, Vanilla Ice threw a towel into the audience. A mother and daughter, injured by fans pressing forward, sued the performer for neglience.[31]

Mrs. Pittman, whose husband died of AIDS contracted through a blood transfusion, tested HIV positive and sued the Red Cross for negligence.[32] Mrs. Pittman won her case. The Ontario Court (General Division), in a 348-page decision, apportioned the fault among the doctor, the hospital and the Red Cross.[33]

Donald Parkes, a 41 year-old man, was brought to the emergency ward of the Cambridge Memorial Hospital unconscious from an overdose of anti-depressant drugs. In an effort to revive him, the nurses hooked up an oxygen line directly from a wall outlet through an endotracheal tube to his lungs. The nurses failed to use a device that would have allowed the patient to exhale as well as to receive the oxygen. Consequently the patients was killed by having his lungs "blown up."

Although a defence was entered, the court found "gross, wanton negligence." The case was interesting to the legal community because of the court's reduction of damages due to the deceased's particular background. He had a history of mental illness which led to two suicide attempts. The court concluded that his life expectancy was lower than that of the average man.[34]

The driver of a garbage truck in Melville, New York failed to see a sunbathing couple and drove over their faces. The couple suffered tire bruises and jaw injuries. The court found more serious damage was averted probably by their having used a sand pillow which gave way under the weight of the truck. The matter was eventually settled out of court for $150,000.[35]

No negligence

Nagy v. Kamloops Cinema Holdings Ltd. et al.

SUPREME COURT OF BRITISH COLUMBIA
KAMLOOPS REGISTRY NO. 15191
NOVEMBER 5, 1990

Robinson, J.:—The plaintiff, an attractive young woman almost 24 years old, received an eye injury while attending at the premises of the defendant, Kamloops Cinema Holdings Ltd., on October 29, 1988. She suffered the injury to her eye as a result of being struck with a flying object. I find that the plaintiff has at this date, fully recovered.

The factual background is somewhat unusual, if not actually bizarre. The premises in question, one of Kamloop's movie houses, ran the film, "The Rocky Horror Picture Show," at or about midnight on October 29th, 1988, that being the Saturday nearest Hallowe'en. This film has achieved a cult status and is often run in movie houses where midnight screenings are conducted. …

The film, "The Rocky Horror Picture Show," in common with some other cult films, involves and invites participation by the audience. The specific manner of participation, with respect to this film, for reasons that need not be detailed, include the spraying of water from water pistols, the throwing of rice, and the throwing of toast.

The manager of the theatre testified that at all previous instances where he had shown the film under these circumstances, this type of participation had successfully gone forward, without undue incident or harm to anyone. To a limited extent, the plaintiff had knowledge of this type of participation and, though knowing nothing else about the film, decided, following an invitation from one or more of her friends, that it would be fun to see the film in these circumstances. Five of the plaintiff's friends accompanied her to the movie theatre, advance tickets having been obtained, and the printed portion of which had been read by the plaintiff. [The ticket stated that "Bottles, candles, cans or drinks of any kind are prohibited. You will be subject to search for admittance."] Approximately five minutes after she had entered the auditorium portion of the theatre, and taken her seat, an unknown object struck her right eye area, causing pain, distress and the protective closing of her eyelids. Almost immediately she was taken to Royal Inland Hospital for emergency treatment, and for several months thereafter was subject to further treatment and examination. …

Three notices of a handmade variety, not normally present during ordinary screenings, were on hand at the theatre that night. The only one of real significance, in my view, is one that read:

> "The following will *not* be permitted inside the theatre:
>
> - *no* water pistols
> - outside food
> - drinks of any kind
> - candles
> - vegetables
> - umbrellas
>
> Any other sharp objects strictly prohibited"

Because, presumably, of the anticipated participation of the audience, as contemplated by the theatre manager, and to control the extent and nature of the participation, he hired additional ushers and security personnel so that there was on hand on October 29th, 1988, four ushers, four security personnel, and the manager and his wife, all of whom were intended to share in the tasks of keeping order and ensuring that the theatre premises would be reasonably safe for all members of the audience. The ushers had been briefed as to the type and extent of the searching processes to be conducted; it included the search of handbags and/or other types of carrying receptacles, and the search of clothing where opportunities for concealment of articles existed. The ushers were given discretion in a general way, and specifically that the searching process was to be directed more to younger members of the audience, presumably at the teenage level and younger. It was the estimate of one of the ushers that a search of one kind or another was conducted with respect to 75 percent of the entering audience, at least with respect to those who were targeted, as it were, for searching. …

The procedures and techniques utilized by the theatre manager in this instance were the same as those he used in all previous instances, except that he allowed entry into the premises by the waiting audience outside the theatre building at least 15 minutes earlier than he had done in previous instances. …

The plaintiff's argument proceeds thusly: The theatre manager allowed the outside audience awaiting entry permission to enter too soon; that there was insufficient security arrangements within the premises, particularly with respect to crowd or audience control; and lastly, that the searching requirements and techniques were insufficient, inadequate, and cursory in the extreme.

Reflection upon the manager's decision to allow the audience into the theatre premises earlier than he had anticipated persuades me that this was an exercise of judgment on his part that does not fall within any accepted concept of negligence; it is simply an exercise of judgment on his part which may have, in the light of subsequent events, been wrong, but he was faced with the unattractive alternative of leaving outside a crowd of people, many if not all of whom had paid for their tickets in advance, in a restive mood, and the probability that serious consequences could ensue outside. Equally, I am satisfied as to the security arrangement in terms of additional personnel hired by the theatre manager for this particular showing, and their use, and the use of the ushers, all involving a primary purpose of ensuring that patrons maintained their seats and conducted themselves in a suitable manner, acknowledging nonetheless the permission, express or implied, to throw certain objects, such as rice or toast, were under all the circumstances, a sufficiency of security arrangements.

Without question, the arrangements for searching did not reveal the many objects, both large and small, which could be carried in one's pocket, and which were found on the theatre premises after the performance [as the plaintiff's lawyer had argued.] The defendant's submission is that the only completely satisfactory search would require the mandatory disrobing of each person, and the seizure of every object potentially capable of causing injury, including of course, coins of various kinds habitually carried by almost everyone.

To recite the obvious, the injury to the plaintiff came about directly as a result of the actions of one of the audience in the theatre, unknown to the plaintiff or the defendant. The question for determination then is: To what extent should the owner of the premises have anticipated that such an action would occur, that is, the random throwing of some object, of sufficient dimension and weight to cause injury? ... [The judge reviewed *Gardener* v. *McConnell* [1946] 1 D.L.R. 730 and *Duncan* v. *Braaten* (1980) 21 B.C.L.R. 368 for the questions to be asked and concludes:] I must then rhetorically query whether the manager of the defendant theatre knew or should have known that potentially dangerous projectiles might be hurled about before or during the performance of the film. At this point it is important to note that the test to be applied is one of reasonableness, not perfection. (*Carlson* v. *Canada Safeway Limited* (1983) 47 B.C.L.R. 252) Applying that test, I am not persuaded that the theatre manager failed to do anything he should have done, in terms of reasonable precaution including the placing of the usher, the use of additional security personnel, the notice warnings, and the searches. There remains only, in my view, the further question whether there being at least an implied permission to the audience to throw non-dangerous objects, that dangerous objects would inevitably be thrown. It is not realistic to deny that possibility, but I place that, in terms of weight, as not higher than a possibility, taking into account the fact that the theatre manager had carried out this manner of showing this film on a number of previous occasions, as did others, without incident; with the onus upon the plaintiff to prove her case on the balance of probabilities, I must conclude that the action be dismissed with costs, if demanded. ...

[Action dismissed]

3. Foreseeable Damage

After the judge found that the accused was guilty of the criminal charges against him, the accused jumped from the window of the courtroom to his death. The widow sued the lawyer representing her husband for negligence in his duties as the legal representative. At the trial the plaintiff's action was dismissed. The court held that the accused's jumping out the window was not foreseeable. *McPeake v. Cannon*[36]

After the funeral service in Dublin, the cars proceeded from the church to the cemetery. The hearse was separated from other cars by a passing train. The driver of the hearse left the hearse running and ran into a store to buy some cigarettes. The hearse was stolen, so the body did not arrive at the cemetery as expected. The wife of the deceased sued the funeral home for negligence.[37]

A baby was put through a baggage X-ray machine at the Winnipeg International Airport.[38]

4. Occupier's Liability

Mr. Faust stopped at a rural canyon construction site to use the outhouse. He fell through a plywood covering into a 12-metre-deep cesspool and, according to the UPI news release, "spent 13 hours fighting off a nasty gopher who fell in with him."[39]

5. Negligent Misstatement

Haig v. Bamford

72 D.L.R. (3d) 68
Supreme Court of Canada
April 1, 1976

Dickson J.: This appeal concerns the liability of an accountant to parties other than his employer for negligent statements. The Court is asked to decide whether there was in the relationship of the parties to the appeal such kind or degree of proximity as to give rise to a duty of care owed by the respondents to the appellant. The damages involved are not large but the question raised is of importance to the accounting profession and to the investing public.

... Siegfried Scholler carried on the business as sole proprietor. In early 1964, following a fire, Saskatchewan Economic Development Corporation (Sedco) agreed to advance Scholler $34,000 for the purpose of establishing a plant to undertake millwork and the manufacture of furniture in Moose Jaw, conditional upon incorporation of the sole proprietorship. Scholler Furniture & Fixtures Ltd. (the Company) was incorporated and the sole proprietorship came to an end. Scholler was an excellent workman but poor financial planner. He evinced a compulsive urge to expand the business of the Company with the result that by January, 1965, a serious shortage of working capital became apparent. Scholler approached Sedco for a further loan of $20,000 which was approved, contingent upon (i) production of a satisfactory audited financial statement of the Company ... and (ii) the infusion of $20,000 of equity capital.

Instructions were issued to the firm of R.L. Bamford & Co. (the accountants), of whom the respondents (defendants) were partners, to prepare the required financial statement and Scholler began a search for an outside investor. He made it known to the accountants that he was seeking an investor. The trial Judge, MacPherson, J. made a crucial finding, not disturbed by the Court of Appeal for Saskatchewan, that the accountants knew, prior to completion of the financial statement, dated June 18, 1965, at the root of the present litigation, that the statement would be used by Sedco, by the bank with whom the Company was doing business, and by a potential investor in equity capital.

The manager of Sedco, a Mr. Wiltshire, helped Scholler in his search for a potential investor, and, with the consent of Scholler, showed a copy of the financial statement to his friend, the plaintiff Haig, who had been looking for a "likely opportunity". Haig discussed the statement with his bank manager and with a chartered accountant. The bottom line of the statement showed that the operations of the Company were profitable; the potential was promising; a $20,000 loan from Sedco and $20,000 of equity money would provide necessary working capital. Influenced by these considerations Haig, an experienced businessman, purchased in mid-August 1965, share in the capital stock of the Company for $20,075 and guaranteed the bank loan to the extent of $20,000. He became president; Scholler became vice-president and operating head. All looking well... But something was wrong ...[T]he Company was again troubled by serious cash shortage. The accountants were consulted and investigation soon disclosed the source of the trouble: a $28,000 prepayment received by the Company... had been treated as if the work had been completed and the moneys earned. The $28,000 had been credited to revenue by the Company's book-keeper rather than shown as a liability. The accountants had failed to spot the error. ... Instead of making a profit in the period, as shown by the June statement, the Company had suffered a loss: instead of buying into a thriving business, as the financial statement of June 18, 1965 would have suggested, Haig bought into a distressed enterprise which never showed a profit...[T]he Company ceased business. Haig lost the $20,075, the loan of $2,500 and $6,500 under the bank guarantee. He sued the accountant, the Company and Scholler to recover $20,075 and $2,500 but later discontinued against Scholler and the Company.

[After concluding that the financial statements provided were done on an audit basis, the judge continued.]

I come then to the question whether Haig, who received the defective financial statements, and relied on them to his loss, has a right of recovery from the accountants. Mr. Justice MacPherson at trial allowed recovery [32 D.L.R. (3d) 66, [1972] 6 W.R.R. 557]. He held that the accountants knew or ought to have known that the statements would be used by a potential investor in the Company; although Haig was not, in the Judge's words, "in the picture" when the statement was prepared, he must be included in the category of persons who could be foreseen by the accountants as relying on the statement and therefore the accountants who owed a duty to Haig. The Judge applied a test of foreseeability.

The majority in the Court of Appeal for Saskatchewan...came to a different conclusion. ...

The outcome of this appeal rests, it would seem, on whether, to create a duty of care, it is sufficient that the accountants knew that the information was intended to be disseminated among a specific group or class, as Mr. Justice MacPherson and Mr. Justice Woods would have it, or whether the accountants also needed to be apprised of the plaintiff's identity, as Mr. Justice Hall and Mr. Justice Maguire would have it. ...

The English Authorities

I do not think one can do better than begin with Lord Denning's dissent in *Candler v. Crane Christmas & Co.*, [1951] 1 All E.R. 426 (C.A.), which later found favour in *Hedley Byrne & Co., Ltd. v. Heller & Partners, Ltd.*, [1963] 2 All E.R. 575 (H.L.). After identifying accountants as among those under a duty to use care, Lord Denning, in answer to the question "To whom do these professional people owe this duty?" said, at p. 434:

> They owe the duty, of course, to their employer or client, and also, I think, to any third person to whom they themselves show the accounts, or to whom they know their employer is going to show the accounts so as to induce him to invest money or take some other action on them. I do not think, however, the duty can be extended still further so as to include strangers of whom they have heard nothing and to whom their employer without their knowledge may choose to show their accounts.

and

> The test of proximity in these cases is: Did the accountants know that the accounts were required for submission to the plaintiff and use by him?

One can find some support in these words for the position taken by the majority in the Saskatchewan Court of Appeal but their effect is tempered by what appears later in the judgment. ...

In the case at bar, the accounts were prepared for the guidance of a "specific class of persons," potential investors, in a "specific class of transactions," the investment of $20,000 of equity capital. The number of potential investors would, of necessity, be limited because the Company, as a private company, was prohibited by s. 3 (1) (o) (iii) of the *Companies Act* of Saskatchewan, R.S.S. 1965, c. 131, from extending any invitation to the public to subscribe for shares or debentures of the Company.

One comes then to the *Hedley Byrne* case. The argument was raised in that case that the relationship between the parties was not sufficiently close to give rise to any duty. Lord Reid dealt with that argument in these words, at p. 580:

> It is said that the respondents did not know the precise purpose of the inquiries and did not even know whether National Provincial Bank, Ltd. wanted the information for its own use or

for the use of a customer: they knew nothing of the appellants. I would reject that argument. They knew that the inquiry was in connection with an advertising contract, and it was at least probable that the information was wanted by the advertising contractors. It seems to me quite immaterial that they did not know who these contractors were: there is no suggestion of any speciality which could have influenced them in deciding whether to give information or in what form to give it. I shall therefore treat this as if it were a case where a negligent misrepresentation is made directly to the person seeking information, opinion or advice, and I shall not attempt to decide what kind or degree of proximity is necessary before there can be a duty owed by the defendant to the plaintiff.

In the present case the accountants knew that the financial statements were being prepared for the very purpose of influencing, in addition to the bank and Sedco, a limited number of potential investors. The names of the potential investors were not material to the accountants. What was important was the nature of the transaction or transactions for which the statements were intended, for that is what delineated the limits of potential liability. The speech of Lord Morris of Borthy-Gest in *Hedley Byrne* included this observation. ...

The American Authorities

Judgment in the two leading cases was written by Mr. Justice Cardozo [as he then was]. In *Glanzer et al. v. Shepard et al.* (1922), 233 N.Y. 236, the defendants, public weighers, at the request of a seller of beans, made a return of the weight and furnished the plaintiff buyer with a copy. The buyer paid the seller on the faith of the certificate which turned out to be erroneous. The buyers were entitled to recover from the weighers. The certificate was held to be the very "end and aim" of the transaction and not something issued in the expectation that the seller would use it thereafter in the operations of his business as occasion might require. ...

The Canadian Authorities

The *Hedley Byrne* case has been considered by this Court in *Welbridge Holdings Ltd. v. Metropolitan Corp.* of Greater Winnipeg (1970), 22 D.L.R. (3d) 470, [1971] S.C.R. 957, [1972] 3 W.W.R. 433 (S.C.C.). Recovery for economic loss caused by negligence has been allowed in *Rivtow Marine Ltd. v. Washington Iron Works et al.* (1973), 40 D.L.R. (3d) 530 at p. 546, [1974] S.C.R. 1189 at p. 1213, [1973] 6 W.W.R. 692, where Mr. Justice Ritchie said:

> ...I am of opinion that the case of *Hedley Byrne* represents the considered opinion of five members of the House of Lords to the effect that a negligent misrepresentation may give rise to an action for damages for economic loss occasioned thereby without any physical injury to person or property and apart from any contract or fiduciary relationship...

See also *J. Nunes Diamonds Ltd. v. Dominion Electric Protection Co.* (1972), 26 D.L.R. (3d) 699, [1972] S.C.R. 769.

In summary, Haig placed justifiable reliance upon a financial statement which the accountants stated presented fairly the financial position of the Company as at March 31, 1965. The accountants prepared such statements for reward in the course of their professional duties. The statements were for benefit and guidance in a business transaction, the nature of which was known to the accountants. The accountants were aware that the Company intended to supply the statements to members of a very limited class. Haig was a member of the class. It is true the accountants did not know his name but, as I have indicated earlier, I do not think that is of importance. I can see no good reason for distinguishing between the case in which a defendant accountant delivers information directly to the plaintiff at the request of his employer (*Candler's* case and *Glanzer's* case), and the case in which the information is handed to the employer who, to the knowledge of the accountant, passes it to members of a limited class (whose identity is unknown to the accountant) in furtherance of a transaction the nature of which is known to the accountant. I would accordingly hold that the accountants owed Haig a duty to use reasonable care in the preparation of the accounts.

I am of the view, however, that Haig cannot recover from the accountants the sum of $2,500 which he advanced to the Company in December, 1965, because by that time he was fully cognizant of the true state of affairs. It cannot be said that the sum was advanced in reliance upon false statements. Haig had the choice of advancing additional money in the hope of saving his original investment. He chose to make a further advance, but the choice was his and not one for which the accountants are liable.

I would allow the appeal, set aside the judgment of the Court of Appeal for Saskatchewan and reinstate the judgment of MacPherson, J., subject only to disallowance of the claim of $2,500, the whole with costs in this Court and in the Courts below. ...

Appeal allowed in part.

Kripps et al. *v.* *Touche Ross & Co. et al.*

57 B.C.L.R. (2D) 291
B.C.S.C.. [IN CHAMBERS]
DECEMBER 31, 1990

Summary of the facts: Between 1982 and 1985 the Victoria Mortgage Corporation Ltd. (V.M.C.L.) offered a series of debentures to the public by way of several prospectuses which were reviewed by the defendant accountants Touche Ross & Co. (Touche), which had consented to the inclusion of their audit report on the company's financial statements for 1980-83. Touche, in the body of its audit reports, expressed opinions, without reservation or qualification, to the effect that the financial statements for the periods noted complied with generally accepted accounting principles. In fact, the financial statements failed to make provision for certain anticipated losses to the mortgage receivable portfolio.

The Superintendent of Brokers issued receipts for the prospectuses and thereby authorized the sale of the debentures. The plaintiffs, some six hundred investors, purchased debentures and received copies of the prospectuses prior to confirmation of their purchases. They lost their investments in 1985 when the superintendent issued a cease trading order. The company went into receivership when $10 million was still owing to the debenture holders. The plaintiffs sued the accountants for negligence in preparing the statements and the superintendent for negligence for failing to scrutinize each prospectus for full, true and plain disclosure of all material facts and for issuing receipts for the prospectuses without first obtaining the express consent of Touche. The accountants and the superintendent applied to the court to strike out the plaintiffs' claim for disclosing no reasonable cause of action.

Note: The following are excerpts from the decision of the judge in chambers on the issue of the liability of the accountants.

Boyd J. As I understand it, before summarily striking any portion of the statement of claim, it must be plain and obvious to the chambers judge "at once" that the pleading cannot stand. Put another way, the court must be satisfied that the outcome of the claim at trial is "beyond reasonable doubt." The issue is whether there is a question fit to be tried. ...

Touche submits that even accepting the allegations of facts pleaded, the statement of claim nevertheless discloses no cause of action against it, since, given the lack of proximity between the parties, there is no common law duty of care owed to any of the individual plaintiffs. ... Touche submits that the "public at large" is too large and unidentifiable a class to form the foundation of a relationship of proximity between the parties. Not only was the class of potential investors unlimited but the amount of money which the public at large might invest was unlimited. Further, the transactions themselves were not limited in time but might continue indefinitely. ... As I understand the thrust of Touch's submissions, it is that no liability for an auditor can arise in the case of a public offering of debentures, since by its very nature the transaction involves an "indeterminate class" of persons who might rely on the audited financial statements supported by the prospectus.

In my view, the identification of the specific plaintiffs or the limited class of plaintiffs has not been the focus of the courts. Indeed, before *Caparo* [*Caparo Indust. plc v. Dickman*, a 1990 decision of the English House of Lords] and in the recent decisions following *Caparo*, our courts have focused upon the nature of the transaction in question and have held that liability of an auditor to persons other than the company for which the statements are prepared can include a third party, the identity of whom is not specifically known to the auditor, provided that the auditor is aware of the nature of the transaction for which the statements were intended: *Haig v. Bamford* [1977] 1 S.C.R. 466, [1976] 3 W.W.R. 331, 72 D.L.R. (3d) 68, 27 C.P.R. (2d) 149, 9 N.R. 43. As Dickson J. stated in *Haig* at pp. 478-79:

> In the present case the accountants knew that the financial statements were being prepared

> for the very purpose of influencing, in addition to the bank and Sedco, a limited number of potential investors. *The names of the potential investors were not material to the accountants. What was important was the nature of the transaction or transactions for which the statements were intended, for that is what delineated the limits of potential liability.*[emphasis added]

This focus upon the auditor's knowledge of the purpose of transaction is seen again in the recent decision of McColl J. in *Surrey Credit Union.* supra. Months before the collapse of the Northland Bank, the bank sought out the Surrey Credit Union (S.C.U.) as a potential purchaser of the debentures. S.C.U. eventually invested $7.5 million in a private offering supported by the financial statements prepared by Thorne Riddell and Clarkson Gordon. At pp. 7-8 [pp. 107-108], the court considered the relationship between the parties:

> The relationship between S.C.U. and the defendants was not, strictly speaking, that of strangers. The defendants were Northland's auditors. Northland sought out S.C.U. as a prospective purchaser of debentures it wished to offer. It could not do so, without, in the case of a public offering, issuing a prospectus which required a disclosure of the last financial statements of Northland, or in the case of a confidential offering, a private offering memorandum which also required the disclosure of the audited statements. In the present case, Northland initially sought to make a public offering. It sought and obtained the consent of the defendants to the disclosure of the audited statements. The defendants knew the purpose for which the consent was being required. They knew that without the consent, the audited statements could not be disclosed. They knew that the debentures could not be issued without the audited statements. Knowing that to be the case, they gave their consent without qualification. When the public offering was later withdrawn by Northland and a private offering put in its place, consent was similarly obtained.
>
> In my view, once the defendants knew the purpose for which the consent to use the audited statements was being sought, they could no longer say that debenture purchasers were strangers. The debentures were being offered for the sole purpose of attracting capital to Northland. The defendants were auditors of international reputation. They knew the circumstances and purpose for which consent was sought.

There, McColl J. held that the only issue to be addressed was whether S.C.U. in fact relied on those financial statements and whether the reliance was reasonable.

Touche submits that this decision is limited to its facts, that is, to the case of a private offering which by definition is an offering to a limited class of persons, and is not authority for the proposition that where an auditor's report is included in a prospectus offered to the public at large, a duty of care will be owed to those persons who acquire the debentures.

I am not satisfied that the decision in *Surrey Credit Union* is so limited. Indeed, in the vast majority of the cases cited by all parties, the courts repeatedly emphasize that the finding of a sufficient proximity will vary with the facts. Accepting the facts pleaded in the amended statement of claim, it follows that the auditor's report was contained in the prospectus of V.M.C.L. with the consent of Touche. I find that there are sufficient facts pleaded which, if proven at trial, will give rise to a duty of care owed by Touche Ross to the plaintiffs.

Whatever the statutory requirements and purposes set out in the Company Act and the Securities Act, Touche was auditing the financial statements not simply for the benefit of the superintendent but for those persons who would acquire the debentures from V.M.C.L. Accepting the pleadings, Touche knew that the financial statements contained in the prospectuses and its consent to use the audit reports contained in the prospectuses allowed V.M.C.L. to issue prospectuses, inviting the public to purchase a series of debentures. Thus Touche was aware of the nature of the transaction and was aware of the fact that an identifiable class of persons (that class of persons who would attend the offices of V.M.C.L. to obtain the prospectuses) would receive the information contained in the financial statements and audit reports and would likely rely on that information in deciding whether or not to purchase the debentures. True, Touche would be unaware of the names of the individual investors. But, as Dickson J. stated in *Haig,* Touche was aware of the "nature of the transaction" or as McColl J. stated in *Surrey Credit Union,* the auditors were aware of the "circumstances and purpose for which consent was sought."

For all of these reasons, those portions of the statement of claim concerning the plaintiffs' claim against Touche based on their actual reliance upon the financial statements and auditor's reports prepared by Touche must stand. In my view, given the facts pleaded, Touch has not succeeded in proving "absolutely beyond doubt" that the pleadings disclose no reasonable cause of action: McNaughton v. Baker, 25 B.C.L.R. (2d) 17 at 25, [1988] 4 W.W.R. 742, 28 C.P.C. (2d) 49 (C.A.)

Note 1: All appeals from this ruling were dismissed (in a fifty-page decision) by the B.C. Court of Appeal on July 8, 1992. *The Lawyers Weekly* August 28, 1992 p. 22

Note 2: Watch for a report of the trial of this case and of *Toronto-Dominion Bank v. Deloitte Haskins Sells* in which Justice Blair of the Ontario Court (General Division) did not strike out the plaintiff's statement of claim alleging the auditor's liability for negligent misstatement. The decision of the judges who try these cases may be significant in settling the law in Canada on the scope of an auditor's liability.

See *The Lawyers Weekly* Oct. 18, 1991 pp. 1 and 9

Queen v. Cognos

SUPREME COURT OF CANADA
99 D.L.R. (4TH) 626
JANUARY 21, 1993

Background facts: Mr. Queen, a chartered accountant, was interviewed for a position as manager, financial standards, for the development of accounting software. He was not told in the interview that the funding for the project was not guaranteed nor that it was subject to budgetary approval by senior management. He left a secure position to join Cognos, Inc. A few months after he signed the employment contract he was told there would be reassignments because of cuts in research and development. Within two years he had received an effective termination notice; the employment contract had allowed for the termination of his employment at any time.

Mr. Queen sued the employer for negligent misstatement. He won at the trial level, but the decision was reversed by the Ontario Court of Appeal.

per Iacobucci J.: — This appeal involves the application of the tort of negligent misrepresentation to a pre-employment representation made by an employer to a prospective employee in the course of a hiring interview. Specifically, the court is being asked to determine in what circumstances a representation made during a hiring interview becomes, in law, a "negligent misrepresentation". A subsidiary question deals with the effect of a subsequent employment agreement signed by the plaintiff, and its provisions allowing termination "without cause" and reassignment, on a claim for damages for negligent misrepresentation. …

This appeal involves an action in tort to recover damages caused by alleged negligent misrepresentation made in the course of a hiring interview by an employer (the respondent), through its representative, to a prospective employee (the appellant) with respect to the employer and the nature and existence of the employment opportunity. Though a relatively recent feature of the common law, the tort of negligent misrepresentation relied on by the appellant and first recognized by the House of Lords in *Hedley Byrne, supra,* [*Hedley Byrne & Co. Ltd. v. Heller & Partners Ltd.* [1964] A.C. 465] is now an established principle of Canadian tort law. This court has confirmed on many occasions, sometimes tacitly, that an action in tort may lie, in appropriate circumstances, for damages caused by a misrepresentation made in a negligent manner: . …

While the doctrine of Hedley Byrne is well established in Canada, the exact breadth of its applicability is, like any common law principle, subject to debate and to continuous development. At the time this appeal was heard, there had only been a handful of cases where the tort of negligent misrepresentation was used in a pre-employment context such as the one involved here: … Without question, the present factual situation is a novel one for this court.

Some have suggested that it is inappropriate to extend the application of *Hedley Byrne, supra,* to representations made by an employer to a prospective employee in the course of an interview because it places a heavy burden on employers. As will be apparent for my reasons herein, I disagree in principle with this view. ...

[T]his appeal may be disposed of simply by considering whether or not the required elements under the *Hedley Byrne* doctrine are established in the facts of this case. In my view, they are.

The required elements for a successful *Hedley Byrne* claim have been stated in many authorities, sometimes in varying forms. The decisions of this court cited above suggest five general requirements:

(1) there must be a duty of care based on a "special relationship" between the representor and the representee;
(2) the representation in question must be untrue, inaccurate, or misleading;
(3) the representor must have acted negligently in making said misrepresentation;
(4) the representee must have relied, in a reasonable manner, on said negligent misrepresentation; and
(5) the reliance must have been detrimental to the representee in the sense that damages resulted.

In the case at bar, the trial judge found that all elements were present and allowed the appellant's claim. ...

[After a lengthy review of the decisions of the lower courts, the relevant case law and the facts, the justice concluded.] In my view, the appellant has established all the required elements to succeed in his action. The respondent and its representative, Mr. Johnston, owed a duty of care to the appellant during the course of the hiring interview to exercise such reasonable care as the circumstances required to ensure that the representations made were accurate and not misleading. This duty of care is distinct from, and additional to, the duty of common honesty existing between negotiating parties. The trial judge found, as a fact, that misrepresentations — both express and implied — were made to the appellant and that he relied upon them, reasonably I might add, to his eventual detriment. In all the circumstances of this case, I agree with the trial judge that these misrepresentations were made by Mr. Johnston in a negligent manner. While a subsequent contract may, in appropriate cases, affect a Hedley Byrne claim relying on pre-contractual representations, the employment agreement signed by the appellant is irrelevant to this action. In particular, cls.13 and 14 of the contract [regarding reassignment and termination] are not valid disclaimers of responsibility for the representations made during the interview.

For the foregoing reasons, I would allow the appeal, set aside the judgment of the Ontario Court of Appeal, and restore the judgment of White J., finding the respondent liable and granting the appellant damages in the amount of $67,224. The appellant should have his costs here and in the courts below.

Appeal allowed

Mr. and Mrs. Wright purchased a house outside London, Ontario only after having been assured by the telephone company that the house would be within the exchange of London, so that calls to friends and family in London would not be subject to long distance charges. The serviceman who came to install the telephone told them that the house was not within the 666 exchange. The Wrights sued the telephone company for negligent misstatement and claimed damages in an amount equal to their telephone charges for calls within the 666 exchange. The judge who first heard the case in Small Claims Court, relying on *Hedley Byrne v. Heller*, held for the plaintiffs. The Wrights returned with another bill and the judge again held for the plaintiffs on the ground that it was a breach of contract and that the damages were continuing. He urged the telephone company to resolve the difficulty. Its failure to do so would lead to the Wrights' return to court.

Wright v. Bell Canada
Summarized from The Lawyers Weekly
July 3, 1987 p.11

6. Voluntary Assumption of Risk / Contributory Negligence

Poirier et al. v. Murphy et al.

36 C.C.L.T. 160
British Columbia Supreme Court
February 17, 1986.

MacKinnon J.: — On June 24, 1982 the plaintiff Peter Albert Poirier (Poirier) and the defendant John Anthony Murphy (Murphy), each 18 years of age, agreed to perform and in fact did carry out a "stunt" which resulted in Poirier being injured by the car driven by Murphy. With Poirier and Murphy, as passengers, were three girls and two boys, all around 17 years of age. They had been driving around with no particular destination and were looking for something to do. A conversation took place between Poirier and Murphy about doing a "stunt." The passengers were unaware of what this meant. However, they did hear Murphy asking Poirier to do it and Poirier refusing twice and then agreeing. The stunt was done in an underground parking lot of the Lougheed Mall in Coquitlam where Poirier would stand underneath a water sprinkler pipe and Murphy, as the driver of the car, from a position about 100 feet away, would drive towards Poirier and at the last moment Poirier would jump up, grab the pipe, do a chin-up, and swerve his hips and legs to one side, and thereby allow the car to pass under him. The expected clearance between Poirier's body and the car would be approximately 4 to 6 inches. It was intended to be thrilling to the participants and anybody watching. It was certainly a dangerous act. In the past, and on the occasion of the accident, the signal indicating that Poirier was ready for the stunt to commence was a slight nod by Poirier. It was to be seen only by Murphy. On observing the signal (the slight nod by Poirier) Murphy would drive the car toward Poirier and expect him to escape any impact. ...

[After reviewing the testimony of the witnesses, the Judge continued:] Thus, on the first run, it would appear the stunt performance went as planned with one exception. It almost failed. Even though Poirier signalled to Murphy his readiness for the commencement he was not able to completely escape contact with the car. His foot or part of his body was hit by the car. That impact did not release his grip on the pipes so as to cause a fall but it was of a sufficient force to be perceived by two of the passengers.

On the second run there are different stories as to what occurred. I do not accept Murphy's evidence that on the second run he backed up and performed the second stunt in the same way as the first. Other witnesses testified that he made a U-turn, headed at Poirier with his back facing Murphy. I have concluded that, after completing his first run, Murphy turned the car around in some manner and immediately commenced his run from the opposite direction. At this time Poirier was still hanging from the pipe. I find Poirier did not signal his readiness for Murphy to start the second run. Notwithstanding Mark Anderson's cry to stop, Murphy proceeded ahead in the belief that Poirier would pull himself up and avoid the impact.

The issues

1. Does the maxim of *volenti non fit injuria* apply to the circumstances of this case?
2. If not, was there contributory negligence?
3. Damages.

Volenti non fit injuria

The defendant submits the plaintiff knew, or ought to have known, the real risk involved in carrying out the stunt and that, when he agreed to do it, he impliedly exempted the defendant from liability. The defendant says that Poirier consented to assume the risk without compensation, and he absolved Murphy from the duty to take care.

Cartwright J., in delivering the majority judgment of the Supreme Court of Canada in *Stein v. Lehnert*, [1963] S.C.R. 38, 40 W.W.R. 616, 36 D.L.R. (2d) 159 said, at p. 620 [W.W.R.]:

> "The decision of this court in *Seymour v. Maloney; Car and Gen. Insur. Corpn. (Third Party)* [1956] SCR 322,...establishes that where a driver of a motor vehicle invokes the maxim *volenti non fit injuria* as a defence to an action for damages for injuries caused by his negligence to a passenger, the burden lies upon the defendant of proving that the plaintiff, expressly or by necessary implication, agreed to exempt the defendant from liability for any damage suffered by the plaintiff occasioned by that negligence, and that, as stated in *Salmond on Torts*,

13th ed., p.44:

> 'The true question in every case is: did the plaintiff give a real consent to the assumption of the risk without compensation; did the consent really absolve the defendant from the duty to take care?' "

In *Lackner v. Neath* (1966), 57 W.W.R. 496, 58 D.L.R. (2d) 662 (Sask. C.A.) Culliton C.J.S., quoted the excerpt from *Stein v. Lehnert*, supra, and then stated at p. 489 [W.W.R.]:

> Clearly, then, to admit the defence of *volenti non fit injuria* there must be established, either by direct evidence or by inference, that the plaintiff: (a) Voluntarily assumed the physical risk; and (b) Agreed to give up his right for negligence, or, to put it more briefly, that the plaintiff accepted both the physical and legal risk. ...

In *Deskau v. Dziama; Brooks v. Dziama*, [1973] 3 O.R. 101, 36 D.L.R. (3d) 36, the plaintiff agreed to assume the risk of riding with the defendant driver whom he knew was driving the car over hills at high speeds so that the car would fly from the crest of the hill with all four wheels off the ground. Keith J. found the nature of the risk voluntarily assumed by the plaintiff was unlimited. He said at p. 106 [O.R.]:

> I respectfully agree with the following statement from Fleming, *Law of Torts*, 4th ed. (1971), pp. 243-4:
>
> 'Formerly it mattered nothing whether a plaintiff was defeated on the ground of voluntary assumption of risk or contributory negligence. Now, however, the distinction has become critical, since the relevant legislation does not purport to extend apportionment to voluntary assumption of risk. All the more reason therefore for the courts to have taken an ever more restrictive view of the defence (sic *volenti no fit injuria*) in order to avoid the distasteful consequence of having to deny the plaintiff all recovery instead of merely reducing his award. In the result, the defence is nowadays but rarely invoked with success.' ...

The defendant submits, and I agree, that had Poirier been injured in the first run the authorities would support the application of the doctrine of *volens*, and his claim would be dismissed. ...

He did not give such approval on the second run. Unlike the first stunt, Poirier was not ready for the second. He did not expect Murphy from that direction. After the first run he may have remained swinging from the water pipes so as to stay out of the way as Murphy was to (but did not) return to the starting position for the second stunt. Had Murphy done so, Poirier could have indicated or withheld his signal to commence the second stunt.

Accordingly, I have concluded that Poirier had not assumed the physical risk of the second stunt and the defence of *volens* does not succeed.

Contributory negligence

Murphy was negligent. As the driver of a motor vehicle, he owed a duty to drive it in a manner different than he did in the underground parking lot where the accident occurred. He was negligent in doing the stunt. He was negligent in failing to hear the noise in the first stunt (Poirier's foot), in failing to pay heed to the passenger's cry to stop, and in failing to recognize that Poirier was not ready for the second stunt. His negligence caused or contributed to the damages suffered by Poirier.

Poirier contributed to his own fate. He failed to take reasonable care for himself. He clearly was negligent in agreeing to the stunt. Though he may not have agreed to the second stunt being done in the manner it was, he placed himself in a hazardous position and failed to remove himself from the risk.

In my view Poirier and Murphy were equally negligent in the first run, and both were negligent in the second. In the second run I attach more blame to Murphy. I apportion the liability two-thirds on the shoulders of Murphy and one-third on Poirier. ...

The plaintiff is entitled to two-thirds of the damages together with court order interest.

Action allowed.

Celebrating the end of the fall term, Mr. Campbell had already had six beers before he arrived with his friends at The Spoke Tavern run by the Student Council. After he had two more beers he was refused more and told he would be asked to leave if he did have more. He returned to the table and continued to drink. He was ordered to leave. While being escorted out, he resisted but was ejected. He sneaked back in, "spoiling for a fight" and was removed once more. He returned and, when pushed through the doorway, he stumbled, his hand went through a small window and he had to undergo surgery to repair a tendon in his wrist and a nerve in his thumb. Mr. Campbell sued the tavern, the bouncer and the student council as operators of the tavern under the *Occupiers' Liability Act.*

The court held that neither the staff nor the principal of the tavern were liable. They had honoured their duty and "Campbell voluntarily assumed the very risk which ultimately befell him by returning as he did."

Campbell v. The Spoke Tavern et al.
Summarized from The Lawyers Weekly
November 27, 1987 p. 31

D. STRICT LIABILITY

Gertsen et al. v. *Municipality of Metropolitan Toronto et al.*

41 D.L.R. (3D) 646
ONTARIO HIGH COURT
AUGUST 21, 1973

[As summarized in the law report:]

By joint agreement, the first municipality brought putrescible organic matter on to the lands of the second municipality in order to dispose of the matter by way of land-fill. Subsequently, as this organic matter decomposed, it generated methane gas which escaped into adjoining lands on which private homes had been constructed and on one occasion caused a fire in a garage which led to the residents being required to park their cars on the street. Still later, however, an official of the municipality which owned the land assured the resident who had suffered fire that the problem had been solved and that garages could again be used. Plaintiffs, having heard this information from its original recipient, began to use their garage again. However, methane gas continued to escape from the land-fill site and filled plaintiffs' garage so that on one occasion when the male plaintiff turned on the ignition of plaintiffs' car an explosion destroyed the garage, damaged the car and injured the male plaintiff.

In an action against both municipalities, *held,* both were strictly liable for the escape of the dangerous substance. A land-fill project as a means of disposing of garbage is a non-natural user [sic] of land in a heavily populated residential district. While the first municipality had statutory authority to pass by-laws for acquiring land for the purposes of dumping and disposing of garbage under s.214b (enacted 1956, c.53, s.23) of the *Municipality of Metropolitan Toronto Act,* 1953 (Ont.), c.73 (now R.S.O. 1970, c.295), the project was not carried out pursuant to that statutory authority.

Furthermore, the continuing generation and escape of gas, with injurious consequences reasonably to be anticipated, constituted a nuisance. It would, however, be impractical and unrealistic to require the second municipality to abate the nuisance by removing the garbage fill. Plaintiffs should be awarded damages for the interference with the beneficial use of their land.

Finally, defendants were liable in negligence for the damage in burying the garbage as they did when they knew or ought to have known that its decomposition would result in the production of gas, in failing to take steps to prevent the escape of the gas, in failing to warn the adjoining owners of the risk and, in the case of the second defendant, negligently misrepresenting that the problem had been solved.

Fletcher v. Rylands (1866), L.R. 1 Ex. 265; affd L.R. 3 H.L. 330; *Hedley Byrne & Co., Ltd. v. Heller & Partners Ltd.*, [1964] A.C. 465, apld; *Read v. J. Lyons & Co., Ltd.*, [1947] A.C. 156; *Dunn et al. v. Birmingham Canal Co.* (1872), L.R. 7 Q.B. 244; *Rickards v. Lothian*, [1913] A.C. 263; *Rainham Chemical Works, Ltd. (in Liquidation) et al. v. Belvedere Fish Guano Co., Ltd.*, [1921] 2 A.C. 465; *London Guarantee and Accident Co., Ltd. et al. v. Northwestern Utilities Ltd.*, [1935] 4 D.L.R. 737, [1936] A.C. 108, [1935] 3 W.W.R. 44, 3 I.L.R. 1; *Pride of Derby and Derbyshire Angling Ass'n Ltd. et al. v. British Celanese Ltd. et al.*, [1953] 1 Ch. 149; *Gadutsis et al. v. Milne* et al., [1973] 2 O.R. 503, 34 D.L.R. (3d) 455; *J. P. Porter Co. Ltd. v. Bell et al.*, [1955] 1. D.L.R. 62, 35 M.P.R. 13; *Esso Petroleum Co., Ltd. v. Southport Corporation*, [1956] A.C. 218; *Newman et al. v. Conair Aviation Ltd. et al.* (1972), 33 D.L.R. (3d) 474, [1973] 1 W.W.R. 317, refd to]

E. Res Ipsa Loquitur

Questions

Because it is so difficult for the plaintiff to prove the elements of negligence, does the law ever allow the plaintiff to shift the burden of proof?

If the court does shift the burden of proof, does the plaintiff automatically win?

Mathews v. Coca-Cola Co. of Canada Ltd.

2 D.L.R. 355
Ontario Court of Appeal
February 29, 1944

Robertson C.J.O.:—This is an appeal by the plaintiff in the action from the judgment of Judge Schwenger, dated July 30, 1943, in an action tried before him at Hamilton, without a jury. The plaintiff's action was dismissed with costs.

On the 12th January 1942 appellant went to a restaurant in Hamilton, and was served with a bottle of Coca-Cola. On proceeding to drink it she noticed an unpleasant taste. She called the attention of the waitress to it, and on examination a dead mouse was found in the bottle. The appellant had some illness as the result, and the learned County Judge assessed her damages at $350 in case it should be found on appeal that she was entitled to damages.

It lies at the threshold of the appellant's case that she must establish that the contents of the bottle of Coca-Cola with which the waitress in the restaurant served her, were the contents of the bottle when it left respondent's hands. Unless this is established respondent is clearly under no liability whatsoever. ...

I do not suppose that anyone would seriously contend that the mouse—alive or dead—got into the bottle during the process of cleansing and filling. This process is carried on with machines, and is a continuous one, the bottles being brought to the machines in regular rotation on conveyors running upon rollers as an endless chain. There are attendants at the various stages of the process to see that things are going as they should. It seems an unlikely time for a mouse to get in. The experts who saw the process in operation say it is impossible. The empty bottles, however, after use are gathered up by respondent from its customers, who are allowed a rebate on their return. It is unlikely that any special care is taken of the bottles once they are empty and are awaiting the gathering up and the process of washing and re-filling. Mice, in their ceaseless search for food, are apt to be about the premises of restaurants and grocery shops, and the other places where such drinks as Coca-Cola are commonly sold, and it is admitted by respondent's foreman that he has seen mice in respondent's premises. It is a likely enough thing that a mouse searching for food should get inside an empty bottle, and perhaps have difficulty in getting out again. It would seem more likely that a mouse would get into an empty bottle at this time rather than at any later time. Whether such a mouse might still remain in the bottle after respondent's process of cleansing and refilling depends on whether the process is so thoroughly efficient as to exclude that possibility.

The experts to whose evidence the learned Judge refers are, one of them a consulting engineer, and the other, a travelling salesman and service-man for a manufacturer of bottle-caps and bottling machinery. These witnesses give a detailed description of the process followed in washing the empty bottles and in refilling them and crowning them ready for sale. They also made tests or experiments by putting foreign substances in bottles at one stage and another. It might have been useful if they had tried a dead mouse, but they did not. These experts commend highly respondent's process, and one of them expresses the opinion that no foreign substance of a substantial size could get through that system and come out in a full bottle of Coca-Cola. In forming this opinion, however, the complete efficiency of respondent's employees whose duty it is to look out for indications of the presence of foreign substances, is assumed. That there is not always that complete efficiency plainly appears by the evidence of another of respondent's witnesses.

There are a number of employees stationed along the line of the conveyor system on which the bottles are carried through the cleansing and filling process. Six of these employees have a duty to watch for defective bottles, bottles that contain foreign substances, and such matters. Five of the six have other functions to perform in the process, but one of them, called the inspector, has only that duty to perform. He is stationed at the point where the cleansing process has finished and the filling process is to begin. There are special lights provided to aid him, and he and another operator alternate as inspectors, in periods of 20 minutes each, because of the strain on the eyes. No doubt, the system is a good one, and that it serves a useful purpose is certain, for the inspectors, as well as others who have a duty to watch, do detect bottles they require to reject. It is highly significant, however, that the attendants further along the line than the inspector, find such bottles. Through some failure on the part of the attendants who have allowed them to pass their inspection, other "rejects" are taken out of the line, even by the last of the six attendants watching for them. Each of the six is supplied with a box in which to place his "rejects", and another employee is assigned the duty of removing these boxes when full, and putting empty boxes in their place. This also is part of the regular routine, and it is, therefore, well within the knowledge of respondent that, mechanically, its process is not completely efficient in cleansing the bottles of all foreign substances, and that the employees make mistakes. There is nothing in evidence to support the view that the last man of the six watching attendants, is infallible, when none of the other five is. ...

With respect to the alterative suggestion that the mouse was placed in the bottle surreptitiously after its processing had been completed, there is not a great deal to be said, for their [sic] is no evidence of any facts that support it. There is no evidence that any person had any motive for doing such a thing, or an opportunity and the facilities for doing it. There is evidence of the keeper of the restaurant, that there were no loose tops on the bottles he put in the cooler. The waitress swears that the contents of the bottle "fizzed" normally, when she opened it. While the evidence may fall short of proving that such an occurrence as is suggested, was impossible, there is an utter absence of evidence of its probability. ...

With great respect for the learned County Judge, I am of the opinion that the balance of probabilities on this question is strongly in favour of the appellant, and as there is no question of the credibility of witnesses involved, I am compelled to the conclusion that the finding of fact should be that the bottle in question, when supplied by respondent to the keeper of the restaurant, contained the dead mouse found in it when served to the appellant. ...

The moot question would seem to be whether the manufacturer sells his products "in such a form as to show that he intends them to reach the ultimate consumer in the form in which they left him with no reasonable possibility of intermediate ," to quote the words of Lord Atkin in *M'Alister (or Donoghue) v. Stevenson,* [1932] A.C. 562 at p. 599, specifically approved by the Judicial Committee in *Grant v. Australian Knitting Mills Ltd.,* [1936] A.C. 85 at p. 102. A "reasonable possibility" denotes an event that reasonably may happen, rather than something that can happen. The sealed bottles of Coca-Cola were delivered by the respondent in cases at the restaurant, the cases being delivered to the "pop-room" in the basement, where they remained until the cooler upstairs in the restaurant required to be re-filled. I find no evidence that would indicate any reasonable possibility of an intermediate examination of the bottle before being served to a customer, although it is not impossible that a suspicious person making a careful examination in a strong light would have discovered the dead mouse.

The appeal should be allowed and the appellant should recover the sum of $350, at which the damages were assessed by the County Court Judge. The appellant is entitled to her costs of the action and of the appeal. ...

Gillanders J.A.:... I take it from these findings that the trial Judge does not doubt that the bottle and the contents, apart from the dead mouse, were supplied by the respondents. Of the two alternatives that the mouse was in the bottle before it went to the washing machine or was placed in the bottle surreptitiously after the processing had been completed, the learned Judge, if necessary, would find the latter. There is no evidence to support such a finding, other than whatever inference, if any, should be drawn if other possibilities can be eliminated. To place a dead mouse in a bottle of soft drink after processing would, under the circumstances here, be highly mischievous. It might possibly make the person responsible, if discovered, subject to criminal prosecution.

There is a presumption against such an act. ... There is, I think, a presumption here which might, of course, be rebutted, against a finding that the dead mouse was mischievously put in the soft drink after processing and after it left the respondents' possession. ...

On all the evidence here the appellant must be held to have sufficiently established her case. The appeal must be allowed with costs, and the appellant should have judgment for $350, the amount at which her damages were assessed with costs on the County Court scale.

Appeal allowed.

Zeppa v. Coca-Cola Ltd.

5 D.L.R. 187
ONTARIO COURT OF APPEAL
OCTOBER 21, 1955

Pickup C.J.O.: —This is an appeal by the plaintiff from the judgment of Moorhouse J. in an action tried by him with a jury at Toronto. The plaintiff's action was dismissed.

The action arises out of injuries sustained by the appellant from particles of glass when drinking from a bottle of Coca-Cola manufactured by the respondent. The bottle of Coca-Cola was one of a six-bottle carton purchased by the appellant from a drug-store in Toronto, and the evidence establishes that the Coca-Cola was manufactured and delivered to the drug-store by the respondent.

Relying upon the findings of the jury that the Coca-Cola was manufactured and sold by the respondent and that the particles of glass were in the bottle when delivered by the respondent to the retailer, the appellant contends that she had made out a *prima facie* case and that the burden was then upon the respondent to show that the particles of glass did not get into the bottle through any negligence of the respondent. Counsel for the appellant asks this Court to reverse the judgment appealed from and to enter judgment for the plaintiff for the amount of damages assessed by the jury.

In the alternative, counsel for the appellant asks this Court to set aside the judgment of the learned trial Judge and direct a new trial on the ground of misdirection on the part of the learned trial Judge in his charge to the jury. In his charge to the jury the learned trial Judge plainly directed the jury that the burden of proving negligence against the respondent was on the appellant throughout but he did not instruct the jury that if they found that the particles of glass were in the bottle of Coca-Cola at the time it left the manufacturer they could presume negligence on the part of the respondent unless the respondent established to their satisfaction that the particles of glass got into the bottle without any negligence on the part of the respondent. ...

[After reviewing the law judge concluded:]

In my opinion the language used by Gillanders J.A. in the *Mathews* case applies in the instant appeal.

Upon consideration of these cases and other cases cited by counsel, which I do not think I need discuss, I reach the following conclusions:

(1) That where a manufacturer delivers a product, such as Coca-Cola, intending it to reach the consumer without intermediate examination before use by the consumer he has assumed a legal duty to the consumer to take reasonable care to see that the product does not contain some substance which may injure the consumer. The degree of care required may vary according to the facts of each particular case but I do not think the manufacturer can escape liability by saying that an intermediary, such as a retailer to whom he delivered his product, might have discovered the injurious substance by an examination which it was never intended he should make.

(2) That when a plaintiff proves that he has been injured by an injurious substance, such as particles of glass, which he would not be expected to observe in a bottle containing a product such as Coca-Cola, he using the product in the manner intended by the manufacturer, and proves that the particles of glass were in the product when it left the manufacturer, there is a presumption of negligence on the part of the manufacturer and a burden upon him of disproving negligence on his part to the satisfaction of the jury. This presumption, in my opinion, applies notwithstanding that the product was furnished through a retailer and not directly by the manufacturer to the consumer. I think prior decisions in this Court, by which I am bound, so hold.

The jury having found that the particles of glass which caused the injury in the instant case were in the bottle of Coca-Cola when it left the manufacturer, a presumption of negligence against the respondent arose, in my opinion, in the facts of this case. It was not a case where one would expect any examination of the product after it left the manufacturer and before consumption in order to ascertain if it contained some injurious substance and it is not, in my opinion, a case where the consumer would be expected to observe the injurious substance. I agree that negligence in a case such as this must be averred and proved but it was averred and, in my opinion, was proved when the appellant proved facts from which it should be presumed, unless it should be found at the end of the case that the presumption has been rebutted to the satisfaction of the jury.

It follows, I think, that the jury were not properly instructed in this case and that their finding that there was no negligence on the part of the respondent cannot be given effect to.

The appeal should therefore be allowed with costs and the judgment of the learned trial Judge should be set aside. It is not a case where judgment should be entered for the plaintiff on the evidence, as the jury have not, in my opinion, passed upon the issue with proper direction as to the law by the learned trial Judge. I would direct a new trial of the action, costs of the former trial to be in the discretion of the Judge presiding at the new trial. I would not limit the new trial to the question of liability but think that it should be a new trial on all issues.

New trial ordered.

The Cohen family had suffered stomach cramps and nausea for a few days before the son noticed white maggots crawling inside the top part of a bottle of Heinz ketchup. The family sued the seller, but also sued H.J. Heinz Co. and argued *res ipsa loquitur.*

The judge did not think that the principle would apply "or even if it did, whether this principle would assist the plaintiffs to any extent, in view of the evidence tendered by Heinz of careful preparation and proper handling of the product, which evidence I have accepted." Heinz submitted evidence showing that a vacuum is created in the bottle before the ketchup is inserted, that the ketchup is inserted at a minimum temperature of 190 degrees Fahrenheit, and that the fruit fly would have had to enter the bottle after it left the manufacturer to have maggots discovered on the date given.

Cohen et al. v. H. J. Heinz Company of Canada Limited and Valdi Discount Foods
Summarized from The Lawyers Weekly
October 17, 1986 p. 7.

Judge O'Regan found no difficulty in applying the principle *res ipsa loquitur* to a case in which the plaintiff alleged she ate glass in a pizza.[40]

Endnotes

1. *The Globe and Mail*, February 9, 1993, p. A12
2. *The Lawyers Weekly,* February 12, 1988, p. 8
3. For more particulars, see *The Lawyers Weekly,* September 15, 1990, p. 8
4. A more detailed account is given in the *Vancouver Sun,* January, 1987
5. A more detailed account is given in the *Vancouver Sun,* March 23, 1982
6. A more detailed account is given in *Newsweek,* June, 1989
7. A more detailed account is given in the *National,* April, 1986
8. A more detailed account is given in the *Vancouver Sun,* December 1, 1987
9. A more detailed account is given in the *Vancouver Sun,* October 24, 1989
10. *The Lawyers Weekly,* August 25, 1989, p. 5
11. *The Lawyers Weekly,* January 19, 1990, p. 23
12. A more detailed account is given in the *Vancouver Sun,* January, 1984
13. A more detailed account is given in the *Vancouver Sun,* April 15, 1985
14. For a more detailed account see the *Vancouver Sun,* January 13, 1993, p. A3
15. *National,* July, 1988
16. *Ontario Lawyers Weekly,* September 6, 1985
17. *Datamation,* 1983

18. *Computer World,* February 27, 1984
19. A more detailed account is given in *Newsweek*
20. A more detailed account is given in *The Lawyers Weekly,* December 17, 1993, p. 14
21. *The Globe and Mail,* November 5, 1992, p. A13
22. *The Globe and Mail,* February 9, 1993, pp. B1, 7
23. For a more detailed account see *The Globe and Mail,* January 6, 1994, pp. 1, 2
24. *The Lawyers Weekly,* September 11, 1992, p. 14
25. *The Globe and Mail,* January 4, 1992, p. A5
26. A more detailed account is given in *Vancouver Sun,* January 14, 1992 p. A5
27. A more detailed account is given in *Newsweek,* April 22, 1991, p. 34
28. A more detailed account is given in *Time* magazine, January 23, 1984
29. A more detailed account is given in the *Vancouver Sun,* July 5, 1993, p. 1
30. *The Lawyers Weekly,* March 8, 1990
31. A more detailed account is given in the *Vancouver Sun,* January 22, 1993, p. C1
32. *CBC Radio,* January 18, 1994
33. A more detailed account is given in the *The Lawyers Weekly,* March 25, 1994, p. 1
34. *Ontario Lawyers Weekly*
35. A more detailed account is given in the *Vancouver Sun*
36. *The Lawyers Weekly,* April 21, 1981, p. 20
37. *The Lawyers Weekly,* May 4, 1990
38. *The Globe and Mail,* January 21, 1989
39. A more detailed account is given in the *Vancouver Sun,* January, 1985
40. Carew v. Midway Gardens Ltd., Supreme Court of Newfoundland, Trial Division file no.: 1990 H.V./G.B. 56 April 29, 1992

III

THE LAW OF CONTRACT

A. Freedom of Contract

Question

What kind of deals are we allowed to make?

The engineering firm SNC-Lavalin Inc. signed a contract with the Thai government to design and build a $3 billion mass transit system in Bangkok, Thailand, one billion of which will be spent in Canada.[1]

The rock group Guns N' Roses insists that reporters and photographers sign a contract which provides that the interviewer must "acknowledge that [the band] shall own all right, title and interest, including, without limitation, the copyright, in and to the interview and all transcriptions or summaries thereof...(it being understood that for the purposes of your services hereunder, you shall be our employee for hire.)" and that the interview be submitted to them for their written approval which can be withheld for any reason. The contract stipulates that any party in breach of the agreement will pay them $100,000 as damages.[2]

B. Formation of Contracts

Question

A contract is often defined as an agreement the law will enforce, but that is not too helpful. What elements in particular must be present before the law will enforce an agreement ?

1. General Duty of Good Faith

In 1967, Gateway Realty Ltd. (Gateway), the owner of a shopping centre, rented space to Zellers, a retail chain. The lease gave Zellers the right to assign or sublet. The store was successful with annual sales over $14 million by the late 1980s. Mr. Hurst, the owner of a rival shopping centre, Bridgewater Mall, persuaded Zellers to open a store in the new mall. Furthermore, Zellers assigned the remainder of its lease in the shopping centre to another of Mr. Hursts's companies, Arton Holdings and LaHave Developments (Arton). When Gateway Realty learned that its lessee had assigned its premises to its competitor it met with Hurst; Arton signed an agreement to use its best efforts to lease the space to suitable tenants. Gateway received inquiries about the space, but despite notices to Arton from Gateway, Arton did not follow up on any leads. Gateway took possession and eventually leased the space to K-mart.

Gateway took an action against Arton for a declaration that Zeller's assignment to Arton was invalid because Zellers had breached its duty of good faith by assigning the remainder of the lease to Gateway's main competitor; or a declaration that Gateway was entitled to terminate the lease with Arton because it had breached its duty of good faith to find a suitable replacement tenant. Arton defended by relying on the lease, which gave an unrestricted right to assign and by claiming that, in Canada, there was no duty of good faith in the performance of contracts. Justice Kelly of the N.S.S.C. found that "the law requires that parties to a contract exercise their rights under the agreement honestly fairly and in good faith." The duty is breached if a party acts contrary to community standards of honesty, reasonableness or fairness.

On the evidence of Arton's actions, the judge concluded there was a breach of its duty of good faith and that the breach was serious enough to allow Gateway the right to terminate the lease. As an alternative reason for his decision, the Judge found that Gateway's agreement with Arton was an amendment to the Zellers lease, and that agreement was breached in such a way to justify Gateway's termination of the lease. He issued the declaration that the leasehold interest of Arton was terminated.

The lawyer for Arton was instructed to appeal.

Gateway Realty Ltd. v. Arton Holding Ltd.
N.S.S.C.
The Lawyers Weekly
October 4, 1991 p. 1

This decision was upheld by the Nova Scotia Court of Appeal. The court found that Gateway was justified in breaking the lease when its competitor failed to find a replacement, but the court did not comment on the trial judge's finding about a general duty of good faith.

The Lawyers Weekly
May 15, 1992. p. 13

2. Offer and Acceptance

SALE OF LAND - Certainty of Terms - Mortgage-Back — The plaintiff sought an order of specific performance of an agreement of purchase and sale of property. The financing was to be payable by: "a morgage (sic) of thirty-two thousand dollars to be paid at ten and one half percent interest for a two year morgage (sic) ammortise (sic) over twenty years Plus a two year additional morgage (sic) option (same) Payment to start on January forth (sic) 1984." Cooper L.J.S.C. held that this memorandum was so unclear as to essential terms to be included in the mortgage as to render the agreement unenforceable at law. It did not say how the interest was to be calculated, how and when the mortgage payments were to be made, whether monthly, quarterly, or otherwise. See *Arnold Nemetz Engineering Ltd. v. Tobien,* (1971) 4 W.W.R. 373 (B.C.C.A.). Here, the absence of essential terms as to the manner of calculating interest and payment of the proposed mortgage rendered the agreement uncertain whether the parties were ad idem on all essential terms in order to make the agreement binding and enforceable in law.

Cooper v. Hawes
Rossland Registry N. SC 59-1984,
January 6, 1986
Reprinted with permission from The Advocate *(published by the Vancouver Bar Association), Volume 44, (1986), Part 6, page 922*

*I*n Louisiana, Ms. Linda Blow sued Jimmy Swaggart, televangelist, in small claims court for the return of her payment of $500. She claims she sent the $500 to the Swaggart Ministries because Mr. Swaggart, in an appearance in December of 1985, said the unsaved could be saved by sending money to the Swaggart Ministries and she wanted her family to change its ways and be saved. After a year had passed and her family had not changed its ways she asked for a refund of the $500.

Campbell v. Sooter Studios Ltd.

MANITOBA QUEENS BENCH
AUGUST 22, 1989
UNREPORTED

Summary of the facts: The lease between the plaintiff lessor and the defendant lessee expired on June 30, 1987. After that date, the lessor sent over a draft of a new lease which provided for a significant increase in the rent and for a three year term commencing July 1, 1987 and ending June 30, 1990. The president of Sooter Studios, the lessee, not satisfied with the document, altered the term of the lease to make it a one year lease ending June 30, 1988, and changed the rent. He then signed it and sent it back to the lessor with no letter or conversation indicating that the terms were changed. The lessor signed it without noticing the alterations, sent it back to the lessee for affixation of the corporate seal. The lessee did affix the seal and returned the lease to the lessor.

The lessor then noticed the changes and argued that there was no new lease; that the lessee should give up possession or pay double rent as an overholding tenant. The lessee maintained there was a lease and it remained in possession until June 30, 1988.

The lessor sued for double rent, for the cost of certain repairs, and for a share of realty taxes.

Jewers, J. ... Counsel for the plaintiffs submitted that there was no concluded contract of lease between the parties...that the plaintiffs were never aware of the alterations made to the draft lease by the defendant, and that there was, therefore, never a true meeting of minds between the parties.

In *Chitty on Contracts* 25th Ed. p. 25 it is stated:

> "The normal test for determining whether the parties have reached agreement is to ask whether an offer has been made by one party and accepted by the other. In answering this question, the courts apply an objective test: if the parties have to all outward appearances agreed in the same terms upon the same subject-matter neither can generally deny that he intended to agree. Hence an unexpressed qualification or reservation on the part of one party to an apparent agreement will not normally prevent the formation of a contract. The theory, popular in England in the nineteenth century, that there can be no contract without a meeting of the minds of the parties, has been largely discredited as it would tend to produce commercially inconvenient results."

The question then is: objectively considered, was there an accepted offer? In my opinion, there was. The original offer was, of course, the draft lease prepared and sent by the plaintiffs to the defendant; this offer was not accepted; the defendant made a counter offer by altering some of the essential terms of the lease, signing the document and then resubmitting it to the plaintiffs for their consideration; the plaintiffs then (objectively at least) accepted the counter offer by executing the lease and returning it to the defendant so that the defendant's seal could be affixed; the contract was finally concluded when the defendant affixed the seal and sent the lease back to the plaintiffs. The defendant had no way of knowing and did not know that the plaintiffs had not noticed the alterations and had not assented to them. The plaintiffs had not agreed to the alterations, but, to all outward appearances, they had. They had signed the document after it had been altered by the defendant and had returned it to the defendant without comment or dissent, except to ask that the defendant's corporate seal be affixed. Subjectively, there was no true meeting of minds, but objectively there was and that is the test. ...

The case could also be approached in another way. The plaintiffs' argument is very much akin to the well known plea of *non est factum*; that is the plaintiffs are saying that their minds did not accompany their deed, and that there was no contract. The plea is commented on by Cote in *An Introduction to the Law of Contract* (1974) 140. ...

The plea then is only available where the mistaken party is under a misapprehension as to the very nature of the document, and not merely as to its terms—no matter how important those terms may be. In this case, the plaintiffs were well aware that they were signing a lease for certain premises, and so knew essentially, what they were signing, although they were mistaken as to some important terms. That is an error which might have been avoided if they had taken care to check over the lease before signing it. This is not a situation where *non est factum* would avail the plaintiffs. ...

I therefore hold that the defendant did enter into a valid and binding lease of the premises expiring on June 30th, 1988: that the defendant was not an over-holding tenant; and that the plaintiffs are not entitled to charge double rent.

[The judge awarded the plaintiffs an amount for a share of the taxes and the cost of repairs to a plate glass window.]

The plaintiffs have been partially successful, but the greater victor has been the defendant...

COUNTER OFFER

Hyde v. Wrench

1840 49 E.R. 132

The Defendant being desirous of disposing of an estate, offered, by his agent to sell it to the Plaintiff for 1200l, which the Plaintiff, by his agent, declined: and on the 6th of June the Defendant wrote to his agent as follows:—"I have to notice the refusal of your friend to give me 1200£ for my farm; I will only make one more offer, which I shall not alter from; that is, 1000£ lodged in the bank until Michaelmas, when the title shall be made clear of expenses, land tax, &c. I expect a reply by return, as I have another application." This letter was forwarded to the Plaintiff's agent, who immediately called on the Defendant; and, previously to accepting the offer, offered to give the Defendant 950£ for the purchase of the farm, but the Defendant wished to have a few days to consider.

On the 11th of June the Defendant wrote to the Plaintiff's agent as follows:—"I have written to my tenant for an answer to certain enquiries, and, the instant I receive his reply, will communicate with you, and endeavour to conclude the prospective purchase of my farm; I assure you I am not treating with any other person about said purchase."

The Defendant afterwards promised he would give an answer about accepting the 950£ for the purchase on the 26th of June; and on the 27th he wrote to the Plaintiff's agent, stating he was sorry he could not feel disposed to accept his offer for his farm at Luddenham at present.

This letter being received on the 29th of June, the Plaintiff's agent on that day wrote to the Defendant as follows:—"I beg to acknowledge the receipt of your letter of the 27th instant, informing me that you are not disposed to accept the sum of 950£ for your farm at [336] Luddenham. This being the case, I at once agree to the terms on which you offered the farm, *viz.*, 1000£ through your tenant Mr. Kent, by your letter of the 6th instant. I shall be obliged by your instructing your solicitor to communicate with me without delay, as to the title, for the reason which I mentioned to you."

The bill stated, that the Defendant "returned a verbal answer to the last-mentioned letter, to the effect, he would see his solicitor thereon;" and it charged that the Defendant's offer for sale had not been withdrawn previous to its acceptance. ...

Mr. Kindersley and Mr. Keene, in support [of the defendant vendor] . ... To constitute a valid agreement there must be a simple acceptance of the terms proposed. *Holland v. Eyre* (2 Sim. & St. 194). The Plaintiff, instead of accepting the alleged proposal for sale for 1000£ on the 6th of June rejected it, and made a counter proposal; this put an end to the Defendant's offer, and left the proposal of the Plaintiff alone under discussion; that has never been accepted, and the Plaintiff could not, without the concurrence of the Defendant, revive the Defendant's original proposal.

Mr. Pemberton and Mr. Freeling, *contra.* So long as the offer of the Defendant subsisted, it was competent to the Plaintiff to accept it; the bill charges that the Defendant's offer had not been withdrawn previous to its acceptance by the Plaintiff; there, therefore, exists a valid subsisting contract. *Kenney v. Lee* (3 Mer. 454), *Johnson v. King* (2 Bing. 270), were cited. ...

[337] The Master of the Rolls [Lord Langdale]... I think there exists no valid binding contract between the parties for the purchase of the property. The Defendant offered to sell it for 1000£, and if that had been at once unconditionally accepted, there would undoubtedly have been a perfect binding contract; instead of that, the Plaintiff made an offer of his own, to purchase the property for 950£, and he thereby rejected the offer previously made by the Defendant. I think that it was not afterwards competent for him to revive the proposal of the Defendant, by tendering an acceptance of it; and that, therefore, there exists no obligation of any sort between the parties. ...

REVOCATION OF OFFER

Mlodinska et al. v. Malicki et al.

60 O.R. (2D) 180
ONT. HIGH COURT OF JUSTICE, DIVISIONAL COURT
JANUARY 26, 1988

Hughes J. (orally):—The order in appeal was made by the Honourable Mr. Justice O'Brien in the course of a case involving a will. It discloses an interesting confrontation having occurred in court in the absence of the learned judge in which the validity of a withdrawal of an offer to settle is in question, and I cannot improve of his concise account in describing what happened.

He says:

> The settlement now in issue occurred following a discussion between counsel. While there is no complete agreement on the facts occurring in court, there is so little difference in the position of counsel I propose to deal with the matter now rather than direct a trial of an issue on that point. I am reluctant to do anything which would increase the expense to the parties.
>
> It appears there had been offers of settlement made by both sides. The defence made one offer on April 2, 1987, which had not formally been withdrawn. There had been a counter-offer from the plaintiff for a larger amount. A further offer had been made by the defence increasing their prior offer but containing a provision that the offer terminated one hour before the trial commenced.
>
> During an intermission of trial counsel for the defendants obtained further instructions from his client. Pursuant to those instructions, he wrote a formal notice indicating any offer of settlement had been withdrawn and formally withdrawing the offer of April 2, 1987.
>
> He walked into the court-room indicating with thumb and forefinger the gesture of a zero, said words to the effect "Now, it's zero," took a few steps to counsel table, where plaintiffs' counsel was sitting, and handed to him the handwritten notice. As he did so, plaintiffs' counsel handed him a typewritten notice purporting to accept the offer April 2, 1987.
>
> The position of counsel for the defence is, while there may have been a very short period of time between his action and that of plaintiff's counsel, there was a time differential, and counsel's position is "first in time, first in right" and the defendants' settlement offer was withdrawn prior to acceptance.
>
> The position of counsel for the plaintiffs is that there has been ongoing settlement discussions, the gesture and statement made by defence counsel as he walked into the court-room was not unequivocal and the exchange of his acceptance and withdrawal was virtually simultaneous.
>
> Plaintiff's counsel also urges it is unseemly to encourage "races" of this type between counsel during the course of a trial.

Then he goes on to refer to rule 49.07 and the case of *Siluszyk v. Massey-Ferguson Industries Ltd.*

(1986), 53 O.R. (2d) 509, 7 C.P.C. (2d) 247, in which the Honourable Mr. Justice Carruthers held that in spite of what the rules said about withdrawals of offers and offers themselves being in writing, or required to be in writing, an unequivocal oral notice of withdrawal was effective.

Speaking for myself, it is not necessary to discuss this case at all, other than to refer to it, or indeed the cases which counsel for the respondents offered which deal in every instance with admissions of service because there is, in my view (and I am advised that my brother Austin will develop the point), an undisputed priority in time, however slight of the presentation of the withdrawal by counsel for the appellants before the handing over of the acceptance by counsel for the respondent.

Nonetheless, the learned judge came to the conclusion that because of the apparent unseemliness of this cut and thrust delivery of papers not, albeit, in his presence, and what Carruthers J. had to say about the policy of the rules being to prevent gamesmanship, that a settlement had been concluded, and he made an order to that effect, which were it not for certain confidential aspects to the amount of money involved in the settlement, would have had to be considered by the Court of Appeal as a final order, but because of the amount involved comes within the jurisdiction of this court. I am more concerned with an aspect other than seemliness involved in this matter, and that is the real purpose, I would have thought, of the rules, in respect of reaching a just result which, I believe, is to be found in rule 1.04(1).

It seems to me that, in addition to the question of who served first, there is an overriding concern of the court to effect that result, and that to impose a settlement upon a party who, when confronted with a counter-offer or a request to consider a higher offer, concluded that not only the existing one should be withdrawn, but none other substituted in its place. To hold on such tenuous grounds that a settlement had been made would, I think, be unfair to the defendants in the case and the appellants here, and produce an unjust result.

In response to the concern of O'Brien J. that he should be given some direction, I am of the opinion that his order should be set aside and that he should continue with the trial.

Austin J. (orally):—It was apparent that, by virtue of the matters set out in the reasons of my brothers, the learned trial judge was in a very difficult position. In his reasons he said:

> It seems to me the purported acceptance and withdrawal were virtually simultaneous. I accept submissions of plaintiffs' counsel it is unseemly for courts to encourage the type of race which might result in gamesmanship in the exchange of paper during the course of trial.
>
> I conclude, therefore, the settlement offer was accepted by the plaintiffs and this litigation is ended.

No one disputes the desirability of settlement. In reaching the result he did, however, the trial judge must have concluded either that the acceptance was given first, or that the exchange was for all intents and purposes simultaneous. In my view, neither conclusion is supported by the evidence.

Counsel for the plaintiffs conceded that counsel for the defendants, "put his piece of paper down on my book prior to me handing mine to him." Leaving aside completely the gesture and oral statement of counsel for the defendants, the uncontradicted evidence is that the defendants delivered their notice of withdrawal before the plaintiffs delivered their notice of acceptance.

The time lapse between the two events may have been very short. Counsel for the plaintiffs described it as a split second. Whatever the length of the period, the withdrawal was first and the acceptance second. In those circumstances it does not seem to me that any offer remained available for the plaintiffs to accept.

It appears that what led to the exchange was the request of counsel for the plaintiffs to counsel for the defendants that he ask his clients to consider increasing their offer. Counsel for the defendants acted on that request. Counsel for the plaintiffs knew, or should have known, that inherent in that exercise was a risk, some risk, that the outstanding offer would be withdrawn. If he was not prepared to run that risk he should not have initiated the exercise. As it was, the risk was realized.

As the evidence stands, it appears that in spite of having initiated the exercise, instead of waiting for the answer, he served or attempted to serve a notice of acceptance. In my view, there was nothing left to accept.

I would allow the appeal and set aside the order of O'Brien J., dated April 24, 1987.

Appeal allowed.

Note: An appeal to the Ontario Court of Appeal was abandoned; the parties settled out of court.

3. CONSIDERATION

Degoesbriand v. Radford

SASKATCHEWAN COURT OF APPEAL
SEPTEMBER 16, 1986
UNREPORTED

Gerwing, J.A. (Orally)

The appellant appeals from a judgment dismissing her claim against the respondent, a shareholder in the company by which she was formerly employed, for a declaration that she was entitled to 5% of the shares owned by him in that company, on the alternate basis of either contract or constructive trust. ...

The appellant had worked for two companies, in which the respondent was interested, between 1979 and 1982. She testified that the respondent had promised to give to her 5% of his shares in the business when he either sold out or retired. Although the respondent denied this the learned trial judge accepted that such promises were made. He said:

> I conclude after considering the testimony of the witnesses, and particularly the evidence of Mr. Wall and Mr. Thomson, that the defendant did indeed state to the plaintiff he would give her five per cent of the shares of the business he was then involved in at some time in the future. I am not satisfied, however, this statement occurred as often as the plaintiff claims and I cannot [accept] her evidence it was made within one week of her becoming employed by the defendant.

The learned trial judge also found that the appellant had worked in excess of reasonable overtime, but then quoted from her examination for discovery: ...

> 280 Q Is it fair to say that you would have worked just as hard at Halmac and Associates L-T-D if you hadn't been promised the five percent of that company as if you had been promised it? Do you see my point?
>
> A Would I have worked just as hard?
>
> 281 Q Yes?
>
> A Yes, I would have.
>
> 282 Q Right, and I take it that it's fair to say that your reason for saying that is that because you were conscientious and work required doing?
>
> A That's right. I believe in doing a good job.
>
> 283 Q Right. So regardless of an offer of five percent of the company, you would have done just as good [a] job as you could have done for all Mr. Radford's work and all Halmac's work during that period of time?
>
> A Yes.
>
> 284 Q Now throughout your dealings with Mr. Radford in the employer/employee relationship from Seventy-nine to, I guess it's about June of Eighty-two when things wrapped up, had you ever thought of leaving his employ or working for someone else?
>
> A Not really.

The learned trial judge concludes that the promise was made after the relationship of employer-employee was already in existence, and also that the promise was not made to induce the appellant to work extra overtime. He concludes that there was no action by the appellant in reliance on, or in consideration for this promise. He also found as a fact that the appellant did not intend any promise he made to create a legal obligation.

This conclusion, however, falls short of holding a legally enforceable contract existed between the parties. The defendant on no occasion stated his promise was contingent on the plaintiff's continuing to work more than reasonable overtime nor did the plaintiff perform these duties as a result of the promise being made. It was only after their cordial relationship cooled, did the plaintiff claim the defendant was legally obliged to give her the shares in return for the hours of extra overtime she provided. The defendant may owe some moral obligation to the plaintiff, however, I am not satisfied the obligation arises from a contract between them.

On the facts as found by the learned trial judge, we are of the view that he was correct to dismiss the contractual claim. He found a bare promise by the respondent to the appellant, with no consideration requested or received by him from the appellant. The suggestion that in some way he made this conditional on performance of extra overtime by the appellant, and that performance of this overtime was a method of accepting this offer, was found by the learned trial judge to be only in the mind of the appellant, arising at a later time after the relationship had terminated.

Further, her services as an employee were already the subject of an employment contract which required her to work a reasonable amount of overtime. There was no evidence she did anything that she was not already contractually obliged to do, or that she was not prepared to do in any event, to do her job properly, in reliance on the promise of the respondent. There was nothing to provide consideration or raise the doctrine of estoppel, and the bare promise remained just that and was unenforceable as a contract. In light of the lack of consideration, it is not necessary to comment on the question of lack of congruence between the offer and acceptance or the question of intention to create a contract.

... In the result, the appeal is dismissed with costs ...

A woman in Kansas was charged with "criminal solicitation to commit murder." In exchange for the killing of her common-law husband she offered to give the killers his baseball card collection. She gave them ten cards as a down payment.[3]

An amendment to the *NWT Maintenance Act*, expected in the fall of 1993, will allow court-ordered support payments to be paid in caribou, seal or other take from hunting and fishing to reflect the fact that these "traditional currencies" are more in keeping with an economy not based on cash.[4]

PROMISSORY ESTOPPEL

Central London Property Trust Limited v. High Trees House Limited

[1947] 1 K.B. 130

Denning J.

By a lease under seal made on September 24, 1937, the plaintiffs, Central London Property Trust Ld., granted to the defendants, High Trees House Ld., a subsidiary of the plaintiff company, a tenancy of a block of flats for the term of ninety-nine years from September 29, 1937, at a ground rent of 2,500£ a year. The block of flats was a new one and had not been fully occupied at the beginning of the war owing to the absence of people from London. With war conditions prevailing, it was apparent to those responsible that the rent reserved under the lease could not be paid out of the profits of the flats and, accordingly, discussion took place between the directors of the two companies concerned, which were closely associated, and an arrangement was made between them which was put into writings. On January 3, 1940, the plaintiffs wrote to the defendants in these terms, "we confirm the arrangement made between us by which the ground rent should be reduced as from the commencement of the lease to 1,250£ per annum," and on April 2, 1940, a confirmatory resolution to the same effect was passed by the plaintiff company. On March 20, 1941, a receiver was appointed by the debenture holders of the plaintiffs and on his death on February 28, 1944, his place was taken by his partner. The defendants paid the reduced rent from 1941 down to the beginning of 1945 by which time all the flats in the block were fully let, and continued to pay it thereafter. In September, 1945, the then receiver of the plaintiff company looked into the matter of the lease and ascertained that the rent actually reserved by it was 2,500£. On September 21, 1945, he wrote to the defendants saying that rent must be paid at the full rate and claiming that arrears amounting to 7,916£ were due. Subsequently, he instituted the present friendly proceedings to test the legal position in regard to the rate at which rent was payable. In the action the plaintiffs sought to recover 625£, being the amount represented by the difference between rent at the rate of 2,500£ and 1,250£ per annum for the quarters ending September 29, and December 25, 1945. By their defence the defendants pleaded (1.) that the letter of January 3, 1940, constituted an agreement that the rent reserved should be 1,250£ only, and that such agreement related to the whole term of the lease, (2.) they pleaded in the alternative that the plaintiff company were estopped from alleging that the rent exceeded 1,250£ per annum. and (3.) as a further alternative, that by failing to demand rent in excess of 1,250£ before their letter of September 21, 1945 (received by the defendants on September 24), they had waived their rights in respect of any rent, in excess of that at the rate of 1,250£, which had accrued up to September 24, 1945. ...

There has been a series of decisions over the last fifty years which, although they are said to be cases of estoppel are not really such. In each case the court held the promise to be binding on the party making it, even though under the old common law it might be difficult to find any consideration for it. The courts have not gone so far as to give a cause of action in damages for the breach of such a promise, but they have refused to allow the party making it to act inconsistently with it. It is in that sense, and that sense only, that such a promise gives rise to an estoppel. The decisions are a natural result of the fusion of law and equity: for the cases of *Hughes v. Metropolitan Ry. Co.* (6) *Birmingham and District Land Co. v. London & Northwestern Ry. Co.* (7) and *Salisbury (Marquess) v. Gilmore* (8), afford a sufficient basis for saying that a party would not be allowed in equity to go back on such a promise. In my opinion, the time has now come for the validity of such a promise to be recognized. The logical consequence, no doubt is that a promise to accept a smaller sum in discharge of a larger sum, if acted upon, is binding notwithstanding the absence of consideration: and if the fusion of law and equity leads to this result, so much the better. That aspect was not considered in *Foakes v. Beer* (1). At this time of day however, when law and equity have been joined together for over seventy years, principles must be reconsidered in the light of their combined effect. It is to be noticed that in the Sixth Interim Report of the Law Revision Committee, pars. 35, 40, it is recommended that such a promise as that to which I have referred, should be enforceable in law even though no consideration for it has been given by the promisee. I seems to me that, to the extent I have mentioned, that result has now been achieved by the decisions of the courts.

I am satisfied that a promise such as that to which I have referred is binding and the only question remaining for my consideration is the scope of the promise in the present case. ...

I prefer to apply the principle that a promise intended to be binding, intended to be acted on and in fact acted on, is binding so far as its terms properly apply. Here it was binding as covering the period down to the early part of 1945, and as from that time full rent is payable.

Judgment for plaintiffs.

Note: Judgment is for full rent from early 1945 but not for the forgiven rent during the war years.

4. CAPACITY

Re Collins

SUPREME COURT OF BRITISH COLUMBIA
VANCOUVER REGISTRY # A913069
OCTOBER 21, 1991

Holmes, J. The Petitioner Andrea Collins ("Ms. Collins") is the mother of the Petitioner [S.] Collins, an infant aged 15. S and his sister [J] Collins, 19 years of age, are parties to a contract dated December 11, 1989 with Ms. Collins the subject matter of which involves the infants interest in a residential property in Vancouver which is owned by a trust created irrevocably by their father Philip Collins. The contract was unenforceable from inception as both S and J (collectively hereafter referred to as "the children") were minors at that date. A letter of August 9, 1991 purportedly affirming the contract and stated to be pursuant to Section 16.2 (1) (b) of the *Infants Act* was signed by J the day after she reached the age of majority. As S remains an infant the contract is unenforceable against him and the purpose of the Petition is to make the contract enforceable by obtaining an Order under Section 16.4 (1) (b) of the *Infants Act* granting to S: "capacity to enter into a contract. ...specified in the order."

Counsel for Philip Collins and the Public Trustee both are opposed to the Court granting the Order. ...

The Facts:

Ms. Collins married Philip Collins in England in September 1975, they separated in 1979, and were divorced in August 1980. ...As a consequence of her divorce from Philip Collins the Petitioner received a lump sum settlement of 100,000£ and spousal support of 8,000£ per annum. ...Ms. Collins wished to move to Vancouver. ... The cost of houses the Petitioner considered suitable were beyond her means and she was "..also concerned about the lack of financial security afforded her by the terms of the previous Orders." Discussions ensued with Philip Collins regarding his possible contribution towards the purchase of a residential property. The Petitioner located a suitable house and Philip Collins paid the $750,000 purchase price and created an irrevocable trust "Collins Children's Trust" to hold title with the Canada Trust Company as Trustee. The purpose of the Trust was to provide a home for J, S and Ms. Collins until S (the youngest child) reached age 20 at which time S and J would receive the property absolutely as tenants in common. Ms. Collins signed a License Agreement requiring her to pay property taxes and cost of maintenance repairs.

... Ms. Collins and the children moved into the house in September 1987 and Ms. Collins remains unhappy about what she considers was a misunderstanding as to the ownership interest she felt was promised in the house. ... The unhappiness and insecurity of Ms. Collins in respect of the property became known to J and S. I am uncertain precisely how that occurred but assume she told them and the three of them discussed the matter. ... [After visiting both a psychologist who assessed the children's' state of mind and a lawyer, the children signed the contract.]

The contract of December 11, 1989 provides that the children transfer their beneficial interest in the Collins Children's Trust to Ms. Collins when their interest vests. In return Ms. Collins agrees to provide financial support for their reasonable maintenance, care, education and benefit until they are age 25. ... Ms. Collins also agrees to create a trust in favour of the children which will see the property, or its remainder, returned to them if she should remarry or die. Ms. Collins is Trustee under the Agreement with extremely wide and unfettered powers, including a power:

3.01 (b) "until the Material DATE (her death or remarriage)...in her absolute discretion, encroach upon the capital of the Trust Property and pay or transfer any amount or amounts of the capital...to or for the benefit of Andrea Collins...as the Trustee, in her absolute discretion, shall determine.

(c) Notwithstanding the generality of clause 3.01 (b), the Trustee may encroach upon the Trust Property to such an extent that the Trust Property is completely distributed and used up.

The Law

The relevant provision of the *Infants Act* is Section 16.4(1)(b) and (2):

> The court may, on an application on behalf of an infant, make an order granting to the infant...capacity to enter into a contract...(but the Court must be) satisfied that it is for the benefit of the infant and that having regard to the circumstances of the infant, he is not in need of the protection offered by law to infants in matters relating to contracts.

It is obvious that the court's power is discretionary, but to grant the infant capacity to contract it is mandatory that:

(a) the contract be for his benefit, and
(b) considering the infant's circumstances does not need the protection accorded by the law to infants relating to contracts.

Counsel advised that they knew of no case law concerning this section which would be of assistance. Counsel also agree that the phrase "...for the benefit of the infant..." is to be given the same meaning at law as "...in the best interests of the infant...". Counsel for the Public Trustee argues there is a presumption in law that an infant is under the influence of a parent or guardian. I agree there is such a presumption however I concur with Petitioner's counsel that is a rebuttable presumption, and the opinion and evidence of Dr. Elterman [the psychologist] and Mr. Martin [the lawyer] supports the view there was no undue influence or pressure by Ms. Collins and both children fully understood the agreement and wished to enter into it.

I accept S is an intelligent young man who does understand the legal implication of his intended contract. He is not under direct compulsion, duress, or undue influence in respect of his agreement to sign. It is my view however that it was Ms. Collins who set a chain of events in motion by in some manner making it known to S and J how unhappy and insecure she felt because Philip Collins had not given her an ownership interest in the property. The inference has to be that in some manner the children received what she was promised and entitled to I have no concern as to whether she is right in a moral context, I do have concern that the remedy for her insecurity has involved the children.

I view the contract of December 11, 1989 as a thinly disguised attempt to vary the trust set up by Philip Collins. ... In my view the Court's discretionary power should not be exercised on a pretext of being for the benefit of the infants when in essence it is to have Ms. Collins achieve financial security.

The consequence of the agreement of December 11, 1989 is essentially that S would be giving up to Ms. Collins an interest in property which will vest in him within 5 years that has a present market value in excess of $700,000. Ms. Collins would have the ability to encroach upon that property for her exclusive benefit so there might be no reversion to him at all ... In my view it is in the circumstances here insulting to suggest that this contract is of any financial benefit to S.

It is suggested that the emotional well being of S is best served by Ms. Collins being happy and secure, and that he genuinely wishes that to be so. I am sure that is true, as it would be in any family relationship. I cannot justify S giving away his interest in the trust to purchase that feeling of security for Ms. Collins. I see no benefit to S in the contract in question. I am of the opinion it is not in his best interest.

The decision to give up as substantial an asset as his interest in this trust is one to be reserved until he reaches the age of majority. Should he feel then, as he does now, he is free to make that gift. If his view, or the circumstances, change in the next five years he is not bound to an improvident contract.

The Petition is dismissed with costs...

5. LEGALITY

Cerilli v. Klodt

(1984) 48 O.R. (2D) 260
ONTARIO HIGH COURT
OCTOBER 17, 1984

Southey J. (orally): — This is an action for specific performance of an agreement for the sale by the defendants to the plaintiff of a house property at 242 Ester St. in Sudbury, owned by the defendants as joint tenants.

The defendants had acquired the property in 1971. The defendants are husband and wife, or were at all material times, and separated in 1977. At the time the agreements upon which the action is brought were entered into, there was a dispute pending between the defendants as to the division of matrimonial assets and other matters arising out of their marriage.

The first agreement referred to in the statement of claim is a handwritten document dated February 27, 1984. It reads as follows:

> *Agreement*
>
> Agreement between John Cerilli and Bob Klodt that on day of 9th March '84 John Cerilli will pay Bob Klodt 4,800.00 by cash for house 242 Esther Rd. plus 45 200 by certified cheque payable to Joe Zito in trust for sale of house by March 9th, '84 sale price of property to be shown at 45 200.00.

The agreement was then signed by Job [sic] Cerilli and Bob Klodt. Mr. Klodt is one of the defendants.

On February 29th, two days later, the two men, John Cerilli and Bob Klodt, attended at the offices of a solicitor, Giuseppe Zito, and signed in his office an agreement of purchase and sale, on a printed form in which Mr. Cerilli, as purchaser, agreed with Mr. Klodt, as vendor, to purchase the property for $45,200. ...

On this evidence, I find as a fact that the plaintiff Cerilli was party to a scheme with the male defendant Robert Klodt whereby a false price of $45,200 would be stated in the agreement of purchase and sale and other formal documents relating to the transaction so that the female defendant Sheila Klodt would be deceived into thinking that Mr. Cerilli was paying only $45,200. The balance of $4,800 was to be paid by the plaintiff directly to the male defendant without the knowledge of Mrs. Klodt, in the hope that Mr. Klodt could thereby avoid her obtaining any portion of that $4,800.

This scheme, in my judgment, was clearly fraudulent, and the result in law is that the agreement between the plaintiff and Robert Klodt is void and unenforceable in the courts. I think it is necessary to refer only to the passage from the decision of the Court of Appeal in England in *Alexander v. Rayson*, [1936] 1 K.B. 169, which was quoted and applied by the Supreme Court of Canada in *Zimmermann v. Letkeman*, [1978] 1 S.C.R. 1097 at p. 1101, 79 D.L.R. (3d) 508 at p. 519, [1977] 6 W.W.R. 741. Mr. Justice Martland, delivering the judgment of the court, quoted from the decision of Lord Justice Romer in the *Alexander v. Rayson* case as follows:

> It is settled law that an agreement to do an act that is illegal or immoral or contrary to public policy, or to do any act for a consideration that is illegal, immoral or contrary to public policy, is unlawful and therefore void. But it often happens that an agreement which in itself is not unlawful is made with the intention of one or both parties to make use of the subject matter for an unlawful purpose, that is to say a purpose that is illegal, immoral or contrary to public policy. The most common instance of this is an agreement for the sale or letting of an object, where the agreement is unobjectionable on the face of it, but where the intention of both or one of the parties is that the object shall be used by the purchase or hirer for an unlawful purpose. In such a case any party to the agreement who had the unlawful intention is precluded from suing upon it. *Ex turpi causa non oritur actio.** The action does not lie because the Court will not lend its help to such a plaintiff. Many instances of this are to be found in the books. ...

**Ex turpi causa non oritur actio* means that from a base matter no action can arise.

...[W]hen the fact that Mr. Cerilli had agreed to pay a total of $50,000 became known, Mrs. Klodt, through her solicitor, Mr. Rivard, confirmed that she was prepared to sell her one-half interest in the matrimonial home to Mr. Cerilli on a basis of a purchase price of $50,000. ...

It is clear from the authorities to which Mr. Humphrey referred, however, that the court is under an obligation to refuse to give effect to an illegal agreement whenever the illegality comes to the attention of the court, even though the parties do not raise it. See the judgment of Mr. Justice Krever in *Menard et al. v. Genereux et al.* (1982), 39 O.R. (2d) 55 at p. 64, 138 D.L.R. (3d) 273 at p. 283, where he quotes from a decision of the Court of Appeal of Saskatchewan in *Williams v. Fleetwood Holdings Ltd. et al.* (1973), 41 D.L.R. (3d) 636 at p. 640 [quoting from *Alexander v. Rayson, supra,* at p. 190]:

> The moment that the attention of the Court is drawn to the illegality attending the execution of the lease, it is bound to take notice of it, whether such illegality be pleaded or not....

Action dismissed.

Note: This case was affirmed by the Ontario Court of Appeal 55 O.R. (2d) 399n.

Lalonde v. Coleman

67 Man. R. (2d) 187
Manitoba Court of Queen's Bench
July 3, 1990

Scott, A.C.J.Q.B.: Prior to June 1982, the plaintiff was a young inexperienced local boxer then fighting under the uninspiring name "Dynamite Donny Lalonde." On June 22, 1982, the defendant promoted a match in which the plaintiff was featured for the first time as the "Golden Boy." Thereafter, a dramatic success story unfolded as the Golden Boy boxed his way up the ladder of success until he attained and then successfully defended in full the WBC light heavyweight world title in 1987 and 1988.

On March 24, 1983, the plaintiff and defendant entered into a document entitled "Preliminary Joint Venture Agreement" (the "agreement") whereby the defendant *inter alia* agreed to produce and promote no less than ten boxing matches as a joint venture with the plaintiff. By May 1, 1984, the parties had come to a parting of the ways. The issue before the court is the legal enforceability of this document. ...

On March 24, 1983, the agreement was executed. It was drawn by the defendant's lawyer who represented him throughout the ensuing years, including these proceedings. Describing the relationship as a "joint venture," it went on to provide for the defendant to promote and produce no less than ten boxing matches. For these matches so produced by the defendant, the plaintiff and defendant were each entitled to share equally in the net proceeds. Even when the defendant did not produce or promote the match, he was entitled to 30% of the total purse earned by the plaintiff. The defendant was under no obligation to produce the matches. The agreement was for an unstated period.

For a number of years now the businesses of boxing and wrestling in Manitoba, and indeed throughout most of North America, have been regulated by government-appointed commissions. Despite argument to the contrary by the defendant, I am convinced that one of the primary purposes for such commissions is to protect the public and boxers against unscrupulous managers and promoters.

Since approximately 1976, there has been such a commission ("the Commission") in existence in Manitoba pursuant to the *Boxing and Wrestling Commission Act*, R.S.M. 1987, c. B-80 (the Act). Section 16(1) of the Act at all material times provided as follows:

> Agreement not binding unless approved by Commission.
>
> 16(1) An agreement entered into for the management or training of a person to take part in a professional boxing contest or exhibition in the province is not binding on the athlete who is to be managed or trained unless it is in writing, signed by all the parties thereto, and approved as being fair and reasonable by

certificate of the Commission under the hand of its chairman or vice-chairman and secretary.

Pursuant to S. 8 of the Act, Regulations were enacted in 1976 and re-enacted without change in 1988. ...

Pursuant to s. 16(1) of the Act, if the agreement in question is an agreement —"for the management or training of a person to take part in a professional boxing contest or exhibition," then it is unenforceable pursuant to statute. On the other hand, if it is simply a promotional agreement or joint venture, then, so argues the defendant, the agreement is not in breach of the section.

In addition to the official regulation, the Commission, approximately one month after the agreement was executed, prepared and distributed guidelines...and rules for professional boxing in Manitoba. These guidelines and rules, while not official regulation of the Commission as duly approved by Order-in-Council, are, I am satisfied, regulations within the meaning of s. 8 of the Act. ...

The guidelines provide by rules 9 and 10 that no promoter shall employ or be in any way commercially connected with any boxer without the written approval of the Commission. ... If the guideline applies, then it matters not whether the defendant is a promoter or manager—the contract is unenforceable as against the boxer. This is the interpretation that in my opinion most closely accords with the principal object of the legislation itself, which is the protection of the boxer.

Having held that the guidelines were regulations pursuant to s. 8 of the Act, then it follows that by virtue of that reason alone the agreement is unenforceable as against the plaintiff because Commission approval was never obtained. Furthermore, as noted earlier, if the contractual obligations by the defendant in the agreement include managerial responsibilities, then it would be invalid pursuant to s. 16 (1) of the Act independent of the provision of the guidelines.

[The judge reviews in detail the nature of the ongoing relationship between the parties.] In essence, then the agreement of March 24, 1983, whatever the original intention, had become a management arrangement because this in fact is what the defendant was doing. In my opinion, this is consistent as well with the provision of paragraph 6 of the agreement which entitles the defendant to 30% of the plaintiff's purse whether he promotes the fight or not. This being so, the agreement not only offends the provisions of the guidelines, ... but also the provisions of s. 16(1) of the Act. For this reason as well it is invalid and unenforceable.

But the problems for the defendant do not stop there. [The judge reviews the performance of the defendant to determine whether or not the defendant breached the agreement sufficiently to give Lalonde the right to terminate the contract.] In this case, in my opinion, in light of the magnitude of the defendant's inability to perform, we are dealing with such a fundamental breach as to entitle the plaintiff to treat the contract as being at an end. Despite the wording of the agreement, the parties must have contemplated performance by the defendant of his essential obligation under the contract. What occurred was a total nonperformance or benefit to the plaintiff. What resulted was something totally different from that which the parties must have contemplated and in my opinion, the plaintiff was quite entitled to walk away from the agreement, assuming it to be enforceable, which I have concluded it was not, in or about May 1984. The defendant deprived the plaintiff of any benefit that might have been obtained under the contract and it is therefore set aside on that ground. ...

In the event, then, the plaintiff's action against the defendant succeeds and the plaintiff is entitled to the declaration sought, namely, that the agreement of March 24, 1983, is neither valid nor enforceable against the plaintiff and has not been so since its inception.

The plaintiff is entitled to costs. ...

Order accordingly.

Boyd v. Newton

SUPREME COURT OF BRITISH COLUMBIA
UNREPORTED NEW WESTMINSTER REGISTRY NO. C90 0402
NOVEMBER 1991

Selbie, J. (In chambers) This action is for negligence in the operation of a motor-vehicle or, in the alternative, damages for assault and battery. I.C.B.C. applies under Rule 18A that the action be dismissed against it on the basis that the claim is barred by the application of the defense *ex turpi causa non oritur* action [out of an illegal consideration no action can arise].

This action is about a drug "rip-off." The plaintiff, Boyd, was trafficking in marijuana at a local billiards arcade in Coquitlam. As usual, while waiting for buyers he was playing the video games. He had been there for about five hours. As well as selling the drug he was performing another function for other traffickers—"I just sit there and play video games all day and so people that deal dope up there used to put their drugs on top of the video games. So I got paid a gram for watching drugs." About nine o'clock a stranger approached him about buying some "grass." Boyd told him he had a gram he could have and the price was settled at $10. The driver of the buyer's car was to pay. Boyd gave over the gram of marijuana and both proceeded outside to a car driven by the defendant Newton. The buyer entered the passenger's seat and Boyd approached the open driver's door to get his $10. He stood in the gap between the door and the car frame waiting for his money. Newton suddenly pushed Boyd away and tried to drive off. Boyd, for the purpose of detaining Newton and getting his money, grabbed Newton by his coat and then grabbed the door frame to keep his balance as the car was driven away. He suffered injuries as he was dragged down the street. In effect, in fighting over the closing of an illegal transaction, he was injured. ... This is not a situation, for instance, where, after a deal was closed, the car in leaving negligently ran over the trafficker's foot. There it could be argued that the injury had no causal connection with the drug deal and the maxim would, arguably, not apply. Here the injuries were directly caused by the action of Boyd in trying to detain Newton in order to complete the transaction.

"No Court will lend its aid to a man who founds his action upon an immoral or an illegal act"—Lord Mansfield in Holman v. Johnson (1775) 1 Cowp 342 as quoted by Gibbs JA in *Hall v. Hebert* B.C.C.A., (unreported), Vancouver Registry #CA010498, February 1, 1991. The principle is founded upon public policy.

Gibbs JA in *Hall v. Hebert* (supra), in discussing the maxim, said at p. 12 of the judgment:

> ... the principle underlying *ex turpi causa* is not limited to circumstances where the injuries were sustained during the course of a joint criminal enterprise. The compass of the defence is much broader. It will be available wherever the conduct of the plaintiff giving rise to the claim is so tainted with criminality or culpable immorality that as a matter of public policy the court will not assist him to recover. The joint criminal enterprise ground is merely an example, and perhaps the most common example, of public policy at work.

In the instant case the injuries *were* "sustained during the course of a joint criminal enterprise" and not "after" as is argued. This then is one of those common examples spoken of by his Lordship which give rise to the maxim as a defense.

Speaking of the doctrine of *ex turpi causa* Taylor J. (as he then was) in *Mack v. Enns* (1981) 30 B.C.L.R. 337 at 344 said:

> The purpose of the rule to-day must be to defend the integrity of the legal system, and the repute in which the court ought to be held by law-abiding members of the community. It is properly applied in those circumstances in which it would be manifestly unacceptable to fair-minded, or right-thinking, people that a court should lend assistance to a plaintiff who has defied the law.

It is proper to apply it here. The application of the Third Party, the Insurance Corporation of British Columbia, is allowed and the action is dismissed as against it.

C. Challenges to Contracts

Question

In what instances will the court allow a party to an agreement to avoid his or her obligations?

1. MISTAKE

carelessness defeats the plea of non est factum.

Marvco Color Research Ltd. v. *Harris et al.*

141 D.L.R. (3D) 577
SUPREME COURT OF CANADA
DECEMBER 6, 1982

Summary of the facts: Mr. and Mrs. Harris were induced to sign a mortgage in favour of Marvco Color Research Ltd. (Marvco) by the representation of Johnston, a man living with the Harrises' daughter. Johnston led them to believe that the document was an unimportant amendment to an existing mortgage when it was, in reality, a second substantial mortgage. Although Mr. and Mrs. Harris did not sign at the same time, neither read the document nor questioned it. When the payments were in arrears, the mortgagee took this action for foreclosure. The sole defence was *non est factum.*

The trial court and the Ontario Court of Appeal held that the plea was effective, that their carelessness did not defeat the defence. The courts were following a precedent set by the S.C.C. in *Prudential Trust Co. Ltd. v. Cugnet et al.* (1956) 5 D.L.R. (2d), (Prudential Trust). This appeal to the Supreme Court of Canada forced a reexamination of the legal principle set out in Prudential Trust in light of an English case, *Saunders v. Anglia Building Society* [1971] A.C. 1004 which held that carelessness would defeat the plea of *non est factum.*

Estey J.:—The decision of the House of Lords in *Saunders* has been considered by a number of Canadian courts. In *Commercial Credit Corp. Ltd. v. Carroll Bros. Ltd.* (1971), 20 D.L.R. (3d) 504*n* (Man. C.A.), the question of whether the principles laid down in *Saunders* are good law in Canada was left open by the court. In a number of more recent decisions, however, the reasoning of the House of Lords has been directly applied. ...

In my view, with all due respect to those who have expressed views to the contrary, the dissenting view of Cartwright J. (as he then was) in *Prudential, supra,* correctly enunciated the principles of the law of *non est factum.* In the result the defendants-respondents are barred by reason of their carelessness from pleading that their minds did not follow their hands when executing the mortgage so as to be able to plead that the mortgage is not binding upon them. The rationale of the rule is simple and clear. As between an innocent party (the appellant) [the mortgagee] and the respondents, the law must take into account the fact that the appellant was completely innocent of any negligence, carelessness or wrongdoing, whereas the respondents by their careless conduct have made it possible for the wrongdoers to inflict a loss. As between the appellant and the respondents, simple justice requires that the party, who by the application of reasonable care was in a position to avoid a loss to any of the parties, should bear any loss that results when the only alternative available to the courts would be to place the loss upon the innocent appellant. In the final analysis, therefore, the question raised cannot be put more aptly than in the words of Cartwright J. in *Prudential, supra,* at p. 5 D.L.R., p. 929 S.C.R.: "...which of two innocent parties is to suffer for the fraud of a third." The two parties are innocent in the sense that they were not guilty of wrongdoing as against any other person, but as between the two innocent parties there remains a distinction significant in the law, namely, that the respondents, by their carelessness, have exposed the innocent appellant to risk of loss, and even though no duty in law was owed by the respondents to the appellant to safeguard the appellant from such loss, nonetheless the law must take this discarded opportunity into account.

In my view, this is so for the compelling reason that in this case, and no doubt generally in similar cases, the respondents' carelessness is but another description of a state of mind into which the respondents have fallen because of their determination to assist themselves and/or a third party for whom the transaction has been entered into in the first place. Here the respondents apparently sought to attain some advantage indirectly for their daughter by assisting Johnston in his commercial venture. In the *Saunders* case, *supra,* the aunt set out to apply her property for the benefit of her nephew. In both cases the carelessness took the form of a failure to determine the nature of the document the respective defendants were executing. Whether the carelessness stemmed from an enthusiasm for their immediate purpose or from a confidence in the intended beneficiary to save them harmless matters not. This may explain the origin of the careless state of mind but is not a factor limiting the operation of the principle of *non est factum* and its application. The defendants, in executing the security without the simple precaution of ascertaining its nature in fact and in law, have nonetheless taken an intended and deliberate step in signing the document and have caused it to be legally binding upon themselves. In the words of *Foster v. Mackinnon* this negligence, even though it may have sprung from good intentions, precludes the defendants in this circumstance from disowning the document, that is to say, from pleading that their minds did not follow their respective hands when signing the document and hence that no document in law was executed by them.

This principle of law is based not only upon the principle of placing the loss on the person guilty of carelessness, but also upon a recognition of the need for certainty and security in commerce. This has been recognized since the earliest days of the plea of *non est factum.* In *Waberly v. Cockerel* (1542), 1 Dyer 51a, 73 E.R. 112. for example it was said that:

> ...although the truth be, that the plaintiff is paid his money, still it is better to suffer a mischief to one man than an inconvenience to many, which would subvert a law; for if matter in writing may be so easily defeated, and avoided by such surmise and naked breath, a matter in writing would be of no greater authority than a matter of fact...

More recently in *Muskham Finance Ltd. v. Howard, supra,* at p. 912, Donovan L.F. stated:

> Much confusion and uncertainty would result in the field of contract and elsewhere if a man were permitted to try to disown his signature simply by asserting that he did not understand that which he had signed.

The appellant, as it was entitled to do, accepted the mortgage as valid, and adjusted its affairs accordingly. ...

I wish only to add that the application of the principle that carelessness will disentitle a party to the document of the right to disown the document in law must depend upon the circumstances of each case. This has been said throughout the judgments written on the principle of *non est factum* from the earliest times. The magnitude and extent of the carelessness, the circumstances which may have contributed to such carelessness, and all other circumstances must be taken into account in each case before a court may determine whether estoppel shall arise in the defendant so as to prevent the raising of this defence. The policy considerations inherent in the plea of *non est factum* were well stated by Lord Wilberforce in his judgment in *Saunders, supra,* at pp. 1023-4:

> ...the law...has two conflicting objectives: relief to a signer whose consent is genuinely lacking...protection to innocent third parties who have acted upon an apparently regular and properly executed document. Because each of these factors may involve questions of degree or shading any rule of law must represent a compromise and must allow to the court some flexibility in application.

The result in this case has depended upon the intervention by this court in the development of the principle of *non est factum* and its invocation in a way inconsistent with that applied many years ago in the *Prudential* case, *supra.* The respondents have pleaded their case in the courts below and in this court consistent with the result in the *Prudential* judgment. In these circumstances consideration can and should be given to the application of the general principle that costs follow the event. The appellant, of course, was required to persevere to the level of this court in order to bring about a review of the reasoning which led to the determination in the *Prudential* case. The respondents, on the other hand, acted reasonably in founding their position upon that decision notwithstanding the revision of the law of England consequent upon the judgments in *Saunders.* In all these circumstances, therefore, I would award to the appellant costs only before the court of first instance with no costs being awarded either party in the Court of Appeal or in this court.

Note: For another application of the plea of *non est factum,* see Campbell v. Sooter. at p. 50.

INTERPRETATION

Implied terms

A contract between a community college and a video game supplier provided that the supplier would supply and maintain tabletop video games and would guarantee a minimum payment to the college of $16,000 a year. The games were installed for the start of the school year. Almost immediately there were problems with vandalism: "machines were overturned, glass was broken, cords and plugs were removed or destroyed, sound equipment was damaged and cash boxes were broken into." The president of the supplier discussed the problem with the operations manager on different occasions and stated that, because the college was not providing security, no money was being earned and no commission could be paid. The supplier agreed to continue on the basis of a 50/50 split of income generated. However, at the end of the term of the contract the college sued the supplier for the full amount owing under the terms of the original contract.

The supplier submitted that the original contract was properly terminated by them because of the college's breach of an essential, though implied term, namely, to provide security for the machines. The court found, on the evidence of several witnesses, that the vandalism was "abnormal, excessive [and] continuous" and that the failure of the college to provide security was a breach of an implied term of the contract entitling the supplier to treat the agreement as at an end. It further held that it was common sense for the college who stood to gain from the games to provide security to prevent the damage. Therefore, the supplier could terminate the contract and need not make the guaranteed payment.

Algonguin College of Applied Arts and Technology v. Regent Vending and Amusement Limited
Summarized from The Lawyers Weekly
May 3, 1991, p. 2

2. MISREPRESENTATION

Rainbow Industrial Caterers Ltd. et al. v. *Canadian National Railway Co. et al.*

54 D.L.R. (4TH) 43
BRITISH COLUMBIA COURT OF APPEAL
SEPTEMBER 15, 1988

Background facts: The plaintiff caterers, relying on an estimate given by the defendant railway on the number of meals required, bid on a contract to supply meals to the railway work gangs. The plaintiff won the contract but suffered losses, part of which were attributed to the error in the defendant's estimate.

The plaintiffs sued the railway and Doroshenko, who was project engineer employed at the railway's head office. At the trial level, both defendants were held liable for negligence and for fraud in failing to disclose the true facts as soon as they came to light. Damages were assessed at the whole of the plaintiffs' loss.

Esson, J.A. …

C.N. concedes error but appeals damages and the finding of fraudulent non-disclosure. …

Fraudulent non-disclosure

…There is no finding that C.N.'s conduct in this regard was deliberately designed to mislead the plaintiffs, or that any of the employees who gave the various assurances did so in other than good faith. In the end, the most that can be said against C.N. is that better "communications arrangements" could have been put in place by it. That may be a legitimate criticism of its conduct of this piece of business but simply is not, in my view, the stuff from which a finding of fraud can be made.

There is much emphasis in the plaintiffs' submissions and in the reasons of the trial judge on the circumstance that this is not a case of fraud "of the usual kind" involving positive misrepresentations of fact but is, rather, one concerned only with non-disclosure by a party which has become aware of an altered set of circumstances. It is, I think, potentially misleading to regard these as different categories of fraud rather than as different factual bases for a finding of fraud. Where the fraud is alleged to arise from failure to disclose, the plaintiff remains subject to all of the stringent requirements which the law imposes upon those who allege fraud. The authority relied upon by the trial judge was the speech of Lord Blackburn in *Brownlie v. Campbell* (1880), 5 App. Cas. 925 at p. 950 (H.L.). The trial judge quoted this excerpt:

> …when a statement or representation has been made in the *bona fide* belief that it is true, and the party who has made it afterwards comes to find out that it is untrue, and discovers what he should have said, he can no longer honestly keep up that silence on the subject after that has come to his knowledge, thereby allowing the other party to go on, and still more, inducing him to go on, upon a statement which was honestly made at the time when it was made, but which he has not now retracted when he has become aware that it can no long honestly perservered [sic] in.

The relationship between the two bases for fraud appears clearly enough if one reads that passage in the context of the passage which immediately precedes it:

> I quite agree in this, that whenever a man in order to induce a contract says that which is in his knowledge untrue with the intention to mislead the other side, and induce them to enter into the contract, that is downright fraud; in plain English, and Scotch also, it is a downright lie told to induce the other party to act upon it, and it should of course be treated as such. …

In seeking to support the finding of fraud, Mr. Roberts relied particularly on *K.R.M. Construction Ltd. v. B.C.R. Co.* (1982), 40 B.C.L.R. 1 (B.C.C.A.). There, relying upon the same passage from *Brownlie v. Campell*, this court upheld the trial judge's finding that the defendant railway was liable for fraudulent non-disclosure. It is worth noting the factual basis for that finding because it illustrates the kind of conduct and mental state which must be present and which is lacking here.

In *K.R.M.*, the plaintiff contractors had been engaged in construction of an extension to the railway. Serious disputes arose, as a result of which the contractor threatened to withdraw and sue for damages. After negotiations, the parties entered into a new agreement on December 10, 1975, which included a release of previous breaches. The contractor by that agreement agreed to continue with its work, it did continue and it suffered a heavy operating loss.

One reason for that loss was that a major revision of the line location, of which the contractor became aware only after the new agreement, rendered impractical the "one camp concept" which was a vital basis for its calculation of costs. Some months before the new agreement, in September 1975, the railway had advised the contractor that a minor revision (which would not have affected the one camp concept) was contemplated. That was a true statement of the railway's intention at the time. The trial judge found, however, on conflicting evidence that the railway officers who negotiated the new agreement were aware before December 10th that the major revision was contemplated and knew of the materiality of that fact to the contractor. …

In other words, there was a deliberate concealment of altered circumstances with the intention of deceiving the contractor and thus inducing it to enter into a new contract. Those elements are entirely lacking here. There was no concealment, no intent to deceive and nothing else which in my view could support the finding of fraud against either Mr. Doroshenko or his employer. ...

It seems, most regrettably, to have become fashionable to allege fraud in commercial cases without much regard for the fundamental rule that fraud must be strictly pleaded and strictly proven. To some extent, this may be an off-shoot of the mistaken notion, to which I referred earlier, that those stringent requirements do not apply to fraud by non-disclosure. However that may be, this is a case in which there was neither a sound factual basis for alleging fraud nor, after C.N. admitted its responsibility for the original error, any practical purpose to be served in pursuing the issue of non-disclosure. ...

In conclusion I would allow the appeal of Doroshenko by dismissing the action against him. I would allow the appeal of C.N. on the fraud issue...and the issue of quantum of damages.

Note: This court remitted the case back to the trial judge to consider the breach of contract claim and to assess the damages. The appeal from the second trial was dismissed by the Court of Appeal. An appeal from the second Court of Appeal decision was dismissed by the Supreme Court of Canada (84 D.L.R. (4th) 291). Despite all the hearings on this matter, the Court of Appeal's ruling that the defendant was liable for negligent misrepresentation and not fraudulent misrepresentation was undisturbed.

Innocent

The National Consumer Council and the Plain English Campaign, which promote the use of clear, straightforward English, gave the 1986 "Golden Bull booby prize for gobbledegook" to a firm which used the following in their share prospectus: "[the signers] agree that without prejudice in any other rights to which you may be entitled, you will not be entitled to exercise any remedy of rescission for innocent misrepresentation at any time after acceptance of your application"

Fraudulent

B.C. Hydro, the defendant, had decided to contract out the construction of transmission lines in a rugged area of British Columbia. B.C. Hydro advertised for tenders. The trial court found as a fact that the defendant had deliberately omitted information from the tender documents about the condition of the right-of-way. The judge stated that the deliberate omission of words of warning amounted to "a form of tender by ambush." In his opinion, the defendant had a duty to make full disclosure of all information relevant to the project, to give the bidders information that accurately reflected the nature of the work to be done so they could prepare a proper bid. He held that the defendant had fraudulently induced the plaintiff to enter the contract and awarded the plaintiff $2.6 million, "the total loss suffered by the plaintiff as a result of being fraudulently induced to enter into this contract."

Summarized from The Lawyers Weekly
July 1, 1988 pps. 6 and 18

B.C. Hydro appealed. After examining the contractual terms relevant to the case, the majority on the B.C. Court of Appeal concluded that the contract meant that the clearing was to have been completed and thus the words constituted a negligent, but not a fraudulent, misrepresentation that induced the plaintiff to enter into a contract at a price less than it would have if it had known the true facts. It reduced the award to $1,087,730 for negligence and remitted the breach of contract issue and the consequent damages back to the trial court.

The court agreed that the law in Canada is still evolving on the question of corporate responsibility for the deceit of its employees, but that fundamental principles still apply, namely, the plaintiff must prove the defendant's intention to deceive. It concluded that the evidence in the case did not show that any of the twelve members of the committee which prepared the tender documents did so with such an intention.

Judge Southin, although dissenting on the finding of negligent misrepresentation, agreed that the plaintiff failed to prove fraudulent misrepresentation. "[I]n my opinion, in the whole of his judgment, the learned judge never came to grips with the issue of who was fraudulent. To say, as the learned judge does, that the defendant did this or that is to ascribe to the defendant a soul which it does not possess. ... I am persuaded that no one had a guilty mind." [At page 189]

BG Checo International Ltd. v. B.C. Hydro and Power Authority
44 B.C.L.R. (2d) 145
B.C.C.A.
March 21, 1990

B.C. Hydro appealed to the Supreme Court of Canada, which dismissed its appeal. All the judges agreed that B.C. Hydro had breached the contract and the majority held that the plaintiff, Checo, could also sue in tort for negligent misrepresentation even though the representations were also stated expressly in the contract. It sent the matter back to the trial court for the assessment of damages and stated that the law should move to reduce the significance of suing in tort rather than in contract. [In tort, the wronged is to be compensated for all the reasonably foreseeable loss that was caused by the tort; in contract the wronged is entitled to damages that would put him in the position he would have been in if there had been no breach.]

The Lawyers Weekly
February 12, 1993
pps. 1, 21.

Note: This case will be remembered less for its finding of negligent rather than fraudulent misrepresentation than for the proposition that a person can bring an action in contract *and* tort, even if the duty in tort is also an express term of the contract, subject only to the limitations set out in the contract.

Ms. Pitt purchased a ticket from a Toronto agent for a three hour flight on the Concorde jet, in response to a newspaper advertisement which urged the reader to "see the curvature of the earth from 60,000 feet," "circle the arctic," "fly to vicinity of the North Pole," and travel at "Mach 2 — twice the speed of sound (1,360 m.p.h.)." Ms. Pitt did not see the curvature of the earth, the flight did not circle the arctic or fly within the vicinity of the North Pole; it went to Goose Bay.

The judge concluded that the misrepresentations were made with reckless disregard for their accuracy and that the defendant was liable for breach of contract. The plaintiff was awarded punitive damages as well as compensatory damages.

Pitt v. Executive Travel (London) Ltd.
Summarized from The Lawyers Weekly
January 12, 1990, p. 4;
January 19, 1990 p. 19.

Note: **See also the tort of Deceit page 21.**

3. Undue Influence

Tannock v. Bromley

10 B.C.L.R. 62
Supreme Court of British Columbia
January 24, 1979.

Bouck J.:—

Synopsis of Claim and Defence

Between approximately July 1974 and January 1977 the plaintiff received treatment from the defendant through the medium of hypnosis. He now says that while he was under her influence he conveyed real estate to her, bought her a car and gave her many other items such as coins, a stereo set, etc. In this action he asks for return of the real property and judgment for the money value of the additional articles transferred to her.

There is not much of a contest over the fact the conveyances occurred and the chattels were given, but the defendant alleges all of this happened by way of gift from the plaintiff to her and so none of the property need be restored. ...

Issue

Must the defendant return to the plaintiff the property or its value?

Law

Where the parties to a contract do not stand upon an equal footing the law has frequently intervened to set aside the contract on the grounds of undue influence by one towards the other. This principle has been applied with particular emphasis in circumstances where there is a fiduciary relationship between the parties. Such a bond has been held to exist between solicitor and client, principal and agent, doctor and patient, priest and penitent, etc.

The main theory of the law is that, when a person who because of his state of mind is incapable of exercising his free will and is induced by another to do an act which may be to his detriment, the other shall not be allowed to derive any benefit from his improper conduct. Conveyances or transfers by the victim are not set aside because of folly or want of prudence but to protect the weak from being forced, tricked or misled into parting with their property.

Once the relationship between the parties is established so that it is clear one has maintained dominion over the other, then a presumption of law arises where a gift is made by the servient to the dominant party. The onus of proof then shifts to the dominant party. The onus of proof then shifts to the dominant party to uphold the validity of the gift. This presumption is to the effect that the dominant party used undue influence over the servient party and consequently the transaction should be set aside unless the dominant party can show the conveyance or gift was a spontaneous act of the donor performed under circumstances which enabled the donor to exercise an independent will.

The authorities on this branch of the law are not altogether consistent and so the textbook discussions of the cases tend to vary from author to author. Nonetheless, in broad outline the principles I have recited seem to be generally accepted: see for example the following texts and cases cited therein: Waters, *Law of Trusts in Canada* (1974), pp. 343-49; Goff and Jones, *Law of Restitution*, pp. 163-68; *Kerr on Fraud and Mistake*, 7th ed., pp. 185-285; and *McKay v. Clow*, [1941] S.C.R. 643, [1941] 4 D.L.R. 273.

On the facts there is no question the defendant controlled the plaintiff in much the same way a solicitor may dominate his client or a doctor his patient. Her position was that of a fiduciary in relation to the plaintiff. Indeed, the influence she held is more profound than in the examples of other situations I have mentioned because of the nature of hypnotism and its method of manipulating the mind through suggestion. The plaintiff was incapable of resisting the defendant's influence and became her obedient servant. She either abused her position of trust or took advantage of the inequality which existed between them. As hypnotist and subject a presumption therefore arose that everything given by the plaintiff to her ought to be set aside unless she could prove the plaintiff's acts were spontaneous and done by him through the exercise of his independent will.

I could not find any solid evidence to support the defendant's cause by way of rebutting the presumption. The conveyances and gifts were voluntary in the sense there was no consideration moving from the defendant to the plaintiff. Furthermore the plaintiff did not receive independent advice so that one could say he was acting outside the influence of the defendant. Because of this the transfers must be set aside. ...

Judgment

By way of summary the plaintiff will recover judgment against the defendant in the following terms:

(a) An order directing the defendant to sign a conveyance of her interest in the Wellington Street farm and in default of her so doing the district registrar of Nanaimo may sign on her behalf;

(b) An order directing that an account be taken as between the plaintiff and the defendant with respect to the moneys received by the defendant on the sale of the Amsterdam house;

(c) An order directing that the plaintiff has a charge against the car in question proportionate to his contribution and that the car be sold;

(d) An order directing the defendant to deliver up the stereo to the plaintiff:

(e) An order that there be an accounting between the plaintiff and the defendant with respect to any loss suffered by the plaintiff as a consequence of the sale of the car, and the value of the rent the defendant must pay to the plaintiff for her use of the car and the stereo;

(f) Costs to follow the event;

(g) Liberty to apply.

Action allowed in main.

An accountant prepared financial statements for a family business and saw the business was in difficulty. The accountant refused to release the statements to an investor intending to buy the company unless the investor signed an agreement to guarantee payment of his accounting fees. The court held the guarantee was obtained by undue influence and the investor was relieved of his obligation.[5]

4. Duress

Mr. and Mrs. B, aged 78 and 72, signed a contract to transfer certain real property to their son Jim. The contract had been prepared by a solicitor. When Jim brought an action for a declaration that he was the beneficial owner of this property Mr. B testified that he and Mrs. B had only signed because Jim had threatened to blow his brother Bill's head off if a family money dispute was not settled. The parents heard this threat through a third brother. Mr. B said that he and his wife, who was very ill at the time and died not long afterwards, were terrified Jim would act on his threat and were prepared to do almost anything to prevent it. Their lawyer had been consulted on how to settle a tangle of money disputes among the members of the family, and he advised that this agreement seemed to be the only way to obtain peace.

Held: the agreement was void for Jim's duress or, alternatively, should be set aside for unconscionability. It was enough if the threat of harm was a reason for executing the document, albeit that the signer might well have done the same if the threat had not been made: *Barton v. Armstrong*, [1976] A.C. 104 (P.C.) A threat of harm to a third party, if acted on by the signer, was duress: *Saxon v. Saxon*, [1976] 4 W.W.R. 300 (B.C. Co. Ct.) Although Mr. and Mrs. B had independent legal advice and chose to sign the agreement, they did so because they feared that Jim would harm Bill unless they signed the agreement. This was a coercion of their will so as to vitiate their consent. Unconscionability was found because through the duress and their lack of understanding of the transaction the parents were in a weak position compared with Jim, and because the agreement was unfairly one-sided.

BYLE v. BYLE et al.
Vancouver S.C. Registry No. C854743 Legg, J.
August 5, 1988
Reprinted with permission from The Advocate *(published by the Vancouver Bar Association), Volume 46, (1988), Part 6, page 986,*

A bank applied for summary judgment against a guarantor who pled duress and *non est factum*. The guarantor alleged that she signed the document unaware that it was a guarantee secured by a mortgage on her home because her husband threatened, among other things, "to open up your belly and drink your blood." The judge concluded a summary judgment was inappropriate.[6] *TD Bank v. Nahmiache*

5. UNCONSCIONABILITY

Turner Estate v. Bonli Estate

77 SASK. R 49
SASK. COURT OF QUEEN'S BENCH
JUNE 2, 1989

[1] Sirois, J.: The plaintiff sues for specific performance of an option to purchase farmland entered into between the purchaser Gordon Turner and the vendor Oli Bonli on the 2nd day of May A.D. 1975. One of the difficulties encountered herein is that both of the main actors are now deceased and their personal representatives stand in their place. It was agreed at trial that the counterclaim would not be proceeded with at this time since there was a likelihood that matters raised therein could either be tried at a later date or settled between the parties depending on the results of the main action. The defendant resists the claim mainly on the basis that the alleged option agreement should be set aside as the entire transaction was unconscionable in that the purchase price of the land and the method of payment of purchase price by installments are gravely inequitable and constitute equitable fraud on the part of the plaintiff. The evidence must be carefully scrutinized. The sole issue is the validity of the option to purchase.

[2] At the time the lease agreements and option to purchase were entered into, Gordon Turner was 47 years of age and Oli Bonli was 88 years of age. Gordon Turner likely typed out the agreement at his residence on the previous night leaving the land description to be filled out later at his office where he had a municipal map to consult. It was executed bright and early around 7 o'clock in the morning. Oli Bonli who lived at the hotel walked over to Turner's office. Alan Pederson who worked at his brother's service station across the road was hailed to come over and sign as a witness. In five minutes or less the deed was done. This is the text of the agreement entered into:

> May 2, 1975
>
> TO WHOM IT MAY CONCERN:
>
> I Oli Bonli do hereby rent all of my land to Gordon A. Turner for the period of five years starting as of today May 2nd 1975. At the end of this time being May 2nd 1980 he may purchase this land for the sum of one hundred thousand dollars, this sum to be paid in twenty equal payments of five thousand dollars each year. This payment to cover principal and interest and there will be no further charges made to him.
>
> If I should decease before the rental agreement is fulfilled, he may purchase the land from my estate under the same terms. The rentor may seed up to four hundred and fifty acres per year and must farm the land in a husbandly manner.
>
> I will receive one third of the crop each year and will pay the taxes on all of this land.
>
> The rentor will haul all my grain to the graneries (sic) and elevator for me at no cost to me, and I in return will let him use any of my machinery that he desires for farming any land at no cost to him.
>
> The rentor will be allowed to store grain in any of my granaries (sic) that I am not using in that crop year at no cost to him.
>
> The legal description of the said land is as follows:
>
> NWquarter Sec. 30-20-14-W3rd
> W1half " 29-20-4-W3rd
> Ehalf " 30-20-14-W3rd
> Pt.NEquarter " 31-20-14-W3rd
>
> I have clear titles to the above land in the Toronto Dominion Bank.
>
> *'Alan Pederson'* WITNESS — *'Oli Bonli'* Oli Bonli
>
> *'G.A. Turner'*
> Gordon A. Turner"

[3] Gordon Turner was in the fuel business all his life. He drove fuel trucks for Texaco, B.A. Oil and finally

Gulf. He was also involved in farming. In 1966-67 he purchased one-half section of land; in 1972 he purchased a further three quarter sections. There was further trading along the way so that by 1975 he owned five quarters of land, besides the Bonli land—the subject of the action. But he had his eyes on this land too. He was very involved in the community. He served on the Town Council for nine years, mayor for two terms and the Elks representative for eight years. In the wintertime he curled for a pastime. From all accounts, he was a mover and doer. He was well-liked and respected in the community. He was married with three children—all boys, with whom he got along well. He enjoyed people and his work. For the last six months of his life his nerves were bad and he suffered from arthritis. He took anti-depressants but finally succumbed, a victim of suicide on the 30th of September 1975.

[4] Oli Bonli appears to have been an entertaining person, always nice, friendly, with a twinkle in his eye. But as a bachelor he kept to himself quite often. He lived on the farm until the winter of 1973-74. He spent his summers on the farm and his winters at the hotel in Kyle. ...

In 1974 and 1975 age was catching up to Oli Bonli. He had good days and bad days when he was very confused. Finally, unable to care for himself properly at the hotel in Kyle, the Social Services Department intervened and he was taken to a nursing home in Langham in the month of November of 1976. In 1980, Oli Bonli was examined by psychiatrists to ascertain the state of his mental condition. In March of 1982 he was declared to be a mentally disturbed person, incapable of managing his affairs through mental infirmity arising from age and the Montreal Trust Company of Canada was appointed Committee of his estate under the *Mentally Disordered Persons Act*, R.S.S. 1978, c. M-4, ss. 5 and 42. He died on the 18th day of February, A.D. 1985 at the age of 98. ...

[13] The leading Canadian case appears to be *Waters v. Donnelly* (1884), 9 O.R. 391, where Fergus, J., held at 409:

> The law which I think applicable to a case of this sort appears to be clearly and briefly stated in a case mentioned by the Chancellor. *Slater v. Nolan* Ir. R. 11 Eq. 386, by the Master of the Rolls, and the decision was afterwards affirmed in appeal. The learned Judge said:—'If two persons, no matter whether a confidential relation exists between them or not, stand in such a relation to each other that one can take undue advantage of the other whether by reason of distress, or recklessness, or wildness, or want of care, and when the facts show that one party has taken undue advantage of the other by reason of the circumstances I have mentioned, a transaction resting upon such unconscionable dealing will not be allowed to stand; and there are several cases to show, even where no confidential relation exists, that where the parties are not on equal terms, the party who gets a benefit cannot hold it without proving that everything has been right, and fair and reasonable on his part.' This decision does not, I think, lay down any new law but rather appears to state concisely what the law was and is. ...

[15] In *Black v. Wilcox*, (1976) 70 D.L.R. (3d) 192; 12 O.R. (2d) 759, at pp. 195-196, Evans, J.A., said:

> In order to set aside the transaction between the parties, the Court must find that the inadequacy of the consideration is so gross or that the relative positions of the parties is so out of balance in the sense that there is a gross inequality of bargaining power or that the age or disability of one of the controlling parties places him at such a decided disadvantage that equity must intervene to protect the party of whom undue advantage has been taken. In considering whether a Court should intervene, it is necessary to look at all the circumstances surrounding the transaction but it is not necessary to find any intentional fraud. The question is whether the transaction reveals a situation existing between the parties which was heavily balanced in favour of the defendant and of which he knowingly took advantage.

[16] If the bargain is fair the fact that the parties were not equally vigilant of their interest is immaterial. Likewise, if one was not preyed upon by the other, an improvident or even grossly inadequate consideration is no ground upon which to set aside a contract freely entered into. It is the consideration of inequality and improvidence which alone may involve this jurisdiction. Then the onus is placed upon the party seeking to uphold the contract to show that his conduct throughout was scrupulously considerate of the other's interests. This is an accurate statement of the law vide: *Mundinger v. Mundinger*, [1969] 1 O.R. 606; 3 D.L.R.(3d) 338, affd. 14 D.L.R. (3d) 256n...*Knupp v. Bell et al.* (1966), 58 D.L.R.(2d) 466, affd. 67 D.L.R.(2d) 256; di Castri, *The Law of Vendor and Purchaser* (2d Ed.), at pp. 205, 206, 207. ...

[17] In the case at bar the 47 year old Turner and the 88 year old Oli Bonli were certainly not par or of equal

bargaining power. Turner drew the agreement himself. ...When questioned by Tony Sander [long time friend, neighbour and helper] about the rumours that his land had been rented to Gordon Turner early in May 1975, Oli Bonli denied that he had either rented or sold any land. On the contrary he declared that he had bought land from Gordon Turner and that Sander would have more work to do for him that spring than he had ever done in the past. Now Oli Bonli was not a liar; he was a nice old man and trickery was not part of his arsenal. I have serious doubts that he really knew all that was contained in Exhibit P-1 or D-2.

[18] Let us look at the agreement itself between this 47 year old active businessman and this failing 88 year old gentleman. The evidence is that he was failing with good days and bad days. One year down the road he could not adequately take care of himself and was taken to a nursing home. This document drawn up by Gordon Turner provides for a five year lease at the end of which, he or his estate could exercise the option to buy. At that time the rentor, Oli Bonli, would be 93 years of age. Then, on the option being exercised over a 20 year period, Oli Bonli would be 113 years of age by the time it was all paid out. The price was $100,000.00 at a time when the land was worth $167,000.00, or was one third more than the purchase price, and at a time when the price of land was ascending rapidly. Furthermore, the agreement makes no provision for interest on the unpaid portion of the purchase price; the five thousand per year would comprise both principal and interest. Gordon Turner knew very well what land prices were doing at this time; this man was world wise and knew what he was after. The agreement moreover provides that the lessee can use any of the rentor's machinery to farm any land free of charge. And again, the lessee reserves the right to use any of the rentor's granaries to store his grain that the rentor was not using at any relevant time.

[19] Can one honestly conceive a more one-sided or improvident agreement than this? To ask the question is to beg the answer. It was all one-sided in favour of Gordon Turner at the expense of Bonli.

[20] Here, there was no independent legal advice given to Oli Bonli; given the respective ages and state of health of both parties there was inequality of bargaining power; the consideration was grossly inadequate and the terms of purchase were very unfair in the light of all circumstances. The transaction resting upon such unconscionable dealing cannot stand. The plaintiff has failed to discharge the onus that rests upon her to show that everything has been fair, right and reasonable on her part. Equity must intervene to protect the defendant's estate when undue advantage was taken of the deceased. The transaction is set aside and specific performance is refused. In effect, the action is dismissed with costs to the defendant. The caveat against the lands is ordered discharged; that is instrument No. 75-MJ-06745 registered on the 2nd day of June A.D. 1975, dated the 30th day of May A.D. 1975. The lands in question are: N half 29-20-14-W3rd; E half 30-20-14-W3rd; half of NE 31-20-114-W3rd; NW quarter 32-20-14-W3rd. Parties have leave to reapply before me if any differences develop with respect to rentals since 1980.

Action dismissed.

Smyth v. Szep

BRITISH COLUMBIA COURT OF APPEAL
VANCOUVER REGISTRY CA012481
JANUARY 21, 1992

Taylor, J.: This is an appeal from a decision on an application for summary judgment on a claim for injuries suffered in an automobile accident, by which the trial court held that a settlement agreement brought about by an Insurance Corporation of British Columbia adjustor amounted to an unconscionable bargain, and was not binding on the plaintiff. ...

[Summary of the facts: A student injured her neck and back in an automobile accident. Some months later, the insurer offered to settle her claim for $2,500 in general damages plus wage loss and special damages of $131. The plaintiff, 19 at the time of the settlement, agreed to the offer and signed a release of all her claims. The next day she attempted to withdraw her consent.]

The Authorities

The leading authority on unconscionable transactions in this jurisdiction is probably *Morrison v. Coast Finance Ltd. & Others* (1965) 54 W.W.R. 25, a decision of this court in a case in which an elderly widow had mortgaged her house to secure a loan for the benefit of one of her lodgers and his partner for no consideration and under circumstances which fixed the mortgage lender with knowledge both of the purpose of the loan and of the mortgagor's very poorly secured position.

This was the context in which Mr. Justice Davey (as he then was) laid down (at p. 259) the rule applicable to unconscionable bargains.

> The equitable principles relating to undue influence and relief against unconscionable bargains are closely related, but the doctrines are separate and distinct. The finding here against undue influence does not conclude the question whether the appellant is entitled to relief against an unconscionable transaction. A plea of undue influence attacks the sufficiency of consent; a plea that a bargain is unconscionable invokes relief against an unfair advantage gained by an unconscientious use of power by a stronger party against a weaker. On such a claim the material ingredients are proof of inequality in the position of the parties arising out of the ignorance, need or distress of the weaker, which left him in the power of the stronger, and proof of substantial unfairness of the bargain obtained by the stronger. On proof of those circumstances, it creates a presumption of fraud which the stronger must repel by proving that the bargain was fair, just and reasonable: *Aylesford (Early) v. Morris* (1873), 8 Ch App 484, 42 L.J. Ch. 546, per Lord Selborne at p. 491, or perhaps by showing that no advantage was taken: See *Harrison v. Guest* (1855), 6 De G.M. & G. 424, at 438, affirmed (1860), 8 H.L. Cas. 481, at 492, 493, 11 E.R. 517.

The reference to "fraud" is explained by Lord Serbourne ... as referring, not to "deceit or circumvention", but to "unconscientious use of power". ...

Taken as a whole, the judgment of Mr. Justice Davey (concurred in by Mr. Justice Bull) stands, in my view, for the proposition that equity will grant relief where there is inequality combined with substantial unfairness, and that in its modern application poverty and ignorance combined with lack of independent advice on the part of the party seeking relief (plus, presumably, some evidence of unfairness) places an onus on the other party to show that the bargain was in fact fair. ...

Another leading authority on the issue in this province is the later decision of this court in *Harry v. Kreutziger* (1978), 9 B.C.L.R. 166, a case in which a native fisherman obtained relief against an improvident sale of his fishboat. Mr. Justice MacIntyre there considered the above excerpts from the judgment of Mr. Justice Davey in Morrison, as well as several other authorities and concluded (at p. 173):

> From the authorities, this rule emerges. Where a claim is made that a bargain is unconscionable, it must be shown for success that there was inequality in the position of the parties due to the ignorance, need or distress of the weaker, which would leave him in the power of the stronger, coupled with proof of substantial unfairness in the bargain. When this has been shown a presumption of fraud is raised, and the stronger must show, in order to preserve his bargain, that it was fair and reasonable.

Mr. Justice Lambert agreed but ... he put the test more broadly.

> In my opinion, questions as to whether use of power was unconscionable, an advantage was unfair or very unfair, a consideration was grossly inadequate, or bargaining power was grievously impaired, to select works from both statements of principle, the Morrison case and the Bundy case, are really aspects of one single question. That single question is whether the transaction, seen as a whole, is sufficiently divergent from community standards of commercial morality that it should be rescinded.

This question must be resolved, he said, with reference to the decided cases, particularly Canadian cases, and principles laid down in statutes dealing with acceptable standard of commercial propriety. ...

Conclusion

In dealing with the Corporation, both as a claimant against one of its insured and also as its insured in respect of her right to Party 7 "no fault" benefits under the scheme, Ms. Smyth was entitled to rely on the corporation to treat her fairly, and the evidence suggests that she did.

There was obvious disparity of bargaining position. There was also, in my view, obvious unfairness in the bargain. ...

The issue is not, in my view, whether a lawyer would have recommended a settlement in that amount — this is made clear in the decision of this court in *Cougle*. The question is whether an adjustor could reasonably consider the offer made here to be fair when he had no basis on which to assess the plaintiff's present condition or future prognosis. A back condition remaining unresolved eight months after the accident might continue to cause pain and disability, and require medical and rehabilitative treatment, either for a few weeks or for years.

If the matter were to be settled at that point, so as to compensate for the whole range of possible eventualities, a settlement figure of $2,613 would have to be regarded by a reasonable adjustor as manifestly unfair.

As the plaintiff had not sought the settlement, and took no advantage of it, and since she was given no opportunity to consider the offer and get advice on it before deciding whether or not to accept it, the bargain must, in my view, be regarded as one which falls short of the community standards relevant to dealings between the Insurance Corporation of British Columbia and members of the public and the judge below was in my view quite correct in holding it to be unenforceable.

I would therefore dismiss the appeal.

Note: Justice Wood concurred with Justice Taylor's twenty-page decision; Justice Gibbs wrote a twenty-three-page dissent which included his apprehension that a test of community standards of commercial morality may induce a trial judge to introduce subjective views as a substitute for the factual tests set out in the Morrison case.

D. Privity and Assignment of Contracts

Two employees of Kuehne & Nagel International Ltd. caused extensive damage ($33,955.41 worth) to a transformer owned by London Drugs Ltd. They dropped it attempting to lift it with two fork lifts, contrary to the method advised. The storage contract included an exclusion clause limiting liability of Kuehne & Nagel on any one package to $40. London Drugs Ltd. sued the defendant in bailment, contract and tort (negligence); it sued the employees personally for the tort of negligence.

At trial the employees were found liable for the full amount of the damage while the liability of their employer company was limited to $40.

The B.C. Court of Appeal found it unreasonable to hold the employees responsible for the full amount of the loss when their employer's liability was limited to $40. The court reduced the employees' liability to $40. After reviewing the existing law, Justice Southin dissented with "regret" because the result is "in a moral sense, unjust," but, she concluded, "it is for judges to state the law and for the legislature to reform it."

London Drugs Ltd. v. Kuehne & Nagel International Ltd. et al
70 D.L.R. (4th) 51
British Columbia Court of Appeal
March 30, 1990

London Drugs Ltd. appealed and the employees cross-appealed, arguing they should be completely free of liability.

The Supreme Court of Canada focused on the issues of whether or not the employees owed a duty of care to their empoyer's customers and whether or not the liability clause contained in the contract between the employer company and the customer could afford any protection to the employees.

The court held that the employees did owe a duty of care to the employer's customer, but found the employees beneficiaries of the exemption clause in the contract between the employer and customer. Thus, the court added an exemption to the privity of contract rule. When a service contract between an employer and its customer contains a clause limiting liability, that clause, if it expressly or impliedly covers the employees, should protect the employees charged with performing the contract. The customer should not be able to circumvent the terms of the contract by suing the employees directly in tort.

London Drugs Ltd. v. Kuehne & Nagel International Ltd. et al
S.C.C.
October 29, 1992 (209 pp.)
Summarized from The Lawyers Weekly *November 13, p. 1, November 20, 1992 p. 15*

A contract by which William Millard borrowed $250,000 from a venture-capital firm, Marriner & Co., allowed the lender to convert the note into 20 percent of the company's stock. The contract was sold to Mr. Martin-Musumeci, who, as the assignee of the contract, claimed the 20 percent of the company, ComputerLand. Millard resisted by claiming he had an oral agreement with Marriner that it could not transfer the right to convert the note. The matter went to court.

The court held that Millard must give 20 percent of his stock to Martin-Musumeci plus punitive damages of $125 million. Twenty percent of ComputerLand, at that time, was estimated to be worth $50 million to $400 million. To appeal, Millard would have to post a cash bond equal to 1 1/2 times the award.[7]

E. Termination of Contracts

1. Performance

Question

Is everybody happy?

Pavel Bure's hockey jersey, one of a limited edition bearing a crest marking the National Hockey League's 75th anniversary, was sold for $4,250. The sheet music for Bryan Adams' song (Everything I Do, I Do for You) was sold for $4,100. (The proceeds of both sales benefited fifteen organizations, including Canuck Place, North America's first free-standing hospice for children.)[8]

Mr. Mateo of New York City bought fifty $100 gift certificates from Toys 'R' Us and offered one certificate for each gun turned in to the police station. Over a few days 375 weapons had been turned in "almost 40 times as many as the precinct has collected in the past year under the department's amnesty program which pays up to $75 a gun." Donations from others allowed the programme to continue.[9]

The Ontario housing ministry ordered a landlord to rebate $2,308.80 to his tenant. The tenant received that amount in change that filled two blue recycling boxes.[10]

2. Agreement

Question

Have the parties contracted to call off the deal?

AMR Corp., the parent company of American Airlines, would invest $246 million in Canadian Airlines if Canadian Airlines and its parent compnay PWA Corp. can withdraw from the Gemini computer system, which PWA co-owns with Air Canada. Canadian Airlines requested the federal Competition Tribunal to hear its submission, but Air Canada challenged the tribunal's right to hear the matter. The Federal Court of Appeal ruled that the Tribunal did have the authority to hear the appeal.[11]

The Supreme Court refused to hear Air Canada's appeal from this decision.[12]

The Competition Tribunal ruled that PWA Corp. can withdraw from the Gemini computer system, and ordered the dissolution of Gemini Group Automated Distribution Systems Inc. if the partners cannot negoiate a settlement by December 8, 1993. The Tribunal held that PWA would likely fail without AMR's investment and that would lessen airline competion in Canada.[13]

Air Canada, with Covia, a third owner of Gemini, appealed the ruling of the competition Tribunal. Before the case was heard, Air Canada abruptly halted its legal fight against PWA.[14]

3. Frustration

Question

Has some unforeseen event beyond the control of either party happened after the contract was formed that makes it impossible or meaningless to perform?

Impala Construction Ltd. v. *Wade*

115 A.P.R. 437
NEWFOUNDLAND DISTRICT COURT
FEBRUARY 10, 1983

Riche, D.C.J. [orally]: In this case the plaintiff, Impala Construction Ltd., ... entered into a contract with the defendant for the performance of certain works consisting of bulldozing a road in the Clarke's Beach area of Newfoundland for a price of $2,000.00 [plus transportation and seeks damages for work done] . ...

What then was the legal position of the parties? There was a contract but it was only partly performed. It was only partly completed because it could not be finished, not because of any action of the parties but because of some outside force. The contract became frustrated because of extreme weather conditions. It wasn't until nearly two years afterwards in the summer of 1981 that the work was actually completed. Even if the defendant had requested the plaintiff to complete the contract in 1981, I do not think the plaintiff would be obliged after such a long delay to go back and complete the contract for the price as stipulated. ... It should be remembered that the contract consisted of only 3-4 days work.

So what we have is a frustrated contract in November, 1979, which cannot be performed and which has been partly performed. In the circumstances I find from the evidence ... that there was at least 50 percent of the work completed and probably something more. The evidence varied the amount from 50 percent to 75 percent. I, therefore, find as a matter of fact that 60 percent of the work was completed. I value the contract at $2,500.00 including transportation; $1,500.00 is the value of the work completed, being 60 percent of the $2,500.00 contract.

In relation to frustration in contracts, I refer to *Canadian Building Contracts*, Goldsmith, (2nd Ed.). It has a fairly concise explanation of frustration, at p. 53 & 54:

> Frustration in the legal sense does not refer to the feeling frequently experienced by both owners and contractors in support of the performance of the work, but occurs when some supervening event for which neither party is responsible and which was not within the contemplation of the parties renders performance impossible. It is always open to parties to provide in their contract what was to happen in such an event, and many contracts contain what is known as a *force majeure* clause. In the absence of any such provision, however, on the happening of such an event the contract will be frustrated, and the parties are released from further performance. The accrued rights and liabilities at the date of frustration remain unaffected, but future or continuing obligations are discharged.

Frustration also occurs if the performance is rendered impossible by an act of God. In this particular case because of the extreme wet weather in the fall of 1979 and 1980 which anyone who has lived in this province knows. [sic] It was an unbelievable year with regards to the amount of rain we had that summer. I hold this contract impossible of performance as the parties contemplated.

By the common law in a contract which is frustrated, by an act of God, neither party would be entitled to recover. However, under the *Frustrated Contracts Act*, R.S.N. 1970, c. 144, s. 4(3). It states: [if]

Before the parties were discharged any of them has by reason of anything done by any other party in connection with performance of the contract, obtain a valuable benefit other than a payment of money, the court, if it considers it just to do so having regard to all the circumstances, may allow the other party to recover from the party benefited the whole or any part of the value of the benefit.

On the basis of this legislation and the law relating to frustrated contracts, I find that the contract here had become frustrated. I find the defendant has benefited from the work done under the contract to the value of $1,500.00 and with respect to the contract I allow the sum of $1,500.00 to the plaintiff in respect of that work.

Judgment for the plaintiff in part. …

Potential causes of contractual frustration:

— frozen waste from an airliner. A large chunk of frozen waste from an airliner smashed through the roof of a home in Seattle.[15]

— a c-130 Hercules cargo plane crashing. Only the chimney was left of Mr. Barnhart's home when such a plane crashed. Mr. Barnhart escaped serious injury.[16]

4. Breach of Contract

Main Line Pictures, an independent film company, sued actress Kim Basinger for breach of contract for failing to star in a film after promising to do so. The company had sold distribution rights for about $10-million when it advertised the film with Basinger's name. The jury ordered her to pay $8.92 million in damages and ruled that she could also be responsible for punitive damages.[17]

Alan Morrison, reluctant to date because of physical disabilities caused by a near-fatal motorcycle accident, hired a dating service which did not do what it promised it would do. Morrison sued for breach of contract. The judge hearing the case was so incensed by the evidence that he adjourned the court until he could suppress his anger sufficiently to write his judgment. He awarded Morrison $3000 for breach of contract and $2,350 for punitive damages.[18]

The judge of the Ontario Court (General Division) found the following as facts: The plaintiff, Ontex Resources Ltd. (Ontex) owned eighteen leasehold mining claims. Mr. Chilian, the president of Metalore Resources Ltd. (Metalore) approached the plaintiff about a possible joint venture, with the result that the companies entered into a contract in 1981. The agreement provided that Metalore would take possession of the property, and that if it would spend $1million, set out a detailed drilling program, and agree to spend a further $5 million, Ontex would either transfer the property to Metalore in return for a 30% net royalty interest, or give Metalore 60% interest in the property and enter into a joint venture agreement.

The contract further provided that Metalore would provide Ontex with information on demand and would provide it with a report by July 1 of each year.

Metalore did provide Ontex with a report in 1982, but it did not disclose a previous and positive report that indicated a potential for a successful gold mine and the areas for exploration. Although Metalore was aware of the industry practice to make full disclosure of all information it possessed about the property, Chilian reported to Ontex that the results were disappointing. Chilian did, however, offer to increase Metalore's interest in the property. Metalore further misled the plaintiff about its drilling plans intentionally concealing its optimistic plans.

In 1983, in response to Chilian's offer, the companies entered into an agreement in which Ontex agreed to assign to Metalore 100% of its interest in the property for $40,000 and a 10% net royalty interest.

In 1984 Chilian received an extraordinary positive report on one drill hole, but those results were not given to Ontex. Chilian secretly purchased stock in both companies; Metalore began staking and acquiring claims. By July 1, 1985 it had acquired 232 claims.

In January of 1986, Ontex demanded reports for 1983, 1984, and 1985 pursuant to the terms of the 1981 agreement. Chilian replied that the 1981 agreement had been replaced by the 1983 agreement but did promise to deliver information. The information provided was confusing, incomplete and inaccurate. Ten days after the information was delivered, Metalore announced its discovery. By then it had acquired another 227 claims.

Ontex sued Metalore and Chilian for breach of contract, fraud, misuse of confidential information, breach of fiduciary duty and claimed ownership of the mining claims.

The trial judge stated the law on the breach of contract as follows:

> *Breach of Contract*
>
> Stephan M. Waddams, *The Law of Contracts*, 2nd ed. (Aurora, Ont.: Canada Law Book, 1984), at pp. 440-442:
>
> A variety of expressions has been used to define the sort of term that, if broken by one party, will excuse the other. "Dependent covenant," covenant which goes to the whole of the consideration," "condition," "condition precedent," "breach going to the root of the contract," "concurrent condition," breach that "terminates" or "frustrates the object" of the contract," "nonseverable breach," "repudiation," "renunciation," "breach of an entire contract," are among the expressions used. Behind them all, it is suggested, lies a single notion—that of substantial failure of performance. Diplock, L.J., said in *Hongkong Fir Shipping Co. Ltd. v. Kawasaki Kisen Kaisha Ltd.*:
>
> > "...in what event will a party be relieved of his undertaking to do that which he has agreed to do but has not yet done?...
> >
> > The test whether an event has this effect or not has been stated in a number of metaphors all of which I think amount to the same thing;

> does the occurrence of the event deprive the party who has further undertakings still to perform of substantially the whole benefit which it was the intention of the parties as expressed in the contract that he should obtain as the consideration for performing those undertakings?"

After his examination of the evidence the trial judge concluded that Metalore had breached the 1981 agreement and that "[t]he 1983 agreement rests for its validity on proper disclosure having been made under the 1981 agreement. Given Metalore's intentional failure to make proper disclosure, the 1983 agreement cannot stand."

With regard to the issue of misuse of confidential information, he stated the following:

> In the course of Metalore's business relationship as operator on Ontex lands, Metalore acquired valuable geological information which led to the Discovery Hole B-31. This was confidential information to be shared by Metalore and Ontex prior to public disclosure. Metalore used this valuable information to the exclusion of Ontex to acquire hundreds of adjacent mining claims.
>
> Chilian, as well, used the confidential information for personal gain.
>
> In *Lac Minerals Ltd. v. International Corona Resources Ltd.*, [1989] 2 S.C.R. 574, 69 O.R. (2d) 287 (note), 44 B.L.R. 1, 26 C.P.R. (3d) 97, 61 D.L.R. (4th) 14, 35 E.T.R. 1, 101 N.R. 239, 36 O.A.C. 57, 6 R.P.R. (2d) 1, all five members of the court agreed that when information of a confidential nature is disclosed by one party to another in circumstances that would lead the reasonable business person to appreciate that the information is confidential and to expect that the recipient would respect that confidence, the confidant is precluded from using the information for personal gain. No evidence has been led to show that Metalore was entitled to use this information for its own benefit.
>
> Mr. Justice La Forest, speaking for the majority on the issue of remedy in *Lac*, held the constructive trust to be appropriate. In my view, the three-part test of breach of confidence (disclosure of confidential information, an awareness on the part of the recipient of the confidential nature of the information and the use of the information to the detriment of the disclosing party) has been met. Although Metalore "developed" the information it was placed in a position to do so by virtue of being Ontex's operator on its lands. I, therefore, conclude that Ontex has established a breach of confidence by Metalore. In my view, the only appropriate remedy is one *in rem*. I conclude that Metalore holds all the staked claims, as described more specifically in my conclusions below, under a constructive trust for Ontex. Mr. Justice La Forest concluded that no major player in the market would be deterred if he knew the alternative was the equal sharing joint venture that would come about had that party not breached its confidence.
>
> The doctrine of breach of confidence has equal application to the 1981 and 1983 agreements.

The trial judge also concluded that the defendant had breached a fiduciary duty. The court terminated the 1981 and the 1983 agreements, held that title to the eighteen leased claims should revert to the plaintiff, that other claims by Metalore are held in constructive trust for the plaintiff, and also awarded punitive damages to the plaintiff because of the improper actions of Mr. Chilian.

Ontex Resources Ltd. v. Metalore Resources Ltd.
75 O.R. (2d) 513
Ontario Court (General Division)
December 18, 1990

On appeal, the Ontario Court of Appeal held that, on the facts, the defendant's breach of the 1981 agreement did not entitle Ontex to terminate the agreement. The court did hold that the "deliberate non-disclosure of information" was a "material misrepresentation which induced [Ontex] to enter the 1983 agreement" and that, therefore, Ontex was entitled to rescission of the 1983 agreement. It therefore held that the 1981 agreement, as per its terms, would be "treated as being renewed as of July 1, 1991."

The Court of Appeal agreed that there was a misuse of confidential information, but overruled the remedy of constructive trust as being unfair on the facts.

Lastly, the court of appeal overruled the judge's award of punitive damages.

Ontex Resources Ltd. v. Metalore Resources Ltd.
103 D.L.R. (4th) 158
Ontario Court of Appeal
June 4, 1993

The plaintiff claimed the Prime Minister and the Progressive Conservative Party were liable for breach of contract. The plaintiff claimed that the defendants failed to honour their election promises to improve postal service and not to enter into a free trade agreement with the U.S. The action was dismissed.[19]

Ruffolo v. Mulroney

In *Lalonde v. Coleman*, (see p. 60 above) the court held that the boxer was not bound by the agreement not only on the grounds that the agreement was illegal but also on the grounds that Coleman's breach of the agreement entitled Lelonde to terminate the contract. Judge Scott wrote: "In this case, in my opinion, in light of the magnitude of the defendant's inability to perform, we are dealing with such a fundamental breach as to entitle the plaintiff to treat the contract as being at an end. ... What occurred was a total nonperformance or benefit to the plaintiff. What resulted was something totally different from that which the parties must have contemplated and in my opinion, the plaintiff was quite entitled to walk away from the agreement. ..."

Lalonde v. Coleman
67 Man. R. (2d) 187 at p. 195

ANTICIPATORY BREACH

Question

What is an "anticipatory breach" and what are the choices of the person faced with such a breach?

Homer et al. v. Toronto-Dominion Bank

(1990) 83 SASK. R. 300
SASKATCHEWAN COURT OF APPEAL
MAY 28, 1990

Sherstobitoff, J.A.: This appeal is from a judgment which awarded damages and interest exceeding $135,000.00 for breach of a lease. The issue was whether the tenant improperly terminated the lease or whether it was entitled to do so by reason of the doctrine of anticipatory breach or repudiation.

In 1978, the appellant bank occupied premises in a shopping centre under the terms of a written offer to lease, signed by the appellant and accepted by the owner of the premises. The offer defined the area to be occupied, fixed the rental to be paid, and fixed the term at ten years, renewable for two ten year periods. The offer was stated, upon acceptance, to be a binding contract and required the tenant to execute the "Landlord's standard form of lease" before occupying the premises, "provided that the lease document shall be in a form mutually satisfactory to both parties." Such a lease was never signed.

In 1980, the respondent became owner of the premises. Over the next four years, the parties negotiated with a view to agreement to the terms of a formal lease, but without success. On October 14, 1984, the respondent, by its solicitors, sent the following letter to the appellant:

> Further to your letter of September 27, 1984, please be advised that I have failed to convince my client that we grant to your client any of the proposed changes contained in your letter of March 22, 1984. My client is most emphatic that they are not prepared to discuss the matter further and have instructed me to advise you that the Lease is either to be executed in the form negotiated between our two respective offices or the Toronto-Dominion Bank is to vacate the premises.
>
> Although I realize you are having difficulty in receiving instructions from your client, I must insist that the matter be resolved on or before the 31st day of October, 1984 failing which I will seek further instructions from my client.

The appellant, by letter of its solicitors dated November 14, 1984, stated that it was terminating the lease as of May 14, 1985, and would vacate the premises on or before that date, which it did.

The respondent sued for damages, alleging the existence of a binding ten year lease. The appellant admitted the existence of such a lease, but relied on the respondent's letter as either an offer to terminate, which it accepted, or a repudiation, which it accepted, in either case terminating the lease. The evidence indicated that the respondent was bluffing when it sent the letter, and had no wish to terminate. However, the respondent also admitted that the appellant had no way of knowing that it was bluffing and that even after the bluff was called, the respondent did not make its position clear to the appellant. The trial judge found a binding ten year lease and ... assessed and awarded damages.

The appeal must be allowed.

The appellant admitted the existence of a binding lease, although that was open to doubt. Because of the admission, it will be assumed, for the purpose of this judgment that there was a binding lease.

The judge, in his decision, overlooked entirely the applicable principles of contract law. The issue was not one of the right to terminate under the terms of the existing lease. Rather, the issue was whether there was an anticipatory breach or repudiation of the existing lease by the respondent, followed by an election by the appellant to accept the repudiation, thereby terminating the contract.

Anticipatory breach occurs when a party by express language or conduct, or by implication from his actions, repudiates his contractual obligations. There must be conduct which evidences an intention not to be bound by the terms of the contract and absence of justification for such conduct. The innocent party may then elect either to preserve the contract and seek to enforce its terms, or to accept the repudiation and terminate the contract. In the latter case, the innocent party is freed from his future obligations under the contract, but may pursue such remedies as would have been available to him if the breach had taken place when performance was due.

The case most close to the point emanating from this jurisdiction is *Canadian Doughnut Co. Ltd. v. Canada Eggs Products Ltd.*, [1954] 2 D.L.R. 77 (Sask. C.A.), affd. [1955] S.C.R. 398. Other judgments of this court dealing with anticipatory breach include *Cowie v. McDonald*, [1917] 2 W.W.R. 356; *Smith v. Crawford*, [1918] 2 W.W.R. 298; and *Sunnyside Nursing Home v. Builders Contract Management Ltd.*, 75 Sask. R. 1; [1989] 3 W.W.R. 721 (S.C.A.). A useful text book analysis of the principles involved is found in Fridman on, *The Law of Contract*, (2nd Ed., pp. 558-571).

The letter of October 15, 1984 demanded that the appellant either sign a new lease or vacate the premises, at the same time foreclosing any further discussion of the matter. Even against the background of four years of fruitless negotiation toward a formal lease, the letter amounted to a clear and unequivocal statement of intention not to be bound by the terms of the existing lease which had three more years to run. No other conclusion is possible because neither of the alternatives given in the letter contemplated continuation of the existing lease. The appellant's letter of reply took no issue with the respondent: it accepted the second of the two alternatives given, that is, to vacate the premises. It was an election to accept the repudiation and to terminate the contract.

The respondent argued that the appellant's letter, which did not agree to give up possession until six months later, May 14, 1985, was not an acceptance of the demands in the respondent's letter, which required a reply by October 31, 1984. That did not change the character of the appellant's letter as an acceptance of the respondents' repudiation. While the respondent may have been entitled to require the appellant to vacate immediately upon receipt of the appellant's letter, it chose not to do so.

Given that both parties accepted the existence of a lease for ten years, there could be no justification for the position taken by the respondent in its letter.

The acceptance of the repudiation was given in a reasonable time.

Although not raised in argument, it should be noted that English authority has held that the doctrine of anticipatory breach did not apply to leases: *Total Oil Great Britain Ltd. v. Thompson Garages (Biggin Hill) Ltd.*, [1972] 1 Q.B. 318 (C.A.). However, the Supreme Court of Canada in *Highway Properties Limited v. Kelly, Douglas and Company Limited*, [1971] S.C.R. 562, took a different view. See Fridman at pp. 563-564 and 576-577.

In light of the above conclusions, we need not consider the appellant's plea of estoppel.

The appeal is allowed with costs under double Column V. The judgment below is set aside and the action stands dismissed with costs.

Appeal allowed.

LACHES

"I say that equity will not leap across an eight-year gulf of acquiescence in what, as a matter of contract, is a clear breach thereof. The right here has been slept on too long; it smacks of a stale claim, and the court will not enforce it."

Logan v. Williams (Logan)
41 B.C.L.R. (2d) 34
B.C.C.A. at p. 39

Judge Anderson, quoting from the reasons for judgment of Judge Drake of the lower court which held that a husband's action, commenced in December of 1987 to set aside a separation agreement breached by his wife in December of 1979, was barred by laches. The Court of Appeal agreed with the lower court's decision.

Alna de Bodisco began an action seeking $2 million from the fashion designer Oscar de la Renta based on an agreement to give her half his wealth. De la Renta admitted signing a letter making the promise. The promise was made on June 22, 1956; the lawsuit was filed April 1979. The court held that the suit was barred by the *Statute of Limitations.*

A cyst removed from a Ms. Argue contained a four-faceted diamond one-third of a centimetre across, which apparently was dropped into her by a careless doctor or nurse during the Caesarean birth of her daughter 52 years ago.

5. Exemption Clauses

Questions

A party to a contract has the right to ask the court for a remedy if the other party is in breach. That is the essence of contract law. How does the court help a person if a clause in the contract states that he agrees not to seek a remedy if the other party is in breach?

Do these exemption clauses illustrate the freedom of contract or are they contrary to the essence of contract law?

Aurora TV and Radio v. Gelco Express

65 Man. R. (24) 145
Manitoba's Queen's Bench
May 10, 1990

Overview

Oliphant, J.: The plaintiff owns and operates an audio and video sales and service outlet at Brandon, Manitoba.

The defendant is a national courier company.

The plaintiff's action is for the recovery from the defendant of the value of a videocassette recorder. The defendant contracted to transport the videocassette recorder for the plaintiff. The videocassette recorder was either lost by or stolen from the defendant.

The defendant does not deny liability. It says its

liability is limited by virtue of the contract between it and the plaintiff.

The Issues

There are two issues to be resolved:

(1) Is there a clause in the contract between the plaintiff and the defendant which limits the liability of the defendant for the loss of the videocassette recorder?

(2) If so, is the defendant entitled to rely upon the clause?

[After reviewing the facts and the case law, the judge concluded as follows.]

Conclusions

On the question of notice of the limitation clause, I agree with and adopt the principles set forth in *Firchuk, supra*. The court must carefully scrutinize any clause in a contract which purports to limit the liability of a party, especially where a limitation clause appears in a standard form contract and purports to limit the liability of the drawer of the contract. Before a party can rely upon a clause which purports to limit his liability, reasonable notice of that clause must be given to the other party to the contract. Also the loss must come within the four corners of the limitation clause.

Here, on the face of the bill of lading, there is a reference to the limitation of the carrier's liability. However, the clause which purports to limit that liability appears on the reverse side of the bill of lading in very small print, buried amongst other words under a heading which is not indicative of a limitation clause.

Notice cannot be said to be reasonable, in my view, if the clause is neither legible nor capable of comprehension.

The clause utilized in the case before me was printed in such a manner that it is difficult, if not impossible, to read without the aid of magnification.

The limitation clause becomes incomprehensible in its attempt to cover almost every possibility in terms of limiting the carrier's liability. The wording of the clause is neither plain nor unambiguous. It is unclear. It is, quite simply, legal gobbledygook.

Even if one accepts the proposition that the requirement of notice is met if the nondrawing party to the contract is given the opportunity to read it, the notice cannot, in my opinion, be said to be reasonable if the clause is unintelligible because of its complexity.

I am not persuaded that any notice of the limitation clause was given to the plaintiff here. If notice were given, then I find that such notice in all the circumstances, was not reasonable.

Accordingly, the defendant is not able to rely upon the clause limiting its liability.

Even if it could be said that reasonable notice of the limitation clause had been given, I would still allow the plaintiff's claim.

The essence of the contract here was that the defendant was to carry certain goods being shipped by the plaintiff from Brandon to Calgary and to deliver the goods to an address in Calgary.

In a contract for carriage, the unexplained disappearance of the goods which are the subject of the contract is in my opinion a fundamental breach of the contract.

Where the goods which are the subject of the contract inexplicably disappear, the possibility of theft is real. As stated by Cory, J. A., in *Punch, supra,* a carrier is liable for loss where theft is a possibility unless there is a clause which clearly exempts the carrier from loss occasioned by theft.

I agree that whether an exclusionary or exception clause is applicable where there is a fundamental breach is to be determined according to the true construction of the contract.

Looking at the contract as a whole and bearing in mind the factual circumstances here, I am not able to say that it is fair and reasonable to attribute to the parties the intention that the limitation clause should survive notwithstanding a fundamental breach by the party in whose favour it was drawn. That is the test applied by Grange, J. A., in *Cathcart, supra*. Is my view it is the correct test.

Cathcart, supra, is also authority for the proposition that in a contract for the delivery of goods, the failure to deliver, though not deliberate, is a fundamental breach. I agree with the correctness of that proposition as well.

I disagree with the reasons for judgment given by Rowbotham, J., in *Lotepro Engineering and Construction Ltd., supra*. He took the view that a failure to deliver does not constitute a breach of the fundamental term of a contract for delivery, rather, it is negligent performance of a contract. I respectfully disagree.

Here, we have a contract for the carriage and delivery of goods. The goods were not delivered and there is no explanation for the disappearance of same. The defendant is liable for the fundamental breach of the contract and because of the lack of clarity in the limitation clause, it cannot, in my opinion, rely upon that clause to escape the consequences of the loss of the goods.

① no reasonable notice
② fundamental breach ∴ interpretation

For the reasons stated, then, there will be judgment for the plaintiff in the sum of $699.95.

The plaintiff is entitled to its costs in the court below in the sum of $88.99. I award the plaintiff costs here in the sum of $250.00.

Additionally, the plaintiff is entitled to interest as is provided for under Part XIV of the *Court of Queen's Bench Act*, S.M. 1988-89, c. 4; C.C.S. M., c. C-280.

Judgment for plaintiff.

The plaintiffs bought a horse for $6,500 at an auction conducted by the Canadian Standardbred Horse Society (CSHS). The very next morning they called their veterinarian to treat it, which he did that day and for the next ten days, at which time it was determined that the horse had rabies. The horse was euthanized a few days later. After revewing the evidence, the judge found it as a fact that the horse had rabies at the time of the sale, which constituted a fundamental breach of the contract as it was not the intention of the seller or the buyers that the subject of the sale was "a dead horse."

The catalogue of the CSHS contained a clause that placed the risk upon the purchaser. The issue of the case was whether or not the clause in the catalogue would block the plaintiff's claim. The judge wrote:

> Although at one time it was felt that when a fundamental breach of contract occurred, an "exclusion clause" contained in the contract ceased to have any effect as a rule of law (see: *Harbutt's Plasticine Ltd. v. Wayne Tank and Pump Co. Ltd.*, [1970] 1 Q.B. 4470, it has now been determined (see *Photo Production Ltd. v. Securicor Transport Ltd.*, above, approved by the Supreme Court of Canada in *Beaufort Realties (1964) Inc. et al. v. Chomedey Aluminum Co. Ltd.*, [1980] 2 S.C.R. 718, 116 D.L.R. (3d) 193, 33 N.R. 460), that whether an exception clause applies when there is a fundamental breach of contract depends upon the construction of the whole of the contract including any exception clause contained in it...
>
> In order to construe the contract, including the conditions of sale, and to determine the intention of the parties, I believe it is proper and necessary to examine and understand the framework in which the transaction materialized and was concluded.

After an examination of facts surrounding the transaction, the judge concluded that it was clear from the evidence that had the parties directed their minds to the risk of rabies both parties would have allocated the risk to the defendant, "seller." He therefore found that the defendant had to bear the risk and gave judgment to the plaintiffs.

Gallant et al. v. Hobbs

(1982) 37 O.R. (2d) 1

Ontario County Court - County of Middlesex

April 26, 1982

The defendant courier company promised delivery within four hours of request. The plaintiff bank called the courier company at 12:08 requesting delivery of municipal tax payments due that day. The driver arrived for the envelopes about 1:30, but they were not ready until 2:00. Three of six deliveries were made by 4 p.m. but at that time the driver was erroneously told by the dispatcher that it was too late to deliver the rest of the cheques. The driver delivered them the following morning. Two of the municipalities did not accept late payment without penalty and assessed fines of $54,089 and $39,407.

After the court concluded that the defendant courier was in breach of contract, the defendant argued, *inter alia*, that the regulations to the *Motor Carrier Act* limited its liability for "any loss or damage" to "$2.00 per pound unless a higher value declared."

In a unanimous decision, the B.C. Court of Appeal upheld the trial judge's interpretation that the regulations only applied to loss or damage to the goods themselves and did not apply to damages arising from delay. The court concluded that the courier must pay the $93,000 penalties which were reasonably foreseeable damages.

Bank of Montreal v. Overland Freight Lines Ltd. *(unreported)*
The Lawyers Weekly
April 21, 1989 p. 2; June 1, 1990 p.19

6. Liquidated Damages

Questions

Can the parties to a contract agree in the contract on the amount of damages to be paid in the event of a breach?
Is such an agreement binding?

Lee v. Skalbania

Supreme Court of British Columbia
Vancouver Registry No. C872510
December 21, 1987

Summary of the facts: Lee and Skalbania entered into a contract for the sale of Lee's property at a price of $975,000, the completion date to be March 31, 1987 and the balance of the cash payment to be paid that day. The vendor Lee was to carry a second mortgage of $200,000. The contract also provided that Skalbania pay a deposit of $50,000 which, at the option of the vendor, would be "absolutely forfeited to the owner as liquidated damages" in the event of his breach. He did breach. He failed to tender the cash payment on the completion date, which was extended to April 1, 1987. Lee refused to grant a further extension of time, cancelled the agreement, and sold the property to another for the same price, but for cash. Lee now claims the $50,000 deposit held in trust.

Gow J.: -... The primary issue is whether the deposit of $50,000 was liquidated damages or a penalty.

The position of the defendant is aptly set out in the affidavits of Skalbania.

In his affidavit filed October 2, 1987 he says:

> 2) That on February 5, 1987 I signed an interim agreement offering to purchase 2487 Point Grey Road, Vancouver, British Columbia ... and at no time was it ever discussed with the plaintiff as to whether the $50,000.00 was or would be a pre-estimate of damages. In fact, the $50,000.00 was not paid until the plaintiff signed the interim agreement on the 10th day of February, 1987. The $50,000.00 was and is not 'non-refundable'.
>
> 3) That the present value of a $200,000.00 mortgage at 9% for two years as at April 1, 1987 is approximately $168,336.00. As a result, the plaintiff by virtue of her sale on April 1, 1987 to new purchasers Mr. Koon Yip Lee and Sau Yung Lee has saved the sum of $31,664.00 with the result the plaintiff has suffered no damages but, in fact, made a profit. Now produced and shown to me and marked exhibit 'A' to this my Affidavit is a true copy of a letter dated October 26, 1987 from Fred Whittaker, Chartered Accountant, setting out the present value of a $200,000.00 mortgage as aforementioned.

In his affidavit filed November 4, 1987 he says:

> 3) That it is unfair that the plaintiff, who has suffered no damages whatsoever, but in reality has made a profit of $31,000.00 by virtue of the fact that the purchase and sale by myself did not take place, to retain the deposit of $50,000.00. It is unconscionable for her to retain the deposit and at no time would I have ever signed or agreed to a deposit of the same had I understood that in the event the Vendor sold the property for the same price and on much more favorable terms to another purchaser, I would lose the $50,000.00 deposit.

Filed on behalf of the plaintiff on October 26, 1987 was an affidavit by one Banu Foroutan, a real estate sales person of Vancouver, who stated "that the usual practice in the real estate business is to obtain a minimum deposit on the sale of residential property of between 5% and 10% of the total purchase price". ...

On the facts I find:

> (1) That the plaintiff was ready, willing and able to complete.
> (2) That the defendant was unable to complete when the time for performance came, namely, April 1, 1987.
> (3) Time remained the essence of the contract.

I hold that the failure of the defendant to perform timeously was a breach of contract on his part which relieved the plaintiff of her obligations to perform under the contract but the contract survived for the purpose of enabling the plaintiff to pursue her remedies thereunder.

I find that she elected the remedy of cancellation of the contract and the forfeiture to her of the deposit as liquidated damages. That is, however, a finding in fact of what the plaintiff did. The question remains is she entitled to that remedy? The answer is "yes" if the $50,000 was a genuine pre-estimate of damages: the answer is "no" if it was a penalty. But even if the answer is a "penalty" the plaintiff will be deprived of the $50,000 only if it were unconscionable for her to retain that sum. *Dimensional Investments Ltd. v. R.*, [1968] S.C.R. 93.

In *Elsley v. J.G. Collins Insurance Agencies Ltd.*, (1978) 2 S.C.R. 916, Dickson J. (as he then was) said at p. 937:

> It is now evident that the power to strike down a penalty clause is a blatant interference with freedom of contract and is designed for the sole purpose of providing relief against oppression for the party having to pay the stipulated sum. It has no place where there is no oppression. ...
>
> Of course, if an agreed sum is a valid liquidated damages clause, the plaintiff is entitled at law to recover this sum regardless of the actual loss sustained.

The facts in *Hughes v. Lukuvka* (1970)–75 (BCCA) bear a striking similarity to the facts in this case.

The headnote reads:

> Appellant had agreed to buy property for $59,500 and time was expressed to be of the essence; he paid a deposit of $5,000. The contract provided that upon failure by the purchaser to pay the balance of the cash payment and to execute formal documents within the time stipulated the owner could cancel the agreement and retain the deposit as liquidated damages. The purchaser failed to complete as stipulated and the vendor elected to cancel the agreement and claimed the deposit, which claim was upheld by Ruttan, J. The substantial question on the appeal was whether the deposit should be regarded as a penalty and its retention by the vendor relieved against as unconscionable.
>
> It was held per curiam, that the appeal must be dismissed; there was no onus on the respondent to prove that the amount of the deposit was arrived at as a result of a genuine pre-estimate by the parties of the actual damage; the fact that it was described as liquidated damages in the contract freely entered into by the parties afforded evidence that it was a genuine pre-estimate of damages especially where, as here, the amount could not be said to be out of all proportion to the damage; while the use of the words 'liquidated damages' was not conclusive, it should not be disregarded without good reason.

The judgment of the Court was given by McFarlane J.A. who concluded his reasons by citing a dictum of Lord Parmoor in *Dunlop Pneumatic Tyre Co. v. New Garage & Motor Co., 1915 A.C.* 79 PC 101:

> No abstract can be laid down without reference to the special facts of the particular case, but when competent parties by free contract are purporting to agree a sum as liquidated damages, there is no reason for refusing a wide limit of discretion. To justify interference there must be an extravagant disproportion between the agreed sum and *the amount of any damage capable of pre-estimate.*

The emphasis added is mine because McFarlane J.A. went on to say:

> Applying these principles to the facts, I am of the opinion that the deposit of $5,000 should not be regarded as a penalty and that its retention by the respondent is not unconscionable.

In that case, the amount of the deposit was approximately 1/12 of the purchase price. In the instant case, the amount of deposit is approximately between 1/19 and 1/20.

Applying the principles discussed to the facts of this case, I find that the sum of $50,000 is not a penalty, but a more than reasonable pre-estimate of damage and, therefore, is liquidated damages. Even if I were in error in making that finding, and the sum was a penalty I would find that it was not unconscionable for the plaintiff to "retain" it.

Does it make any difference that the plaintiff was fortunate enough to re-sell for the same price?

Again, the decision in *Hughes v. Lukuvka*, supra, is most helpful. There, in the original contract, the price was $59,500, payable $38,500 in cash and the balance by assumption of an existing mortgage for approximately $21,000 with interest. The completion date was June 30, 1969. Before June 20, 1969, the purchaser informed the vendor that he would not have funds by the completion date and requested an extension of time. The request was refused and on July 22, 1969 the vendor gave the purchaser written notice of her election to exercise her contractual right to cancel the agreement and claim the deposit. On July 25th, she accepted an offer from other purchasers to buy the property for $59,500.

The reason is plain. The test of reasonableness is at the date of the making of the contract and not at the date of the breach or any subsequent date. The reason for that reason is also plain, namely, that at the time when the agreement about liquidated damages is made, each party takes a risk, the vendor that the damages he may in fact suffer from failure on the part of the purchaser to complete will be very much greater, and the purchaser, that the vendor may not suffer any damage at all, or if he does suffer damage that damage is much less in amount than the amount stipulated as liquidated damages.

Nor does it matter that the plaintiff as vendor was to take a mortgage back of $200,000. First of all, that was an advantage to the defendant and a disadvantage to the plaintiff because she could not put that part of the price into her pocket. Secondly, even with respect to the cash balance of $775,000, the $50,000 was only 1/15. ...

I dismiss the counterclaim and application of the defendant.

Judgment for plaintiff.

7. DAMAGES

Question

How does the court approach the problem of determining the amount of damages to be paid by the party found to be in breach of contract?

Parta Industries Ltd. v. Canadian Pacific Ltd. et al.

48 D.L.R. (3D) 463
BRITISH COLUMBIA SUPREME COURT
JULY 4, 1974.

Summary of the facts from the law report, reprinted with permission of Canada Law Book Inc., 240 Edward Street, Aurora, Ontario L4G 3S9.

The defendant carriers agreed to ship from Montreal to British Columbia certain goods imported from Belgium, described as construction material. The bill of lading was marked "RUSH." The goods consisted of equipment essential to the plaintiff's plan to bring into operation a manufacturing plant. Owing to the derailment of three railway cars the goods were damaged, and as a result, the plaintiff had to reorder the goods from Belgium, and the opening of its plant was delayed for 105 days. [The plaintiffs sued] for damages caused by the delay. ...

Craig, J.:—The plaintiff commenced an action against the defendants (hereinafter referred to as "the defendants") claiming

(a) Special and general damages for breach of contract entered into between the Plaintiff and the Defendants on the l2th day of September 1969, by which contract the Defendants, common carriers, contracted to deliver goods for and to the Plaintiff, and did fail to do so in accordance with the terms, express and implied, of the said contract. Which failure caused financial loss to the Plaintiff.

(b) In the alternative, damages against the Defendants for negligence in the performance of the aforementioned contract, which negligence caused financial loss to the Plaintiff.

The defendants have denied the plaintiff's claim, generally, and have counterclaimed for the sum of $1,548.59 which, they allege, is the net amount owing to them after making financial adjustments between the parties relating to this incident. ...

Mr. Moran contends that the failure of the defendant to deliver the equipment in usable condition on or before September 19th, or within a reasonable time of this date, was a breach of the contract to "rush" delivery and that the plaintiff suffered damages totaling $129,705. He filed a schedule as ex. "4" which representatives of the plaintiff had prepared, showing how damages were calculated and what items were included. He submitted that these items of damages and the amounts claimed for these items are such damages:

(1) "...as may fairly and reasonable be considered as...arising naturally...", or at least,
(2) "...as may reasonable be supposed to have been in contemplation of both parties, at the time they made the contract, as the probable result of the breach of it".

citing *Hadley v. Baxendale* (1854), 9 Ex. 341, 156 E.R. 145, and the well-known judgment of Asquith,

L.J., in *Victoria Laundry (Windsor) Ltd. v. Newman Industries Ltd.; Coulson & Co. Ltd. (Third Parties),* [1949] 2 K.B. 528, [1949] 1 All E.R. 997. ...

In the *Victoria Laundry (Windsor) Ltd. v. Newman Industries Ltd.* case, *supra,* Asquith, L.J., listed six propositions applicable to damages for breach of contract. His judgment has been referred to on numerous occasions. These propositions are as follows [at pp. 539-40]:

> (1) It is well settled that the governing purpose of damages is to put the party whose rights have been violated in the same position, so far as money can do so, as if his rights had been observed: (*Sally Wertheim v. Chicoutimi Pulp Company,* [1911] A.C. 301). This purpose, if relentlessly pursued, would provide him with a complete indemnity for all loss *de facto* resulting from a particular breach, however improbable, however unpredictable. This, in contract at least, is recognized as too harsh a rule. Hence,
>
> (2) In cases of breach of contract the aggrieved party is only entitled to recover such part of the loss actually resulting as was at the time of the contract reasonably foreseeable as liable to result from the breach.
>
> (3) What was at that time reasonably so foreseeable depends on the knowledge then possessed by the parties or, at all events, by the party who later commits the breach.
>
> (4) For this purpose, knowledge "possessed" is of two kinds; one imputed, the other actual. Everyone, as a reasonable person, is taken to know the "ordinary course of things" and consequently what loss is liable to result from a breach of contract in that ordinary course. This is the subject matter of the "first rule" in *Hadley v. Baxendale.* But to this knowledge, which a contract-breaker is assumed to possess whether he actually possesses it or not, there may have to be added in a particular case knowledge which he actually possesses, of special circumstances outside the "ordinary course of things," of such a kind that a breach in those special circumstances would be liable to cause more loss. Such a case attracts the operation of the "second rule" so as to make additional loss also recoverable.
>
> (5) In order to make the contract-breaker liable under either rule it is not necessary that he should actually have asked himself what loss is liable to result from a breach. As has often been pointed out, parties at the time of contracting contemplate not the breach of the contract, but its performance. It suffices that, if he had considered the question, he would as a reasonable man have concluded that the loss in question was liable to result (see certain observations of Lord du Parcq in the recent case of *A/B Karlshamms Oljefabriker v. Monarch Steamship Company Limited,* [1949] A.C. 196).
>
> (6) Nor, finally, to make a particular loss recoverable, need it be proved that upon a given state of knowledge the defendant could, as a reasonable man, foresee that a breach must necessarily result in that loss. It is enough if he could foresee it was likely so to result. It is indeed enough, to borrow from the language of Lord du Parcq in the same case, at page 158, if the loss (or some factor without which it would not have occurred) is a "serious possibility" or a "real danger." For short, we have used the word "liable" to result. Possibly the colloquialism "on the cards" indicates the shade of meaning with some approach to accuracy.

In his judgment, also, Asquith, L.J., said that the case of *British Columbia Saw-Mill Co. v. Nettleship* (1868), L.R. 3 C.P. 499, annexed a rider to the principle laid in *Hadley v. Baxendale* to the effect

> ...that where knowledge of special circumstances is relied on as enhancing the damage recoverable that knowledge must have been brought home to the defendant at the time of the contract and in such circumstances that the defendant impliedly undertook to bear any special loss referable to a breach in those special circumstances. The knowledge which was lacking in that case on the part of the defendant was knowledge that the particular box of machinery negligently lost by the defendants was one without which the rest of the machinery could not be put together and would therefore be useless.

Having regard to the evidence in this case and the circumstances generally, I find that the only knowledge possessed by the defendant was that he was to

"RUSH" delivery of 77 packages of "construction material." There is nothing in the contract to indicate the nature of the material, nor the use to which it was to be put. Certainly, there is nothing to indicate that it was to be used in a large manufacturing plant and that the plant could not operate without the equipment. In other words, the defendant did not have knowledge of the special circumstances of the situation which would bring into operation the second branch of the rule in *Hadley v. Baxendale*. That being so, what damages, if any, in this case should be considered as "...such as may fairly and reasonably be considered as...arising naturally i.e. according to the natural course of things from the breach of contract..."? In my opinion, the defendant could have reasonably foreseen on the facts which were known to it in this case that a delay in delivery, or a failure to deliver was liable to result in:

(a) a delay in actual construction;
(b) extra labour costs;
(c) interest;
(d) depreciation of equipment;
(e) additional overhead expenses;
(f) cost of repairing and replacing equipment.

While I think that the defendant could have reasonably foreseen a delay in construction, I do not think that the defendant could have reasonably foreseen a delay of 105 days. ...

A woman injured in two automobile accidents had worked full time in a bakery co-owned with her husband, and approximately 40 hours a week at home. She appealed from the trial judge's award of damages which she argued were "inadequate." The Saskatchewan Court of Appeal held that she was entitled to an award of damages that would compensate her not only for loss of earning capacity, pain and suffering and loss of amenities, but also for the impairment of her housekeeping capacity. The court would take into account the cost of employing someone to provide the services she had performed, including the value of management.

Dean v. Fobel; MacDonald v. Fobel
Saskatchewan Court of Appeal
83 D.L.R. (4th) 385
August 27, 1991

The Supreme Court of Canada refused leave to appeal in March of 1992.

The Lawyers Weekly
September 18, 1992 p. 3

Note: This "landmark" decision has now been followed in numerous cases. Watch for further cases on and discussion of compensation for lost "housekeeping capacity."

Penzoil successfully sued Texaco for interfering with its planned merger with Getty Oil and was awarded $10.53 billion by a jury, the largest award in U.S. history. Texaco subsequently filed for bankruptcy. Later the companies reached a settlement by which Texaco would agree to pay to Pennzoil the sum of $3 billion in cash.[20]

Mr. Oshry contracted with the City of Edmonton for an advertisement to be placed in the Yellow Pages. He alleged the contract was breached, for one reason, because of the misspelling of his name. By spelling his first name as Aaroon rather than Aaron he could lose potential clients who would think him Arabic rather than Jewish. The trial judge awarded him a refund for the price of the advertisement, $900. On appeal the court held that the misspelling was not a breach of an essential term which would allow the plaintiff to terminate the contract. The plaintiff's loss was merely the waste of some time answering calls about his name. The award was reduced to $150, the hourly rate for an experienced lawyer and $10 nominal damages.

Oshry v. City of Edmonton
Summarized from The Lawyers Weekly
November 29, 1991 p. 28.

DIFFICULTIES IN ASSESSING QUANTUM OF DAMAGES

When Judge Taylor of the B.C. Supreme Court had to assess damages to be awarded to an 88-year-old plaintiff seriously injured when struck by a car, he found the principles for assessing damages "sadly inadequate to the task." The life expectancy tables were not especially helpful to determine the loss to a man of that age who had been active and robust before the accident. Furthermore, the judge did not feel that the practice of awarding a lump sum was appropriate. Nevertheless, following established procedures, he awarded the plaintiff $50,000 non-pecuniary damages.

Olesik v. Mackin et al.
Summarized from The Lawyers Weekly
March 27, 1986 p. 18

A dispensing error by a pharmacist in Vancouver resulted in a fatal dose of an anti-psychotic drug being given to a 94-year-old woman.

In Louisiana, a coroner deliberately dropped a dead baby to examine the results of a fall on her head. The information would help him as an expert witness in an infant mortality case.

Punitive Damages

The National Bank of Canada was sued because of its role in diverting funds from a public company to a rogue and his companies. The Ontario Court of Appeal found that the bank had conspired to deplete the company's assets and awarded the plaintiff $4.8 million dollars in punitive damages, in addition to the $7 million awarded for compensatory damages. The judges reviewed the law with regard to punitive damages as follows:

"In the words of Schroeder J.A. in *Denison v. Fawcet*, 1958 O.R. 312 at pp. 319-20, 12 D.L.R. (2d) 537 at p. 542 (C.A.), exemplary or aggravated damages may be awarded:

> [i]f, in addition to committing the wrongful act, the defendant's conduct is "highhanded, malicious, conduct showing a contempt of the plaintiff's rights, or disregarding every principle which actuates the conduct of a gentleman"...

In *Robitaille v. Vancouver Hockey Club Ltd.* (1981), 124 D.L.R. (3d) 228 at p. 251, [1981] 3 W.W.R. 481, 30 B.C.L.R. 286 (C.A.), it was pointed out that aggravated damages may be awarded on the basis of circumstances which accompany or are associated with the tortious conduct.

A further principle for consideration comes from *Cassell & Co. Ltd. v. Broome*, [1972] All E.R. 801 (H.L.) at pp. 830-31. In an exhaustive analysis of exemplary, punitive or aggravated damages, Lord Hailsham observed, citing Lord Devlin in *Rookes v. Barnard*, [1964] 1 All E.R. 367 (H.L.), that '[e]xemplary damages can properly be awarded whenever it is necessary to teach a wrongdoer that tort does not pay'."

Claiborne Industries Ltd. v. National Bank of Canada
(1989) 59 D.L.R. (4th) 513

Note: See also *The Lawyers Weekly* (July 14, 1989 p. 1, 15) which quotes the winning counsel as saying "it was by far the largest punitive award in the history of this country".

In 1984, The U.S. Supreme Court reinstated a $10 million punitive damages award won by the estate of Karen Silkwood. In Oklahoma a jury had awarded her children $500,000 in actual damages and $10 million in punitive damages. The U.S. Circuit Court of Appeals had overturned the punitive damage award on the basis that the federal government's exclusive regulation of radiation hazards precluded any punitive damage award based on state law.[21]

In 1986 it was reported that the estate settled for $1.38 million.[22]

8. Contempt of Court

Question

Equitable remedies are one type of orders of the court. What can be done if a person ignores an order of the court?

See p. 173 for the consequences imposed for failing to obey an injunction.

Faye Leung, the person who arranged the sale of former B.C. premier Vander Zalm's Fantasy Garden theme park, was sued by former business associates who alleged that she had fraudulently induced them to participate in a real estate investment. The court ordered Leung to produce a list of her assets. She not only failed to provide the list, but also violated a court order by attempting to remove "a major asset" from the province. Her conduct was held to be in contempt of court.

At the hearing in which the Supreme Court Judge was attempting to determine the appropriate remedy, the lawyer for the former associates referred to her as a "whirling dervish of deceit" and in response to the judge's suggestion that she do community service, the lawyer answered "not to be unkind or flippant, but I have some concerns about loosing this woman upon the world."[23]

In his judgment released February 17, 1992, the judge described her as "obstructive, uncooperative, and dishonest," but suspended her sentence with a two-year probation. He stated that he had considered a sentence of imprisonment with a recommendation for electronic monitoring, "but concluded she is likely to become too much of a nuisance to the corrections authorities."

Her former associates won their case against her.[24]

Lyndon LaRoche, a controversial political figure in the U.S. frequently cited for contempt of court, ran for the U.S. presidency and was quoted as saying "It's a terrible inconvenience running a presidential campaign from prison."[25]

Criminal Contempt

An inmate, protesting his transfer to a different jail, plugged the toilet in the cell directly above the courtroom so that the overflowing water would fall on the judge below. It was reported that the judge, to continue on with his cases, merely ordered a bailiff to hold an umbrella over his head. The inmate was charged with contempt of court, but the judge, after receiving an apology from the inmate, imposed no sentence.[26]

Endnotes

1. Summarized from *The Globe and Mail,* February 10, 1992, p. B1
2. *The Lawyers Weekly,* May 24, 1991, p. 2
3. *The Lawyers Weekly,* October 2, 1992, p. 17
4. Summarized from *The Globe and Mail,* April 23, p. 1
5. Summarized from *The Lawyers Weekly,* October 23, 1992, p. 16
6. Summarized from *The Lawyers Weekly,* September 27, 1991, p. 24
7. A more detailed account is given in *Newsweek,* March 25, 1985, p. 72
8. A more detailed account is given in the *Vancouver Sun,* November 19, 1992, p. B7
9. Summarized from *The Globe and Mail,* December 29, 1993 p. A9
10. A more detailed account is given in the *Vancouver Sun,* December 15, 1993, p. A16
11. Summarized from *Maclean's,* November 22, 1993, p. 37
12. A more detailed account is given in the *Vancouver Sun,* October 15, 1993, p. D1
13. Summarized from *The Globe and Mail,* November 25, 1993, p. B2
14. For a more detailed account see the *Vancouver Sun,* January 27, 1994
15. Summarized from *The Globe and Mail,* November 17, 1992, p. A9
16. A more detailed account is given in the *Vancouver Sun,* October 8, 1992, p. A10
17. A more detailed account is given in the *Vancouver Sun,* March 25, 1993, p. A18
18. A more detailed account is given in the *Vancouver Sun,* November 1, 1993, p. A4
19. *The Lawyers Weekly,* July 29, 1988, p. 2
20. More detailed accounts of this case can be found in *The New York Times.* See, for example, December 20, 1987, p. 1
21. Summarized from *The Globe and Mail,* January 12, 1984, p. 8
22. *The Globe and Mail,* August 23, 1986
23. A more detailed account is given in the *Vancouver Sun,* January 29, 1992, p. 1
24. A more detailed account is given in the *Vancouver Sun,* February 18, 1992, p. 1
25. A more detailed account is given in the *Vancouver Sun,* October 29, 1992, p. A14
26. *The Lawyers Weekly,* June 6, 1986

IV

LEGISLATIVE INTERFERENCE IN THE CONTRACTUAL RELATIONSHIP

A. Sale of Goods Act

Questions

What types of contracts are covered by the Sale of Goods Act?
What contractual terms are implied by the statute?
What additional remedies does the statute give the unpaid seller?

1. Scope of the Statute

Mr. Gee and Mr. and Mrs. Pan, customers of White Spot restaurant, claimed they suffered botulism poisoning from food eaten at the restaruant. They sued the restaurant for breach of the implied term of the contract that the food was fit for purpose. The defendant argued that the contract was one for services and not goods and was not properly covered by the *Sale of Goods Act.* The first question the plaintiffs put before the court was whether or not the *Sale of Goods Act* applied to the purchase of a meal from a restaurant.

The B.C. Supreme Court had no binding precedent before it. The Justice reviewed cases from Canada, the United Kingdom and the United States and concluded that "an item on the menu offered for a fixed price is an offering of a finished product and is primarily an offering of the sale of goods and not primarily an offering of a sale of services." In answer to the second question as to what must the plaintiff prove to establish the liability of the defendant restaurant, the court answered that to establish an impled condition of resonable fitness three requirments must be met:

"First, the goods in question must be of a kind in which the seller normally deals in the course of his business. ...

The second requirement is that the proposed use of the food is made known to the seller so as to show the plaintiff's reliance on the seller's skill and judgment...

The third requirement is that the contract is not for sale of a specified article under its patent or other trade name."

Applying the law as stated to the facts of the case, the court held for the plaintiffs. The defendants were liable under s. 18(a) of the *Sale of Goods Act* (the fit for purpose provision).

Furthermore, the facts supported a claim under s. 18(b), namely, the defendants were liable for breach of the implied condition that the goods were of merchantable quality.

The judge commented that fourteen other actions were pending against White Spot on similar allegations.

Gee v. White Spot Pan et al v. White Spot
32 D.L.R. (4th) 238
British Columbia Supreme Court
October 27, 1986

2. Implied Terms

Fit for Purpose/Merchantable

Sigurdson et al. v. *Hilcrest Service Ltd., Acklands Ltd., Third Party*

73 D.L.R. (3D) 132
SASKATCHEWAN QUEEN'S BENCH
DECEMBER 21, 1976.

Estey, J.:—This action arises out of a single vehicle accident in which the plaintiffs allege that they did suffer personal injuries. The said vehicle was owned by the plaintiff Mr. K.E. Sigurdson. The plaintiffs allege that the cause of the accident was a faulty brake hose installed on the vehicle in the defendant's garage. The defendant joined Acklands Limited as a third party as Acklands supplied the defendant with the two hydraulic brake hoses which the defendant through its employees installed on the said vehicle.

The plaintiff Karl Edward Sigurdson stated that he was on June 16, 1973, operating a 1963 Ford vehicle owned by him and had as passengers his wife Hannelore and his children Christopher and Michael.

At approximately 4:30 p.m. on June 16, 1973, Mr. Sigurdson was approaching the intersection of Avenue H and 20th St. in the City of Saskatoon intending to make a right-hand turn onto 20th St. when he was confronted with a red stop-light at the said intersection. Mr. Sigurdson stated that pedestrians were crossing the intersection in front of his vehicle and when he applied the brakes they failed to operate. He immediately swung his vehicle to the right hitting a power pole. Mr. Sigurdson stated that at the time of the accident his speed was 15 to 20 m.p.h. and that the brakes of the vehicle had up until the time of the accident been operating in a proper manner. The vehicle as a result of the accident was damaged beyond repair. A few days prior to May 1, 1973, Mr. Sigurdson took his vehicle to the defendant's service station for certain repairs as the defendants had previously serviced his vehicle. Exhibit P.10 dated May 1, 1973, is the invoice which Mr. Sigurdson received from the defendant covering the repairs and labour performed on his vehicle immediately prior to the said date. This exhibit shows that two brake hoses were on this occasion installed by the defendant on Mr. Sigurdson's vehicle. Mr. Sigurdson as a result of the accident had three teeth removed and now has a partial denture. His son the plaintiff Michael received minor scratches while the plaintiffs Christopher and Mrs. Hannelore Sigurdson received injuries to which I will later refer. Mr. Sigurdson stated that after receiving his vehicle from the defendant's garage on or about May 1, 1973, the brakes on the said vehicle did until the time of the accident operate in a proper manner and that from May 1, 1973, to the date of the accident he had travelled approximately 1,300 miles. Mr. Sigurdson takes the view that the cause of the brake failure was due to a faulty brake hose. Counsel agreed that the brake hose removed from Mr. Sigurdson's vehicle is ex. P.11 and that exs. P.12, 13, 14 and 15 which are portions of a brake hose were cut off P.11 for purpose of examination.

Professor C.M. Sargent, from the faculty of mechanical engineering at the University of Saskatchewan in Saskatoon, examined the said brake hose by means of cutting off portions and found therein at least two particles which were composed of what he described as a "glassy material". His opinion was that due to the operation of the motor vehicle these particles tended to work towards the outside of the brake hose permitting the brake fluid to escape. His evidence was that in order for a garage operator to discover the presence of these "glassy particles" the hose would have to be cut and thereby destroyed. ...

[After reviewing the reports of injuries suffered by the plaintiffs the judge turned to the evidence of the defendant.]

Evidence on behalf of the defendant was given by Mr. A.P. Halseth who in May, 1973, was an officer of the defendant company and worked in the company's service station. Mr. Halseth admitted that just prior to May 1, 1973, Mr. Sigurdson's vehicle was in the defendant's service station and that the two new brake hoses were installed on the said vehicle. The said brake hoses were obtained by the defendant from the third party Acklands Limited which company had been a supplier to the defendant since 1958. Mr. Halseth stated that the defendant company relied on the third party to supply proper brake hoses. Exhibit D.3 is an invoice from the third party referring to two brake hoses. Mr. Halseth stated that after the accident he inspected the plaintiff's vehicle to determine the cause of brake failure. He filled the master brake cylinder with brake fluid but found there was no build-up of pressure and on examining one of the brake hoses which had been installed by the defendant he found that brake fluid was dripping from the brake hose in the location immediately adjacent to the male end of the hose. The witness stated that he has had considerable experience with brake hoses but does not know of a method of testing a brake hose for leaks prior to installation. Mr. Halseth stated that after installing new brake hoses he puts the fluid under pressure and inspects for leaks. The witness denied that any member of the defendant's staff did anything in the installation of the brake hose which contributed to the rupture of the hose.

The plaintiffs in their statement of claim allege that the cause of their injuries was the failure on the part of the defendant's employee or employees to properly service and repair the vehicle and failure to test and examine the repairs to the vehicle. The plaintiffs also allege the use of defective materials by the defendant in effecting the repairs. The statement of defence pleads the provisions of the *Contributory Negligence Act,* R.S.S. 1965, c.91, and in the alternative that if liability is found the responsibility for such injuries and damages rests with Acklands Limited as its supplier of automotive parts. The third party's statement of defence admits that the said party is engaged in the wholesale automotive parts business and did on or about May 1, 1973, sell and deliver to the defendant's place of business two brake hoses priced at $6.60. The third party also alleges that the hydraulic brake hoses were supplied to it by a firm know[n] as Echlin Limited and that if there was negligence in the "supply and manufacture of the said brake hose, it was the negligence of Echlin Limited the supplier and manufacturer". It should be pointed out that at the time of the trial of the action the manufacturer of the said brake hoses was not a party to the action.

I will first deal with the actions of Mrs. Sigurdson and her son Christopher. My understanding of the law is that in order for these parties to succeed against the defendant they must establish negligence on the part of the defendant in the repair of the vehicle. I am satisfied from the evidence that one of the brake hoses installed by the defendant was defective in that it contained at least two foreign objects as determined by Professor Sargent and that due to the operation of the vehicle these objects moved causing a rupture in the hose which permitted brake fluid to escape. I am further of the view that the cause of the accident was brake failure caused by the escape of the brake fluid. If there be negligence on the part of the defendant it must be carelessness on the part of its employee or employees in the installation of the brake hose or in the installation of the brake hose which the defendant's employees knew or should have known was defective. From the evidence I am unable to find that there was any negligence in the installation of the brake hose. The evidence further established to my satisfaction that no inspection by an employee of the defendant of the brake hose prior to installation would have determined the defects other than that of cutting the hose as was done by Professor Sargent. Indeed the professor stated that he knew of no test which could be made in the garage which would determine the presence of foreign objects in the hose other than by the destruction of the hose. The question of the necessity for an inspection of the brake hose by the defendant is dealt with in *Charlesworth on Negligence*, 5th ed. (1971), para. 654, pp.405-6, when the author writes:

> A retailer is under no duty to examine goods for defects before resale, in the absence of circumstances suggesting that they might be defective, when he obtains them from a manufacturer of repute. ...

Placing the defendant in a position of a retailer I take the view that there were no circumstances in the present case which would suggest to an employee of the defendant that the brake hose was or might be defective when it was delivered to the defendant's place of business by the third party. Indeed there was, prior to installation of the brake hose, no test or examination which could be conducted by the defendant which would locate the foreign object short of destruction of the brake hose. Moreover, the operation of the vehicle from May 1st to June 16th suggests in itself that the actual installation of the brake hose was proper. There is therefore in my opinion no negligence on the part of the defendant in either the installation of the break hose or in the failure to inspect such hose prior to installation. As I have held that there is no negligence on the part of the defendant, I dismiss the actions of the plaintiffs Mrs. Sigurdson and her son Christopher.

The liability of the defendant towards the plaintiff Mr. Sigurdson involves other considerations. While I have already held that the defendant's employees were not guilty of negligence the defendant, in so far as the plaintiff Mr. Sigurdson is concerned, is faced with the provisions of the *Sale of Goods Act*, R.S.S. 1965, c. 388, s. 16, which reads:

> 16. Subject to the provisions of this Act and of any Act in that behalf there is no implied warranty or condition as to the quality of fitness for any particular purpose of goods supplied under a contract of sale except as follows:
>
> 1. Where the buyer expressly or by implication makes known to the seller the particular purpose for which the goods are required so as to show that the buyer relies on the seller's skill or judgment and the goods are of a description that it is in the course of the seller's business to supply, whether he be the manufacturer or not, there is an implied condition that the goods shall be reasonably fit for that purpose;
>
> 2. Where goods are bought by description from a seller who deals in goods of that description, whether he is the manufacturer or not, there is an implied condition that the goods shall be of merchantable quality:
>
>   Provided that if the buyer has examined the goods there shall be no implied condition with regard to defects which such examination ought to have revealed;
>
> 3. An implied warranty or condition as to quality or fitness for a particular purpose may be annexed by usage of trade;

Waddams in his text *Products Liability* (1974) suggests that even in the absence of negligence a repairer may be liable to the plaintiff Mr. Sigurdson for breach of the implied warranty as set out in said s. 16 when the author writes at pp. 18-9:

> However, insofar as the defect complained of is caused by defective materials supplied by the installer or repairer, there may be liability even in the absence of negligence for breach of an implied warranty that the materials used are reasonably fit.

The said author points out at p.76 of his text:

> ...liability for breach of the implied warranties is strict liability in the sense that it is no defence for the seller to show that he exercised reasonable care or that the defect in the goods was undiscoverable.

I am of the view on the facts of the present case that there was by virtue of the *Sale of Goods Act,* an implied warranty or condition that the brake hose would be "reasonably fit" for the purpose for which it was intended. I find that the said brake hose was not "reasonably fit" in that it contained foreign bodies which eventually caused a rupture and brake failure which failure was the cause of the accident.

The defendant's plea of contributory negligence appears to be based on Mr. Sigurdson's failure to keep a proper look-out. The plaintiff was in the situation described by Hodgins, J.A., in *Harding v. Edwards et al.,* [1929] 4 D.L.R. 598 at pp. 599-600, 64 O.L.R. 98 at p.102 [affd 1931] 2 D.L.R. 521, [1931] S.C.R. 167], when he wrote:

> ...hence I cannot convince myself that he was sufficiently recovered from the shock of the emergency to be judged by standards involving deliberation and opportunity for conscious decision, or by what is called by Lord Sumner "nice judgment, prompt decision:" *SS. "Singleton Abbey" v. SS. "Paludina",* [1927] A.C. 16, at p. 26.

The plaintiff when confronted with pedestrians in front of him and a failure of his foot-brakes was faced with an emergency and he chose to turn to his right. There was no time for a "conscious decision" to the effect that he should try the hand-brake for by turning right he would hit a power pole. I do not think that contributory negligence attaches to the plaintiff on the facts of this case.

The question now arises as to the damages to which the plaintiff Mr. Sigurdson is entitled. Counsel for the parties agreed to special damages in the amount of $2,079.56. I therefore award to the plaintiff Mr. Sigurdson special damages in the amount of $2,079.56. I award the said plaintiff general damages in the amount of $2,000. The plaintiff Mr. Karl Sigurdson shall be entitled to his tax [sic] costs in this matter, such costs to be taxed in accordance with column 4 of the Queen's Bench tariff of costs. ...

The third party did not take an active part at the hearing. The reason being no doubt that it admitted selling two brake hoses to the defendant. My view is that the defendant may successfully recover from its supplier the third party for a breach of warranty, *i.e.,* that the brake hose was defective or not reasonably fit for the purpose for which it was intended. This point is dealt with by Waddams at p. 189 when the author writes:

> Although it is doubtful that one held liable for breach of warranty has a claim for contribution against the manufacturer of the defective goods as a joint tortfeasor, he may have a remedy against his own supplier (whether manufacturer or other distributor) for breach of implied warranty.

I therefore award judgment in favour of the defendant against the third party in the amount of the judgment recovered by the plaintiff against the defendant, together with the taxed costs paid by the defendant to the plaintiff.

Judgment for the plaintiff

A woman, shopping at Safeway, bought a 7-Up which she began to drink while the cashier packed her other groceries. The can contained a small dry cell battery which had made the fluid toxic. The woman suffered a severe burning of the lining of her mouth, throat and stomach. She sued Safeway for breach of contract, namely, breach of the implied term that the goods were fit for purpose. In the alternative, she sued the manufacturer and bottler and distributors of 7-Up for negligence.

Estrin v. Canada Safeway Ltd., 7-Up Vancouver Ltd., and Gray Beverage Co. Ltd.
A more detailed account is given in the Vancouver Sun, *November, 1979*

Note: Robert Gardner, the lawyer for the plaintiff, confirmed (January 18, 1994) that this matter was settled out of court.

Exemption Clauses in Contracts for the Sale of Goods

"... TO THE MAXIMUM EXTENT PERMITTED BY APPLICABLE LAW, MICROSOFT DISCLAIMS ALL OTHER WARRANTIES, EITHER EXPRESS OR IMPLIED, INCLUDING BUT NOT LIMITED TO IMPLIED WARRANTIES OF MERCHANTABILITY AND FITNESS FOR A PARTICULAR PURPOSE, WITH RESPECT TO THE SOFTWARE, THE ACCOMPANYING PRODUCT MANUAL(S) AND WRITTEN MATERIALS, AND ANY ACCOMPANYING HARDWARE... "

From the license agreement accompanying the computer program EXCEL.

3. Unpaid Seller's Rights

The defendant supplied a company with canola meal in installments as per the contract between them. After some of the meal had been delivered, the purchasing company made an assignment in bankruptcy. The bankrupt company owed $236,858 to the supplier. The trustee in bankruptcy pressed the supplier to continue to supply the meal. When it refused to do so, the trustee petitioned the court, which held that the purchasing company's breach was not sufficient to give rise to the right of the supplier to repudiate. The supplier appealed.

The B.C. Court of Appeal, in a 52-page decision, allowed the appeal. The supplier could retain the canola meal. Pursuant to the *Sale of Goods Act* the unpaid seller had a right to withhold delivery of the goods. Furthermore, the Act provided that a seller could retain the goods if the buyer became insolvent and that a seller had these rights even if he had made part delivery of the goods.

Coopers & Lybrand Ltd. v. Canbra Foods Ltd.
Summarized from The Lawyers Weekly
February 27, 1987 pp. 11, 13

B. Other Consumer Protection Legislation

Labels on Batman products warn the buyer that the "Armor does not provide actual protection and cape does not enable wearer to fly."[1]

Competition Act R.S.C.

Donald Cormie, the former president of defunct Principal Group Ltd., was charged under the *Competition Act* with misleading advertising and deceptive marketing practices. He pleaded guilty to misleading investors in the company's 1985 annual review. He was fined $500,000, the largest fine imposed on an individual under the Act. With the

1987 collapse of Principal Group Ltd., a group of more than one hundred thirty companies, some 70,000 investors were affected. These investors are suing Mr. Cormie for about $130 million in civil actions.[2]

"Damages Awarded: To the major-league baseball players union, $102.5 million in lost salaries for the 1987 and 1988 seasons; to be paid by the 26 club owners for conspiring to fix the market for free agents."[3]

Nintendo did not admit to any wrongdoing, but agreed to send $25 million worth of $5 discount coupons to registered users of Nintendo games who purchased games between June 1, 1988 and December 31, 1990; $1.75 million to the states of New York and Maryland where most of the legal work was done; and $3 million to other states. The company paid these sums to settle charges that it pressured dealers who wanted to sell below the suggested retail price by threatening to slow or reduce delivery of the games.[4]

FOOD AND DRUG ACT R.S.C.

Jim Pattison Industries Ltd. was fined $5,000 for violations of the *Food and Drug Act* R.S.C. The bakeries operated by Overwaitea Foods claimed the baguette bread had "no preservatives or fat". In fact, it had the same amount of fat as regular bread.[5]

Beech-Nut Nutrition Corp. (owned by Nesfood Inc. a subsidiary of Nestle S.A. of Switzerland) pled guilty to 215 counts of intentionally shipping millions of jars of bogus apple juice for babies. The juice was sold as pure apple juice, but, in fact, was mixed with other juices, beet sugar, corn syrup and other ingredients. The U.S. District Judge imposed a $2-million U.S. fine,, the largest ever paid under the U.S. *Food, Drug and Cosmetic Act.*[6]

BUSINESS PRACTICES ACT/TRADE PRACTICE ACT

Schryvers and Schryvers v. Richport Ford Sales Limited et al.

BRITISH COLUMBIA SUPREME COURT
VANCOUVER REGISTRY NO. C917060
MAY 18, 1993

Tysoe, J.: —On May 15, 1991 Mr. and Mrs. Schryvers acquired two vehicles from Richport Ford Sales Limited ("Richport Ford") through its salesperson, Mr. Stehr. They had intended to purchase the two vehicles in cash but the transactions were ultimately structured as leases with options to purchase. The aggregate amount payable by the Schryvers under the leases is greater than the sale prices of the vehicles plus a financing charge. …

Did the lease transactions involve a deceptive or unconscionable act or practice in contravention of the Act? [*Trade Practice Act* R.S.B.C. 1979, c 406]

Section 22 of the Act authorizes the Court to grant relief in a case where a consumer has entered a consumer transaction involving a deceptive or unconscionable act or practice by the supplier of the goods. Section 3(1) of the Act states that a deceptive act or practice includes any representation or conduct that has the capability, tendency or effect of deceiving or misleading a person. Subsection (3) of s. 3 lists instances of deceptive acts or practices, including a representation that is such that a person could reasonably conclude that a price benefit or advantage exists when it does not (clause j) and the failure to state a material fact in making a representation which makes it deceptive or misleading (clause r).

Section 4 of the Act deals with unconscionable acts or practices. There is no statement as to what constitutes an unconscionable act or practice. Subsection (2) states that a court shall consider all of the surrounding circumstances and it lists five types of circumstances that should be considered (e.g., undue pressure). Mr. Schryvers was an experienced businessman who has been involved in the purchase of over 100 vehicles in the past [from Richport]. Although the Schryvers may have been getting tired by the end of the dealings, they were not forced to continue. It may be argued that it was unconscionable for the Schryvers to be persuaded to enter into leases when they were too tired to realize that they were leases. However, I believe that Mr. Schryvers did appreciate that he was entering into leases and that he had second thoughts at a later time. In any event, it is clear that the Schryvers appreciated that they were entering into some kind of financing arrangement and I do not think that it would be unconscionable for the Schryvers to have entered into a financing arrangement by way of a lease with an option to purchase rather than a more conventional financing arrangement.

There is more merit in the claim that there was a deceptive act. In *Rushak v. Henneken* (1991), 84 D.L.R. (4th) 87 the B.C. Court of Appeal commented on the wide scope of the Act at p. 95: . …

It is my view that Richport Ford committed deceptive acts with respect to the lease transactions in at least two respects. In view of the fact that Mr. and Mrs. Schryvers had indicated their intention to purchase the vehicle with cash, it was incumbent on Mr. Stehr to have properly explained the financial differences between a lease and a cash purchase. Mr. Stehr failed to state a material fact when he did not advise the Schryvers that the cost of acquiring the vehicles by way of the lease/options was greater than the cost of purchasing the vehicles in cash (after taking into account the savings on the taxes under the lease and the saving of interest by leaving their money in the bank). I believe that Mr. Stehr intentionally left the impression that there was a price advantage by acquiring the vehicles through lease/options when such an advantage did not exist. Even if the "guaranteed" price or the availability of the three options at the end of the terms of the leases represents a significant benefit, the Schryvers should have still been properly advised on the financial comparison so that they could decide whether they were prepared to pay the extra amount for this benefit.

The second deceptive act relates to the position of Richport Ford that the sale prices of the vehicles is no longer relevant when it has been decided that the transaction is to be structured as a lease/option. In the words of counsel for the Schryvers which were adopted by Mr. Stehr, it is like comparing apples to oranges because the transactions are so different. Whether this position is right or wrong, Richport Ford had an obligation to disclose its position to the Schryvers so they would be aware that the two types of transactions could not be compared. I have no doubt that, to the knowledge of Mr. Stehr, the Schryvers believed that the plan was equivalent to a method of financing the purchase of the vehicles in a manner that was advantageous to an outright purchase. Mr. Stehr had a duty to point out to the Schryvers that the two methods of acquisition were not comparable and that the negotiated sale prices would not be utilized for the purposes of applying the lease rate factors to determine the amounts payable under the leases. …

[After lengthy discussion and calculation of damages the court concluded] The total of the general damages in respect of both vehicles is $4,948.31 + $6,630.16 = $11,578.47.

The Schryvers also seek punitive damages in the amount of $10,000. Counsel for the Schryvers relied on the following passage from *Novak v. Zephyr Ford Truck Centre Ltd.* (unreported, B.C.C.A., November 24, 1988, No. CA008534) at p. 7:

> Secondly, I wish to add that while the power of the court to award punitive damages should always be exercised with extreme caution and care, I note in this case that the learned trial judge found not only that there had been a deceptive trade practice, he also specifically found that upon this matter being questioned the de-

> fendant then adopted a series of stalling tactics which led to a heated confrontation and other unpleasantness. In those circumstances it seems to me that the learned trial judge had ample reason to make an award of punitive damages if he thought as he did, and we ought not to interfere.

Counsel for the Schryvers pointed to the fact that Mr. Schryvers complained about the leases well within the 15-day period during which Ford Credit would have allowed Richport Ford to cancel the assignment of the leases.

If the deceptive act committed by Richport Ford was restricted to a failure to properly explain the financial differences between a lease and a cash purchase, I may not be inclined to award punitive damages. However, I have also found that Richport Ford intentionally committed a deceptive act by structuring the leases without regard to the sale prices that were listed on the vehicles. Richport Ford received from the Schryvers and Ford Credit the following amounts (net of taxes) in comparison to the agreed sale prices (as adjusted to reflect the extended warranty, the undercoating and the freight and inspection charges):

	Amount Received	**Sale Price**
Explorer	$28,244	$26,080
Escort	$19,258	$15,220

Little wonder Richport Ford had a contest for the salesperson who could persuade the most customers to acquire their vehicles by way of a lease transaction. I consider the actions of Richport Ford to be sufficiently flagrant and high handed to warrant an award of punitive damages.

There must be a disincentive to suppliers in respect of intentionally deceptive trade practices. If no punitive damages are awarded for intentional violations of the legislation, suppliers will continue to conduct their businesses in a manner that involves deceptive trade prices because they will have nothing to lose. In this case I believe that the appropriate amount of punitive damages is the extra profit Richport Ford endeavoured to make as a result of its deceptive acts. I therefore award punitive damages against Richport Ford in the amount of $6,000.

Conclusion

I grant judgment against Richport Ford in the amount of $17,578.47 plus costs. ...

The plaintiff purchased a truck which the dealer had said had not sustained damage over $2,000. In fact, the truck's original owner had rolled the truck and the repairs to the bent frame had cost $34,000. After learning the story, the plaintiff complained several times to the seller who refused to deal with the matter. The buyer returned the truck, sued for rescission of the contract, return of the purchase price of the truck and punitive damages.

The court found for the plaintiff.

Novak et al. v. Zephyr Ford Truck Centre Ltd.
Summarized from The Lawyers Weekly
January 22, 1988 p. 12

The plaintiff learned that Mr. McGuire had a dormant account at the bank. He then contacted McGuire and identified himself as an estate locator finding heirs for unclaimed estates. He told him that he had good news for him, but he must first sign an agreement which provided that Mr. McGuire would pay him a fee. After being given the information, Mcguire refused to pay the fee; he maintained that he had known all along about the dormant account.

The court held for the defendant. The plaintiff had not provided McGuire with means of obtaining money unknown to exist. The agreement was a misleading and deceptive document and one which could be rescinded under the *Ontario Business Practices Act* because it was designed to make Mr. McGuire believe that he was entitled to some benefit from an estate when in fact he was being offered his own money for a fee.

Estate Locators v. McGuire
Summarized from The Lawyers Weekly
December 16, 1988 p.24

Someone sanded off the original grade stamps on millions of board feet of lumber and replaced the stamp with a higher-quality label. The lumber was sold by a B.C. supplier throughout the Seattle area. Some apartments will have to be dismantled to find and replace or reinforce the inferior wood.[7]

The Texas Attorney General began an investigation of televangelist, Robert Tilton, who professed to be the "Prophet of God," for deceptive trade practices. Tilton urges viewers to send him prayers they want answered with their donations. It is estimated that Tilton receives about $80 million a year, but a report by ABC (American Broadcasting Corporation) suggests that the money is taken from the envelopes but not the letters. Its reporters found the envelopes had been opened, the donation apparently taken and the letters left unread.[8]

The revelation that Milli Vanilli, a "singing" group, had not actually sung the songs on its best-selling album resulted in more than the rescinding of its Best New Artists Grammy. In California, Sheila Stalder, mother of 14-year old David, who felt "hurt, cheated" after learning that the group merely lip-synched the songs, began a class action suit asking for restitution to any California consumer who bought its album of performances. The pleadings alleged that "the entire Milli Vanilli success story is a fake foisted upon unsuspecting consumers by the defendants in the action who bilked untold numbers of consumers, many of them children, out of tens of millions of dollars."[9]

Note: *The New York state legislature is considering a bill which would make it mandatory for promoters of concerts to state in their advertising whether or not the concert contains pre-recorded music. This concern for truth in the advertising of concerts is in response to groups such as New Kids on the Block and Milli Vanilli.*[10]

Luciano Pavarotti, renowned tenor, agreed to refund money paid by the BBC for broadcast rights to a concert in Modena Italy when it was learned he had lip-synched his performance.[11]

The Attorney General in Texas challenged a Volvo ad in which the car withstands the crush of a huge truck. It was learned that the car in the ad had been reinforced with steel or wood. Volvo agreed to run a newspaper ad correcting the false ad, to make no unproved claims and to pay the state $316,250 for the costs incurred investigating the matter.[12]

"*Dear* PowerBar consumer,

Consumer and Corporate Affairs Canada (CCA) is threatening to pull PowerBars from the marketplace.

After having approved our PowerBar label in April of 1991, the CCA now believes that we are misleading you, the Canadian consumer, with the word "Power" on our label. In their opinion, the term Power is an inherently misleading term that:

> connotes a time/energy relationship, and is fundamentally different from the term 'energy'. Foods cannot provide power; they can provide the energy component thereof. Therefore the word Power is misleading to Canadian consumers and must be deleted from your product.

What are your feelings about this department's ruling?

Please write to: Minister of Consumer and Corporate Affairs ..."[13]

Laidlaw Inc., a company based in Burlington, Ontario, agreed to pay $3 million to settle a consumer protection action commenced in California. The customers alleged that they were sent forms with removable stickers which said the forms should be signed for insurance purposes or as pledges not to dispose of hazardous waste in the companies' garbage bins. In fact, the forms were used by Laidlaw as long-term contracts. Customers who complained were told that they would have to continue with the company or pay a six-month service charge to cancel the contract.[14]

ENDNOTES

1. Adapted from *The Globe and Mail,* October 16, 1990, p. A18
2. Summarized from *The Globe and Mail,* January 23, 1992, pp. A1, 5
3. From *Newsweek,* October 1, 1990 © 1991, Newsweek, Inc. All rights reserved.
4. A more detailed account is given in *Newsweek,* April 22, 1991, p. 48
5. A more detailed account is given in the *Vancouver Sun,* January, 1990
6. A more detailed account is given in the *Vancouver Sun*
7. A more detailed account is given in the *Vancouver Sun,* November 21, 1990
8. A more detailed account is given in *Newsweek,* January 6, 1992, p. 43
9. A more detailed account is given in the *Vancouver Sun,* November 20, 1990
10. *The Lawyers Weekly,* 1990
11. A more detailed account is given in the *Vancouver Sun,* October 23, 1992
12. A more detailed account is given in the *Vancouver Sun,* November 6, 1990
13. *Fittingly Yours,* Aug/Sept/Oct, 1992, p. 47
14. Summarized from *The Globe and Mail,* January 11, 1991

V

PRIORITY OF CREDITORS

Questions

In contracts for loans the debtor promises to repay the creditor, but if the creditor wants more than just the promise what else can he take as security?

What can this secured creditor do if the debtor doesn't pay?

How does the procedure work?

A. Secured Transactions

In Boulder Colorado, the bank ordered a tractor be repossessed because James Futhery missed his payments. In response, Futhery drove the tractor through the front entrance of the bank, causing several thousand dollars worth of damage.

Mr. Martins bought a $47,000 Canon laser photocopier. He gave the seller a $25,000 cheque as a down payment. The cheque was returned NSF (not sufficient funds) three weeks after the buyer had taken possession of the copier.

When the seller repossessed the machine, a piece of paper containing three $50 Canadian bills was discovered. In all, $24,240 in $20, $50, and $100 counterfeit bills had been made using the machine. Despite the arguments of the accused which included his allegation that he was merely testing the colour of the reproduction, he was found guilty and sentenced.[1]

R. v. Martins Ontario District Court

PERSONAL PROPERTY SECURITY ACT

Glenn v. General Motors Acceptance Corporation of Canada

ONTARIO COURT OF JUSTICE (GENERAL DIVISION)
FILE NO. 5274/92
JULY 7, 1992

MacLeod, J.

This is an application brought by Robert Glenn against Canadian Motors Acceptance Corporation of Canada Limited for the return of the applicant's 1990 Mercedes-Benz 500 SL automobile, and for compensations and damages, pre-judgment interest and costs.

On or about the 4th of June, 1992, the respondent, or its agents, repossessed the automobile which was the subject of a conditional sales contract between the applicant and the respondent. On June the 8th and 9th of 1992, Mr. Glenn tendered, or attempted to tender, upon the respondent the sum actually in arrears, pursuant to the conditional sales contract, plus a sum equal to the respondent's reasonable expenses of repossession, pursuant to section 66, subsection 2 of the *Personal Property Security Act*. To date, the respondent has refused to reinstate the security agreement and to return the vehicle to Mr. Glenn.

The issue for the court to determine, on this application, is the interpretation of section 66, subsection 2 of the *Personal Property Security Act*. In particular, that section states as follows:

> Where the collateral is consumer goods, at any time before the secured party, under section 63, has disposed of the collateral or contracted for such disposition, or before the secured party under subsection 65(6) shall be deemed to have irrevocably elected to accept the collateral, the debtor may reinstate the security agreement by paying,
>
> (a) the sum actually in arrears, exclusively of the operation of any other default which entitles the secured party to dispose of the collateral; and
>
> (b) a sum equal to the reasonable expenses referred to in clause 63(1)(a) incurred by the secured party.

The section provides, in section (3), that this remedy may only be exercised once during the term of the security agreement, unless leave of the court is obtained.

The issue to be determined by me is whether or not Mr. Glenn can reinstate the security agreement by paying the arrears and the expenses due to the respondent, which is his position on the application. The respondent's position is that they are opposing the reinstatement of the security agreement in relation to the second part of clause 66(2)(a), which is:

> ...by curing any other default which entitles the secured party to dispose of the collateral...

Counsel for General Motors Acceptance Corporation refers, specifically, to two paragraphs of the terms of the conditional sales contract between Mr. Glenn and G.M.A.C. In the additional terms and conditions of the contract, which is page 2, paragraph 2, in relation to the section, "Default and Repossession" states, in part, that:

> ...should the Seller deem itself insecure the unpaid balance of the Total Time price and all other amounts owing under this contract shall immediately become due and payable and the Seller take possession of the vehicle where it may be found, so long as repossession is done peacefully.

The second aspect of the contract referred to by counsel is paragraph 7, which states that:

> You ... [shall] not ... permit to continue any charge, lien or encumbrance of any kind upon the vehicle, and shall not use it illegally or for hire.

The respondent's position on the application is that Mr. Glenn has caused the respondent to deem him insecure and, secondly, that he has operated, or allowed the vehicle to be operated, illegally.

The cross-examination of Mr. Glenn satisfies me that, in fact, he allowed the motor vehicle licence plates, and registration of the vehicle, to expire in June of 1991. It is clear, from his evidence given on that examination, that he has allowed the vehicle to be operated on the roads and highways in Canada and the United States without it being legally licensed. In my view, that clearly is an illegal operation of the vehicle, entitling the respondent to repossess the vehicle and prevent reinstatement of the security agreement.

Secondly, the respondent alleges that Mr. Glenn is deemed to be insecure. I accept Mr. Glenn's counsel's submission that G.M.A.C. cannot, capriciously, or of its own volition, decide whenever it likes that a creditor [sic] is deemed insecure; but having had the full benefit of argument, and the examination of the parties in this case, I am satisfied that the respondent has made its case that Mr. Glenn is, in fact, insecure. There is no reasonable prospect that he will maintain the currency of the contract. There is also a risk to the creditor of removal of the vehicle from the province of Ontario and a history, at least on one occasion, of refusing to advise the respondent of the actual location of the vehicle.

The cross-examination of Mr. Glenn indicates that there are extensive executions registered against him, totalling several hundred thousand dollars, and that he has no present means of income from his corporation, which was his principal business operation, being a numbered company operating "Bandito Video." He refused, on his cross-examination, to disclose his other sources of income.

The *Personal Property Security Act* has a clear legislative policy in favour of reinstatement of security agreements for consumer goods, such as a vehicle, if all of the expenses and amounts owing, "except for an acceleration clause," are paid by the debtor. This is a policy that has been implemented in subsection 2 of section 66 of the Act. Clearly, however, the creditor is not without remedy in a situation where they have established, to the satisfaction of the court, that the deemed insecurity provisions of the contract have, in fact, been met on a reasonableness basis. The creditor also has a remedy for illegal operation of this vehicle.

I find that the respondent, on the facts of this case, is entitled to refuse to reinstate the security agreement. Counsel have advised me there is no law on this section of the *Personal Property Security Act*. The legal argument was novel. I am dismissing Mr. Glenn's application for return of the vehicle, and I am making no award as to costs.

B. Builders' Liens

Dominion Bridge (of United Dominion Industries Limited) placed two construction liens against the property of Skydome (the Stadium Corp.). The liens totalled more than $46 million. Skydome wanted the liens removed and, pursuant to the provisions of the *Construction Lien Act* of Ontario, asked the court for orders to "vacate" the liens upon its posting security . Dominion Bridge brought a cross-motion for an order under the statute to require Skydome to post security not only for the full amount of the liens but an additional 25% as security for costs which it anticipated to be approximately $6 million. The Master concluded that to remove the liens, Skydome should pay into court the full amount of the liens plus an amount of $50,000 for costs for each lien.

Dominion Bridge appealed; Skydome moved to "quash" the appeals.

The wording of the statute regarding the vacating of a lien is as follows:

s. 44 (1) Upon the motion of any person, without notice to any other person, the court shall make an order vacating,

(a) ...the registration of a claim for lien ... or,

(b) ...the claim for lien,

where the person bringing the motion pays into court, or posts security in an amount equal to, the total of,

(c) the full amount claimed as owing in the claim for lien; and

(d) the lesser of $50,000 or 25 per cent of the amount described in clause (c), as security for cost.

(2) Upon the motion of any person, the court may make an order vacating the registration of a claim for lien, and any certificate of action in respect of that lien, upon the payment into court or the posting of security of an amount that the court determines to be reasonable in the circumstances to satisfy the lien.

s. 71 (3) No appeal lies from,

(b) an interlocutory order made by the court.

The judge quashed the appeals. The court held that the order relating to costs was interlocutory and furthermore, that s. 44(2) could not override the mandatory provisions of s. 44 (1). With regard to costs, Skydome would only have to post $50,000 for each lien, considerably less than 25% of the liens.

United Dominion Industries Ltd. v. Ellis-Don Limited et al.
Ontario Court of Justice (General Division)
File numbers 405/92 and 406/92
January 12, 1993

C. Bankruptcy

Olympia & York Developments Ltd. (O&Y), a Toronto-based company, averted bankruptcy in the U.S. when the Swiss Bank Corp., a judgment creditor to whom it owed $8 million, agreed not to enforce the deadline set for 5 p.m. November 24, 1992.

O&Y still teeters on the brink of bankruptcy; its U.S. division is in default of most of its $6-billion debt.[2]

In February of 1993 the creditors approved a plan of corporate restructuring, perhaps the largest in Canadian or world history, which was done in accordance with the *Companies Creditors Arrangement Act.*[3]

The Finnish Communist Party, filed for bankruptcy. Some of its $19.06 million U.S. debt was incurred by "share investments gone bad".[4]

Nearly $200 million in debt, Henry Birks & Sons Ltd. filed documents under the new federal *Bankruptcy and Insolvency Act.* After filing with the bankruptcy branch of Consumer and Corporate Affairs Canada, the company has 30 days to make a restructuring proposal to its creditors.[5]

After the court decision finding Kim Basinger liable for $8.1-million for breach of contract [see p.80 above], the actress declared bankruptcy, but the bankruptcy judge rejected her plan for paying her debts as being too vague. A new plan is to be resubmitted by January of 1994.[6]

It was reported that Ms. Basinger changed her bankruptcy petition, a change that necessitates her selling many of her assets.[7]

D. Fraudulent Conveyances Act/Fraudulent Preference Act

Question

How can the family home be protected from the creditors of the husband's business, or from the creditors of the wife's business?

In October of 1990 Lajos Solar obtained a default judgment against Joseph Kovacs for $250,612.13 plus costs. On March 4, 1991, four and one-half months after the judgment, the judgment debtor transferred both of the existing shares in a company to his wife. The sole asset of the company was the family home.

Solar, the judgment creditor, took an action under the *Fraudulent Conveyances Act* to set aside the transfer. Kovacs argued that back in 1982, when he and his wife lost everything to the real-estate crash, they decided that if they built another family home it would be put in the wife's name to protect it. Thus, he argued, there was an automatic trust attached to the home acquired in 1987, that is, the company, the registered owner of the home, was really holding it for the wife. In the alternative, he argued that there was a constructive trust [one the law should infer] when the holding company was acquired and the company bought the house. He further argued that he had no intention to defraud the judgment creditor.

The judge examined but rejected all arguments. He found that they "simply agreed between themselves that any future home should be put in the wife's name," but that agreement did not create an enforceable contract, nor was any express trust created. There was no trust property in existence at that time to be the subject of a trust. Furthermore, when the home was acquired years later (at least partly from money inherited) the actions of the husband belied any intention to create an express trust. He used the equity in the home to finance his business endeavours and did not transfer his share to the wife when she requested that the house be put in her name. In short, he used the company and the house as his own. The judge found no evidence of the husband's intention to hold the property in trust for his wife. Furthermore, because the wife had made no contribution with labour or money to the acquisition or improvement of the shares in the company or its asset, the house, the judge found no constructive trust. With regard to the third argument the judge stated "I also reject the proposition that the husband had forgotten a $250,000 debt which had been several times demanded of him and in respect of which he had been served with a writ within the six months previous to the transfer."

Finally, finding there was no good consideration given by the wife for the shares, the judge concluded: "I hold therefore that this transfer of the two shares was void under the *Fraudulent Conveyances Act* as against the plaintiff. An order will go directing the wife to re-convey the shares to her husband."

Solar v. Kovacs et al.
Supreme Court of British Columbia
Vancouver Registry No. C917141
October 18, 1993

Question

How angry can the court be when assets are moved to defraud creditors?

In the Matter of:

Babbitt and Paladin Inc., Gary Husbands and Excalibur Technologies Inc.

ONTARIO COURT (GENERAL DIVISION) IN BANKRUPTCY
TORONTO FILE NO: B274/92
NOVEMBER 26, 1992

The background facts are as follows: The plaintiff , Babbitt, had successfully sued Paladin Inc. and Gary Husbands, its majority shareholder. At the examination in aid of execution it was learned that the defendant Husbands had shut down Paladin and transferred all its assets to a newly created company, Excalibur Technologies Inc. The plaintiff then applied to have the transfer of assets set aside under the *Fraudulent Conveyances Act.* As a creditor of a corporation, the plaintiff used the oppression remedy under s. 248 of the *Ontario Business Corporations Act.*

Summarized from *The Lawyers Weekly* February 26, 1993 p. 21

Carruthers, J. (given orally) This matter comes before the Court by way of a motion within an action which was terminated by a Judgment in favour of the plaintiff against the defendants, Paladin Inc. and Gary Husbands. It was with a view to satisfying this Judgment that this motion has been made pursuant to the provisions of the *Business Corporations Act.*

The basic issue concerns the fact that all the business and assets of Paladin, of which the defendant Husbands at all relevant times had the majority interest and was its sole operating mind, have ended up with a company known as Excalibur Technologies Inc. This company was the creation of Husbands and at all relevant times was also under his sole control and direction.

Essentially what happened was that Husbands shut down Paladin and started Excalibur, and in the process of doing so took all of the assets of Paladin, including 45 service contracts, all of the employees required to service those contracts and its goodwill and gave or transferred them, without cost, to Excalibur. As a result Paladin was left as an empty shell, thereby rendering the claims of outstanding creditors, and in particular the plaintiff, Cynthia Babbitt, unenforceable.

There appears to be no disagreement between counsel that all of the circumstances surrounding these dealings between Paladin and Excalibur, all of which are not disputed, give rise to a presumption in favour of the plaintiff against the validity of the transaction between Paladin and Excalibur. ...

In the course of testifying the defendant Husbands said without any reservation or qualification that a factor, if not the factor, in changing his business operations from Paladin to Excalibur was his inability to overcome what he described as being "a mountain of debt" that had been generated on behalf of Paladin. He testified that he could see "no way out of the situation" but to start a new business in the manner in which he did.

It is said on behalf of the defendants that there was no intention to defeat creditors of Paladin because Husbands only intended to start a new business because the situation with Paladin rendered a desired new business relationship ... impossible. ... As I said to counsel during argument, what Mr. Husbands had to say comes about as close to an admission that he intended to defeat or defraud Paladin's creditors as one could expect in a case of this kind.

Frankly I am surprised and concerned that any business man in this Province would not understand that what was done here is wrong. Surely Husbands had to know that one cannot by simply organizing a succession of new companies, utilizing new labels and transferring assets, without any consideration avoid the indebtedness of those left behind. That surely is a simply straightforward common sense basic principle. To permit what Husbands did would create havoc in the business and commercial world.

In my opinion the defendants have not succeeded at all in rebutting the presumption which the circumstances of this case give rise to. ...

[H]ad there been a claim for punitive damages, I would have most probably assessed punitive damages against the defendants. This is just absolutely a case in which we have someone who is virtually thumbing his nose at the Law and the rights of others, and abusing the processes of this Court in the process. It is very difficult for me to understand how anyone of his apparent intelligence can think that he is entitled to do what he has done and then come to this Court and say, it is right. And, I might add at this point, bring with him a strong attitude, as well, that it is wrong to criticize him for what he did.

While lots of people might do these things, it is rare that they would then try and justify them in a Court of Law. The whole thing is just an absolute waste of everyone's time, except of course for the defendants. I am sure they thought time was in their favour. ...

I have endorsed the record for oral reasons given, Judgment for the plaintiff against Paladin Inc., Gary Husbands and Excalibur Technologies Inc., for $31,339.85, and costs on a solicitor and client basis at $16,330. The liability of each of the parties, Paladin Inc., Gary Husbands and Excalibur Technologies Inc., is on a joint and several basis.

Judgment for the plaintiff

Endnotes

1. Summarized from *The Lawyers Weekly,* August 25, 1989, p. 20
2. Summarized from *The Globe and Mail,* November 25, 1992, p. B18
3. *The Lawyers Weekly,* April 9, 1993, p. 16
4. *The Globe and Mail,* November 16, 1992
5. Summarized from *The Globe and Mail,* January 12, 1993, p. A1, 2
6. Summarized from *The Globe and Mail,* November 11, 1993, p. A13
7. A more detailed account is given in *The Miami Herald,* December 29, 1993, p. 2A

VI

EMPLOYMENT LAW

A. Terms of the Employment Contract

Questions

When you say "yes" to a job offer, what are you promising your employer?

What is the employer promising you?

Drexel Burnham Lambert Inc. sued its former employee Michael Milken "junk bond pioneer" for more than one billion dollars, the compensation he received from the company over a four-year period. Milken is serving a ten-year prison sentence after pleading guilty to federal securities law violations. The lawsuit against Milken and other former employees is part of an agreement that would free the company from bankruptcy proceedings.

Summarized from *The Globe and Mail* September 12, 1991 p. B6

Details of the proposed $1.3 billion settlement indicate that Milken would retain about $125 million.[1]

(The prison term was reduced by a U.S. Federal Court in August of 1992.)

The head office introduced a non-smoking policy, but it was not implemented at Ms. Scholem's centre in a suburb of Sydney, Australia. Ms. Scholem, in her action against her employer for failure to provide a smoke-free working environment, stated that her centre was a "tobacco-laden environment" and she was obliged to take part in consulting sessions with heavy smokers in a room with closed windows and doors. She alleged that the passive smoke, which she had to endure for her 12 working years, aggravated her asthma, led to bronchial spasms, shortness of breath and caused her to be on constant medication. The court held in her favour and awarded her about $80,000 (Can) in damages. Ms. Scholem, a psychologist, worked with the New South Wales health department.[2]

B. Just Cause/Wrongful Dismissal

Questions

In a non-union situation, does your employer owe you your job?
Can the employer fire you for any *reason?*
For any reason not prohibited by the Human Rights Code*?*
What does the employer owe you?
If your contract is silent on the matter, what are the implied terms about dismissal?

John Pultitzer, the U.S. publisher, in whose name the Pulitzer prize for journalism is awarded, fired several employees because of the way they ate soup.[3]

Durand v. The Quaker Oats Company of Canada Ltd.

45 B.C.L.R. (2d) 354
British Columbia Court of Appeal
February 21, 1990

Locke J.A.: The plaintiff/respondent in this appeal [from 20 C.C.E.L. 223] commenced employment with the Quaker Oats Company of Canada in 1968 and he held positions of ever increasing responsibility until April 1986. His progress had been steady throughout the company. At the time of which we speak, he was the sales planning and development manager for the western region and throughout this time he reported to the western region manager, one Ken Vaillant. One of Durand's duties was to assist Vaillant in putting together advertising programs for the company's products. In November 1985 one Neil Soper of *T.V. Week Magazine* made a presentation to Vaillant and Durand. Included in this package was a trip for two of Quaker Oats' employees to Las Vegas. This type of scheme is apparently common in the advertising industry and is known as a trade trip.

As a result of Soper's presentation, Quaker Oats purchased two packages and made it possible for four employees of Quaker to take the proposed trip planned for early April 1986. Quaker Oats had a policy in regard to the use of these trade trips and it was one of what I call openness. Whether or not the company intended to use the trips was a question for the region or zone manager. Vaillant generally used trips for awarding long service employees or for his own or others' pleasure. All this was carried on with the knowledge and consent of head office.

In mid-March 1986 Vaillant and Durand had a meeting to discuss the sales meeting in April. Durand pointed out that the proposed meeting conflicted with the time of the trade trips offered by *T.V. Week Magazine*. Unknown to Durand, Vaillant had cancelled the trips in the previous month because Quaker Oats was not doing well financially. In response to a question, or in the course of the conversation between Vaillant and Durand regarding this, Vaillant said that the trip would be "too much of a hassle" or some such words and that the matter was no longer an issue.

Subsequent to this Durand, without telling Vaillant or anyone else in the company, contacted Soper to make some inquiries and asked if a trip could be arranged for another person. Eventually, he or his nominee were put on the waiting list of this, I gather, chartered airplane. Subsequently, Soper advised Durand that there had been a cancellation and Durand made arrangements for his wife and a friend of hers to use the tickets while he himself attended the scheduled sales meeting.

Within some weeks of the completion of the trip Vaillant learned, by accident and for the first time, of Durand's actions with respect to the cancelled trip. He had a meeting with Durand, faced him with this and Durand's reply was to the effect that Vaillant—who was going to be replaced as the region manager shortly—had no authority to cancel the trip. His conduct was described as "belligerent." There was however no further conversation. Vaillant reported the matter to head office and subsequently in the middle of April 1986 a meeting was held with the new region manager, a Mr. Bruce Barbour and Vaillant. The Durand story was listened to. He gave the same reason, that he did not think that Vaillant has any authority to cancel the trip and he was then summarily told he would be discharged or was discharged then.

Subsequently (the decision had been made solely by Mr. Barbour) a letter was delivered at the time of termination and it said:

April 18, 1986

H.L. Durand
[Address]

Dear Sir:

This is to confirm that your employment with Quaker has been terminated for cause.

We have discussed with you in detail our concern, and have listened carefully to your comments on the matter.

It is clear that you have broken the bond of trust required between us.

You have breached specific provisions of our Conflict of Interest Rules. Further, you have committed an act of direct insubordination in order to derive personal gain.

Your conduct with regard to this matter leaves us no choice.

Yours truly,
"Bruce E. Barbour"
Bruce E. Barbour
Zone Manager
Western Canada

Quaker Oats had, for all its employees, conflict of interest rules and guidelines. They are comparatively detailed and the respondent, when he was employed, signed certain documents and among the guidelines which each employee got was a general statement that no officer or employee should have any personal interest outside the company which in any way conflicts with the interest of the company or puts the employee in a position where he or she could use company's connection for personal or family gain to the possible detriment of the company. ...

[After a review of precedents, Locke, J.A. concludes:]

The evidence establishes clearly that there was secrecy, that there was insubordination, that there was a conflict of interest and that there had been an acquisition of a "perk" by Durand for his own or his family's personal advantage.

It was because, I think, of the trial judge's original error in characterizing the breach of the conflict of interest rules as "technical" that led him, in my view, to the decision he enunciated. In my opinion, on the facts and on the law there were substantial reasons for the executives of the Quaker Oats Company determining that the taking of the unauthorized trip had placed the company in a sense in hostage to a potential contractor for advertising and that the confidence that they would feel in Durand in handling advertising matters in the future could not be justified any longer.

I think that the express and implied terms of the contract of employment were breached and that the discharge was justified. I would correspondingly allow the appeal and dismiss the action.

Seaton J.A.: I agree.

Southin J.A.: Mr. Justice Locke has stated the facts and I agree with him that the appeal must be allowed. I would like to put my legal foundation for that opinion in my own words.

The appeal is from a judgment granting judgment for what is called wrongful dismissal. What such an action is usually, and is in this case, is an action for damages for breach of the implied term of a contract of employment which lacks an express term on the point that it can only be terminated by either side on reasonable notice, and that in itself leads to the action being founded on the proposition that the employer's act in not giving reasonable notice was itself a repudiation. But here the employer says that the employee repudiated and thus its notice of dismissal was in law an acceptance of that repudiation.

As my learned brother has referred to the implied term of the contract of employment, however one puts it, it is a promise by the employee that he will faithfully, honestly and diligently serve his employer. If he commits a fundamental breach of that term the employer is entitled to say "I have no further obligations to perform and that includes the obligation of giving you reasonable notice."

I approach the matter this way because, despite much of the language in the cases, contracts of service are not governed by any different legal principles from those governing all other contracts. (See on that point, *Laws V. London Chronicle [(Indicator Newspapers) Ltd.*, [1959] 1 W.L.R. 698, [1959] 2 All E.R. 285 (C.A.)]). What constitutes a fundamental breach of the implied term is not always easy to determine, but it must be determined objectively. It is not a question of the intention, necessarily or at all, of the employee—that is, did it ever occur to him that he was about to be in breach of an implied term is not material. It may well be in this case that the respondent never thought for a moment that anything that he was doing was in breach of the implied term of his contract of employment.

The learned judge below called what the respondent did deceptive, dishonest and bordering on insubordinate. Those terms are descriptive. They do not come, in my opinion, to grips with the issue. The gravamen of the appellant's case is that the respondent obtained for his wife and a friend from a supplier to the company, two tickets for a trip to Las Vegas worth about $800 each, without the knowledge of his superiors, and that is the kind of conduct that an employer can look upon as a fundamental breach because it exposes the employee to the importunings, possibly of the supplier, in connection with his duties.

Thus, in my view, that sort of thing, even if it did not occur to Mr. Durand (as I hope that it did not) that it was dishonest, is in fact a fundamental breach. Where, in my opinion, the learned judge erred was first, in not asking himself whether to do this thing was a fundamental breach and secondly, in considering that the company was under any legal obligation to choose a different way of dealing with this fundamental breach than the course it did choose. The company was under no obligation to choose any other course once there was a fundamental breach and for that, of course, I need only refer to *Port Arthur Shipbldg. Co. v. Arthurs*, [1969] S.C.R. 85, 70 D.L.R. (2d) 693 [Ont.]. I would therefore allow the appeal.

Seaton J.A.: The appeal is allowed. The action dismissed.

Appeal allowed

Stanley Scott Werle v. SaskEnergy Incorporated

SASK. QUEEN'S BENCH
FILE NO. 1215-003
JUNE 3, 1992

Kyle J.: The defendant, SaskEnergy Incorporated ("SaskEnergy"), conducted a search for a Vice-President of its Sales and Marketing Department in September of 1990. The plaintiff, Mr. Stanley Scott Werle, was the successful applicant. Fifty-one people had applied. SaskEnergy is a public utility which sells natural gas to residents of Saskatchewan. It had recently been separated from SaskPower, the provincial electrical utility, and though it was a Crown corporation, it had plans to become privately held, plans which had excited some political controversy. When Mr. Werle sought the position of Vice-President of Sales and Marketing Department, it was a new position and the advertisement described aspects both of sales and of marketing as being part of the job.

Mr. Werle sent an application letter with a resume attached. In the resume he detailed his background as a salesperson with Xerox. He had been most successful in that role, and he was hoping that the new job, if he got it, would entitle him to a salary at or near the $100,000 level which he had attained at Xerox. In his resume he outlined his level of education which was stated to be a Bachelor of Commerce (Marketing) from the University of Saskatchewan. In fact, Mr. Werle had tried for four years to get his Bachelor of Commerce, but he had never passed even one year and he had certainly never been granted a degree. Mr. Werle has advanced no explanation for this misrepresentation which he says was an error resulting from a failure to carry forward some qualifying words which appeared in an earlier version of the resume.

Mr. Werle was hired after a number of interviews and a newsletter announcing his hiring was sent to the 500 or so employees of the company. It mentioned a Bachelor of Commerce and he noticed it, but did nothing. After a month or two, the personnel department asked him for a record of his university training, either a statement of marks or a copy of the diploma. After some delay, he indicated that he could not find his diploma. The personnel officer said: "Didn't you have it framed?" and he answered: "I am not a plaque collector."

When the personnel officer's suspicions were aroused, she called the University and discovered the truth and advised her superiors.

Mr. Bill Baker, President of the company, testified that he had hired Mr. Werle because of his sales experience and background of education in marketing at the University of Saskatchewan. He says he would not have hired Mr. Werle had he known that he did not have a degree. When he found out that indeed he did not have the education, his concerns were twofold. First he felt that Mr. Werle could not do the marketing work he was, in part, hired to do. Secondly, he was concerned that they had hired someone who had lied about his credentials. He was disappointed by this turn of events. He liked Mr. Werle, although some doubts as to his ability in the planning area had started to surface. He says that to have someone in the company who would do such a thing was simply unacceptable. It was something that everyone would know about and it would be a terrible precedent or signal. Mr. Baker was most sympathetic with Mr. Werle. He respected the effort which Mr. Werle had made to get where he was, he respected the success he had achieved, and he liked his motivated style. He would have liked to have been a forgiving boss in these circumstances, and he toyed with the idea. He was, however, fully aware that his duty to the company was on a higher level and he felt that dismissal was required.

Mr. Werle's testimony was not convincing, not only could he not explain how the inaccuracy occurred, but when the newsletter announced that he had a degree, he did nothing and when personnel asked for his diploma he prevaricated. One can only conclude that he was living a lie, if not from the beginning when he filed the false resume, at least from the time of the newsletter. It is not surprising that the company would find this to be evidence of a lack of the integrity requisite in a vice-president. The fact that he allowed the error, as he called it, to continue is quite clearly consistent with the view that the original misrepresentation of his educational status was intentional, a conclusion which the company reached. I find that the company was fully entitled to conclude, as it did, that it had a dishonest employee. Its reluctance to fire him is understandable—his wife was expecting, he was remorseful, and he was a valuable employee, notwithstanding his shortfall in the marketing area. The transfer to a lower position as opposed to termination would, of course, have constituted constructive dismissal so his consent would be essential if that were to be done. Mr. Labas, President of a subsidiary of SaskEnergy, was really in charge of resolving the problem which had arisen. Against Mr. Baker's better judgment, he made an offer of a much reduced status for Mr. Werle, one which would have allowed him to regain the company's confidence. He did not accept the terms proposed and accordingly his employment was terminated for the cause referred to above.

That the company would dismiss a vice-president for what can only be described as fraud, is not surprising. Indeed, the willingness of the company to give Mr. Werle a second chance is surprising; it can only be related to a humane and forgiving nature on the part of the officers of the company. It was in no sense a condonation of Mr. Werle's misdeeds. It would have involved a reduction in salary of some $35,000 and a significant loss of status. In Mr. Werle's action for wrongful dismissal, he claims that the misstatement in the resume was inadvertent, that in ignoring the newsletter, he simply fell prey to the pressure of other matters, and that in his evasion of the personnel department's requests, he was unaware that his resume contained the aforementioned error.

There are no cases where an employee whose dishonesty was so clearly established has been found to have been wrongfully dismissed. The cases cited by Mr. Werle which raise the level of proof to a higher level than that of balance of probabilities, are not relevant here as I am in no doubt as to the dishonesty of Mr. Werle in respect of his credentials. His efforts to rationalize his behavior as presented at trial were not credible and they simply reinforce the impression of dishonesty which the events themselves had justified. His decision to bring this action was simply another example of his bad judgment. Accordingly, the action is dismissed and SaskEnergy is entitled to its costs.

[*The plaintiff's action for wrongful dismissal is dismissed*]

Kim v. Wray Energy Controls Ltd.

ONTARIO COURT (GENERAL DIVISION) TORONTO REGION
JUNE, 1992

His Honour's Reasons for Judgment:

In this action the plaintiff sues for damages for wrongful dismissal along with other relief. As counsel for the plaintiff submitted in argument, the only issue is whether or not the plaintiff was fired without cause or whether he quit. ...

On such a simple issue of fact, I find it difficult to understand why it took three days of evidence in this trial. The essential issues of fact are that on February 3rd, 1988 the plaintiff had an interview with the president of the defendant corporation concerning his job performance concerns and advised that he should take the balance of the day off, that he would be paid for that day, and requiring him to comment in writing to Mr. Gibson, the president of the corporation, on the following Monday, February 6th. The plaintiff attended at the defendant's premises on the following Monday, at approximately 11:00 o'clock in the morning. The general manager, Mrs. Greig, placed him in what is known as the integration room and asked him for something in writing.

Tab 14 is a handwritten note to Mr. Gibson by the Plaintiff which says:

"Let's discuss this in an open forum that involves the whole company." And at tab 15, also in his handwriting, a letter headed: "What I did during summer vacation", and goes on "Concerning My Remuneration."

Not having given a written response as requested, Mr. Gibson sent the letter at tab 16, dated February 6, 1989, which states: "I cannot condone wilful misconduct, disobedience or wilful neglect of duty as described in our letter of February 3, 1989. Because of the gravity of this situation I have decided to suspend you without wages for a period of two weeks effective this date."

In addition, I should refer to the memorandum of October 18, 1988 to the plaintiff from Mr. Gibson with respect to the job description and performance. The plaintiff denies that he ever saw that memorandum before this action was commenced. But Mr. Gibson testified that he gave it to him and asked him to review it at his leisure and respond to it. He said he subsequently got it back from him with what appears, and what he thought would have been the plaintiff's initialling, on both the first and second pages. The plaintiff denies that that is his signature.

I can say this, from having heard all of the evidence: To a large extent, it is essentially a question of credibility. I accept the evidence of Mrs. Greig and the evidence of Mr. Gibson and I reject entirely the evidence of the plaintiff on that issue in particular. But throughout his whole evidence he was completely evasive and seemed to have felt hard-done by. Indeed, I almost wonder why the case is before me because even the plaintiff admits that Mrs. Greig and Mr. Gibson reiterated throughout that his employment was not terminated. And when he finally returned or, at least, made an appearance on February 22nd, two days after the two-week period of suspension ended, and then kept insistently asking for a letter of termination, he is repeatedly told by Mrs. Greig: "You are not terminated." He left and he never returned.

Counsel for the plaintiff made some issue as if the company should have made arrangements for his return to work. He was due to return to work on Monday, the 20th of February, at the normal hour of 8:30 a.m.; and he didn't show up on Monday, he didn't show up on Tuesday, he finally shows up on Wednesday. Why would the company have to make any special arrangements for his return to work, like some grand homecoming?

The unusual aspect of this case, having regard to all the evidence which was before me on the performance of the plaintiff, is: Why didn't the company fire him months previously? But they never did, previously, or even at the very end. And the explanation was very simple: He was a computer programmer, and only he knew what he had done, even though Mr. Gibson and Mrs. Greig repeatedly asked him to document it. The company had invested a tremendous amount of money into the program, and only he knew the answers, or the keys, or the passwords. And as Mrs. Greig said: He was holding us up to ransom. They leaned over backwards in a desperate effort to get him to comply with their requests, but he responded to their requests with derision, insubordination, and laughter, and then had the unmitigated gall to ask, at the final time he returned to the office, for a letter of termination notwithstanding that he was told then and many times before that he had not been terminated.

Counsel for the plaintiff raised the question in cross-examination: What would have happened if he produced the documentation that they required, having regard to his performance? and Mrs. Greig responded: Well, it would have depended on his attitude. Counsel for the plaintiff suggested: If you got the documentation and, having regard to his attitude, therefore, in all probability you would have then fired him. You got what you wanted. Wouldn't that have been a dirty trick? In the circumstances of this case, it wouldn't have been a dirty trick at all. He would have deserved exactly that.

This is one of the simplest cases I have ever had to decide in eleven years as a judge. I can't believe this is before me. ...

The testimony of the defendant was that they had to hire additional programmers after he left in order to find out what were the keys to the kingdom. ... I haven't the slightest hesitation in dismissing the action. In my humble opinion, in all the circumstances, it should never have come before this court.

I should add that although the defendant was held at ransom, they ultimately had to pay the ransom price; and I guess it was wishful thinking on their part, or hopes. But I commend the defendants to that extent, although as they look back on it now they may well wonder, why did they ever do it. But they were tolerant. They had a vested interest in it; and the officers of the defendant seriously tried to resolve the difficulties and all they got was utter disdain and insubordination from their employee. ...

I have endorsed: For reasons dictated, action dismissed. Costs to defendant on a party and party basis up to trial and on a solicitor and client basis thereafter. Anything else?

Counsel for the plaintiff did refer me to the case of *Baichan v. Peca Bros. Auto Collision Ltd.*, 31 C.C.E.L., 261, at tab 1 and referred to the test set out by Callaghan J. in the case of *Rajput v. Menu Food Ltd.* (1984), 5 C.C.E.L. 22 at 27:

> It seems to me that in deciding whether or not a person was entitled to think that he had been fired, or whether in fact the person had resigned, a Court ought to ask itself: What would a reasonable man understand from the words used in the context in which they were used in the particular industry, in the particular working place, and in all the surrounding circumstances?

And I subscribe to that reasoning that a reasonable man, in the circumstances of this case, when it was reiterated constantly that he was not terminated, should come to the conclusion that he was fired, is totally contradictory.

[*The plaintiff's action for wrongful dismissal was dismissed*]

A production manager, Mr. Kennedy, the highest level employee who had to punch a time card on arriving and leaving work, had a co-worker punch his time card for him each morning, contrary to the company rules. He and the co-worker were told to stop the practice and were warned that failure to do so could result in dismissal. After a time the practice resumed, but with a different co-worker punching his time card. This came to light when Kennedy called in to say he wouldn't be reporting to work that day because of a car accident; his time card, however, was punched by his faithful but uninformed co-worker. The company dismissed Kennedy and alleged it had just cause because he had persisted to do what he had been ordered not to do. Kennedy sued for wrongful dismissal.

The court dismissed the action; instant termination was justified. The judge stated that Mr. Kennedy would have been entitled to pay in lieu of 15 months notice if there had been no just cause for dismissal.

Kennedy v. MTD Products Ltd.
Ontario Court (General Division)
Summarized from The Lawyers Weekly *April 12, 1991 p. 16*

A co-worker reported some irregularities in the procedures of a cashier at Canadian Tire Corp. An outside security specialist conducted a discreet surveillance and documented that she was allowing her friends to take away items that were not paid for or were entered under improper codes. She was dismissed for her dishonesty. She sued for wrongful dismissal. The court concluded "The plaintiff was dishonest. She was caught out but was acquitted of whatever criminal charge was laid. She is bitter. Her action would better have been discontinued. The Defendants having proved dismissal was for 'just cause' this action is hereby dismissed with costs to Defendants. ..."

Murphy v. Canadian Tire Corp.
Ontario Court of Justice (General Division) Registry no. 25752.
Unreported. November 25, 1991

Mr. Caruso, the chauffeur for the senior executives of Northern Telecom Ltd., claimed neck and back injuries after a minor accident. The company paid him disability payments equivalent to full salary. The company later dismissed him without notice and alleged it was for just cause because he had defrauded its sickness and disability plan. Mr. Caruso sued the company for wrongful dismissal. The court found as facts that while receiving the disability payments he played golf, did renovation work, loaded wood and had driven or sat in cars for several hours at a time. The court dismissed Mr. Caruso's action concluding that by failing to return to do work for the company when he was capable, he had not acted in good faith and thus had given the company just cause for dismissing him.

Caruso v. Northern Telecom Ltd.
Ontario Court (General Division)
Summarized from The Lawyers Weekly *January 25, 1991*

C. Damages for Wrongful Dismissal

Question

What factors does the court consider in determining what constitutes reasonable notice?

Ansari et al. v. *British Columbia Hydro and Power Authority*

(1986) 2 B.C.L.R. (2D) 33
SUPREME COURT OF BRITISH COLUMBIA
APRIL 3, 1986.

McEachern C.J.S.C.:—The separate actions of these four plaintiffs against the defendant for damages for wrongful dismissal were tried summarily together under R. 18A.

I. *General*

In 1984 a great many graduate engineers employed by B.C. Hydro were deemed surplus to its requirements and they were terminated without cause and without reasonable notice. They were given a severance allowance based upon years of employment with B.C. Hydro plus a percentage allowance of 25 per cent or 30 per cent for benefits. I understand that about 660 employees not covered by collective agreements were terminated in this way and some of them have brought actions for damages for wrongful dismissal. ...

The present four cases have been chosen not as test cases, for no other plaintiffs are bound by the result except, of course, by the possible application of *stare decisis* (the doctrine of precedence in which courts consider themselves bound by some previous decisions), but rather to explore the question of notice and to obtain a judgment on the questions of pensions and other benefits that were not specifically decided in the other four cases. ...

The principles relating to the assessment of damages for wrongful dismissal, which has been too much before the courts during the recent economic unpleasantness, are well established. These are stated and restated in case after case. In fact, in *Nicholls v. Richmond*, 60 B.C.L.R. 320, [1985] 3 W.W.R. 543, 50 C.P.C. 171 (S.C.), Mr. R.H. Guile, Q.C., furnished a 100-page summary of nearly 500 recent Canadian reported wrongful dismissal cases. It is not my function to rationalize the law but it is obvious that the profession is urgently in need of guidance.

The underlining principle which arises out of the law of master and servant (as they were called at common law) is that, absent contractual provisions, the master who terminates the employment of a servant must give reasonable notice and, upon doing so, he is not required to compensate the servant in any way. If the master does not give reasonable notice, then the law requires him to compensate the servant by an award of damages that is intended to put the servant in the position he would be in if he had received proper notice. In the assessment of these damages, the recovery of lost income is not limited to salary, but includes other benefits incidental to the employment being terminated: *Lawson v. Dom. Securities Corp.*, [1977] 2 A.C.W.S. 259 (Ont. C.A.).

It is not the function of damages for wrongful dismissal to penalize the employer for the manner of dismissal nor to compensate the employee over and above the damages flowing from the breach of the contract of employment for his loyal or useful service to the employer. This had been settled law since at least 1883 when the Supreme Court of Canada held that vindictive damages cannot be awarded for breach of contract: *Guilford v. Anglo-French SS. Co.* (1883), 9 S.C.R. 303 [N.S.].

The House of Lords reached a similar conclusion. ...

In short, damages for wrongful dismissal are founded in contract and the focus of the inquiry is what damages, assessed in accordance with the principles I shall discuss, flow from the breach.

II. *The period of reasonable notice*

In what is often regarded as a leading case, *Bardal v. Globe and Mail Ltd.*, [1960] O.W.N. 253, 24 D.L.R. (2d) 140 (H.C.), McRuer C.J.H.C. said at p. 145:

> There can be no catalogue laid down as to what is reasonable notice in particular classes of cases. The reasonableness of the notice must be decided with reference to each particular case, having regard to the character of the employment, the length of service of the servant, the age of the servant and the availability of similar employment, having regard to the experience, training and qualifications of the servant.

In *Gillespie v. Bulkley Valley Forest Indust. Ltd.*, [1975] 1 W.W.R. 607, 50 D.L.R. (3d) 316 (B.C.C.A.), it was said that the factors enumerated by McRuer C.J.H.C. should not be regarded as exhaustive but, with great respect, they are indeed the most important factors, and other matters which have crept into the assessment of this kind of damages are not of great significance.

[After reviewing the other matters which he does not consider useful, Judge McEachern concludes:]

At the end of the day the question really comes down to what is objectively reasonable in the variable circumstances of each case, but I repeat that the most important factors are the responsibility of the employment function, age, length of service and the availability of equivalent alternative employment, but not necessarily in that order.

In restating this general rule, I am not overlooking the importance of the experience, training and qualifications of the employee but I think these qualities are significant mainly in considering the importance of the employment function and in the context of alternative employment.

What all this means, in my view, is that the general statement of factors quoted above from *Bardal* are the governing factors, and it would be better if other individual or subjective factors had not crept into the determination of reasonable notice. In my view such other matters are of little importance in most cases.

I turn to a consideration of the individual cases...

An action in California for wrongful dismissal by Jeffrey Collins against the pharmaceutical company Triton Biosciences Inc., a subsidiary of Shell Oil Co. resulted in an award of $5.3 million dollars. The former top manager was dismissed after his secretary discovered a private memo outlining rules for a gay "safe sex" party. The judge of the Alameda County Superior Court found the firing a "totally inappropriate over-reaction" to the memo.[4]

MITIGATION

Question

How can an employee wrongfully dismissed mitigate his losses?

Mifsud v. MacMillan Bathurst Inc.

63 D.L.R. (4TH) 714; 70 O.R. (2D) 701
ONTARIO COURT OF APPEAL
NOVEMBER 21, 1989

Summary of the facts and of the judgment of the trial court given in the law report, reprinted with permission of Canada Law Book Inc., 240 Edward Street, Aurora, Ontario, L4G 3S9.

The plaintiff had been employed by the defendant for 18 years, and had been promoted first to the position of foreman, and later to that of supervisor. After some dissatisfaction with the plaintiff's work, the defendant reassigned him to the position of foreman. There was no reduction of salary, but the new position involved shift work and had reduced prospects of promotion and reduced responsibilities. The plaintiff started work in the new position, but left after a few days. An action for wrongful dismissal succeeded at trial on the basis of constructive dismissal. The defendant appealed to the Ontario Court of Appeal.

McKinlay J.A.:—The defendant, MacMillan Bathurst Inc., appeals a judgment in favour of the plaintiff, Frank George Michael Mifsud, awarding him the sum of $38,332.13 plus costs as a result of a finding that he was constructively dismissed from his position as a shift superintendent at the appellant's Etobicoke plant on September 4, 1984. This sum represents a notice period of 10 months. ...

Counsel for the appellant argues that where there is a constructive dismissal, but where the new assignments involve no subjection to degrading work or humiliating relationships, the employee is obliged to mitigate his loss by accepting the position that was offered to him, and to work out his period of reasonable notice in that position. ...

The doctrine of mitigation was concisely stated by Chief Justice Laskin in *Red Deer College v. Michaels* (1975), 57 D.L.R. (3d) 386 at p. 390, [1976] 2 S.C.R. 324, [1975] 5 W.W.R. 575 (S.C.C.):

> The primary rule in breach of contract cases, that a wronged plaintiff is entitled to be put in as good a position as he would have been in if there had been proper performance by the defendant, is subject to the qualification that the defendant cannot be called upon to pay for avoidable losses which would result in an increase in the quantum of damages payable to the plaintiff. The reference in the case law to a "duty" to mitigate should be understood in this sense.
>
> In short, a wronged plaintiff is entitled to recover damages for the losses he has suffered but the extent of those losses may depend upon *whether he has taken reasonable steps to avoid their unreasonable accumulation.*
>
> (Emphasis added.)

There is no doubt that the duty of the plaintiff to take steps to mitigate his damages applies in all wrongful dismissal cases. The question is simply whether or not the steps taken by the plaintiff were reasonable.

When an employer wishes to dismiss an employee (other than for cause) the employer may choose either to give the employee reasonable notice of his termination date and require that he work out the notice period, or he may require the employee to leave immediately, thus rendering the employer liable for damages equal to the employee's remuneration and benefits for the reasonable notice period. If the employee leaves immediately, he is required to take reasonable steps to mitigate his loss and, barring any agreement to the contrary between the parties, any moneys earned in mitigation must be credited against his damages.

Is the situation substantially different when an employer does not wish to dismiss an employee but, being unsatisfied with his performance, or for some other valid reason, wishes to place him in a different position at the same salary? Why should it not be considered reasonable for the employee to mitigate his damages by working at the other position for the period of reasonable notice, or at least until he has found alternative employment which he accepts in mitigation?

The fact that the transfer to a new position may constitute in law a constructive dismissal does not eliminate the obligation of the employee to look at the new position offered and evaluate it as a means of mitigating damages. In all cases, comparison should be made to the contractual entitlement of the employer to give reasonable notice and leave the employee in his current position while a search is made for alternative employment. Where the salary offered is the same, where the working conditions are not substantially different or the work demeaning, and where the personal relationships involved are not acrimonious (as in this case) it is reasonable to expect the employee to accept the position offered in mitigation of damages during a reasonable notice period, or until he finds acceptable employment elsewhere.

It must be kept in mind, of course, that there are many situations where the facts would substantiate a constructive dismissal but where it would be patently unreasonable to expect an employee to accept continuing employment with the same employer in mitigation of his damages.

In this case, Mr. Mifsud improperly rejected the opportunity to mitigate his damages by maintaining an employed status from which to seek a preferable position elsewhere.

I would allow the appeal, replace the judgment of the trial judge with a judgment dismissing the plaintiff's claim, and allow the appellant its costs here and below.

Appeal allowed

D. Wrongful Resignation

Question

If you are not a member of a union and your employment contract is silent on the point, how much notice must you give your employer if you want to quit your job?

Systems Engineering and Automation Ltd. v. Power et al.

78 Nfld. & P.E.I.R. 65
Newfoundland Supreme Court
October 12, 1989

Wells, J.: The parties, I will refer to as SEA, Power, Guy and Avalon, respectively. SEA is a Newfoundland company, incorporated in 1983 and is a "high tech" supplier of services and hardware to other companies which require design, installation, and repair services for computer and control systems. Messrs. Power and Guy are technicians who were employed by SEA until May 7, 1987. Avalon was incorporated in May of 1987, and is owned by Messrs. Power and Guy.

SEA says that Messrs. Power and Guy, acting in concert, resigned from their employment on May 7, 1987 without notice and that in so doing they seriously prejudiced the work of SEA and caused it severe financial losses in the amount of $171,974.00.

SEA says that Messrs. Power and Guy secretly and improperly formulated a plan to incorporate Avalon to compete with it, and to take its customers, and that they asked fellow workers to leave SEA and work for the new company. It also says that Messrs. Power and Guy removed documents and records from the offices of SEA when they left.

Messrs. Power and Guy admit that they resigned without notice, however they say that SEA's demands upon them were such that their personal and family lives were being destroyed, and that they were justified in resigning without notice.

Avalon denies all allegations against it, and says that it did not commence business until more than two months after its incorporation which was at the time of the resignations of Messrs. Power and Guy.

The main issues are:

(a) were Messrs. Power and Guy justified in leaving the employ of SEA without notice?
(b) did Avalon do anything improper, and is it liable to SEA as a result of its entry into a similar business?
(c) If the defendants are liable, what is the measure of damages?
(d) who should bear the costs of this action?

In order to clarify the allegations, it is necessary to review the history of SEA, and the work histories of the individuals concerned.

[The judge reviewed the struggle of the company and the work and contributions of the defendants.]

A variety of reasons caused SEA to demand such working hours of Mr. Guy, but in my opinion the main reason was that the company could not afford to hire and train the number of technicians that it needed. Consequently it placed an increasingly heavy burden on the technicians which it already had, of whom Mr. Guy was the most senior and experienced. ...

Although Messrs. Power and Guy did not work together, their work histories at SEA somewhat paralleled each other and the company's records show that Mr. Power also worked as much as fifty, sixty, seventy and even eighty hours per week, mostly away from home and living in hotels. ...

By the spring of 1987, Messrs. Power and Guy found themselves vis-a-vis their employment and their family lives, in roughly comparable situation, which were far from satisfactory. [They talked about their frustrations and eventually they incorporated a company and resigned from SEA]. ...

The evidence indicated that the resignation enraged the management of SEA. ...

The first issue is whether or not Messrs. Power and Guy were justified in leaving their employment without notice.

I have no doubt that their working conditions which included long hours and the frustrations of working away from home, were difficult. Neither of them could have been expected to continue indefinitely to work these hours under these conditions. Nevertheless they were well aware that their particular jobs were important to their employer, and despite the frustrations which they felt, they must have known that to leave their employment without notice, would cause some difficulties and expense for SEA. Furthermore, nothing new or startling had taken place, for they had been working under similar conditions for months prior to May 7th.

[Their solicitor advised] that in the circumstances, they would have been justified in giving the minimum notice required by law.

It is agreed that there were no written contracts between the parties nor was their employment governed by a collective agreement. For these reasons it was argued that the *Labour Standards Act* applies, and I accept that argument as it applies to the minimum requirements.

Section 48 says:

> Subject to sections 49 and 50, no employer or employee shall terminate a contract of service unless written notice of termination is given by or on behalf of the employer or employee, as the case may be, within the period set out in paragraph (a) or (b) of Section 51.

Section 51 says in its relevant parts:

> The period of notice required to be given by the employer and employee under section 48 is
>
> (a) one week, if the employee has been continuously employed by the employer for a period of one month or more but less than two years; and
>
> (b) two weeks, if the employee has been continuously employed by the employer for a period of two years or more, ...

Accordingly I find as provided for in the Act, that Mr. Power should have given at least one week's notice and Mr. Guy, two.

[The Judge reviewed various projects on which the defendants were working at the time of their resignations to determine the extent of damages suffered by the plaintiffs because of their resigning without notice].

In summary therefore, I am prepared to allow under the various headings of damage:

(a) $2,000.00 for lost profits from Marystown Shipyard Limited,
(b) $3,000.00 for additional expenses in completing projects on which Mr. Power might have been able to assist,
(c) $5,000.00 for additional expenses in completing projects on which Mr. Guy might have been able to assist.

Total $10,000.00 ...

The evidence of Messrs. Power and Guy was to the effect that considerably more than $1,000.00 was owed to each of them, but they did not have records from which the amounts owing could be calculated. On a balance of probabilities, I am satisfied that they are owed at least $1,000.00 each, so that the sum of $2,000.00 should be deducted from the sum of $10,000.00 to which I have found the Plaintiff is entitled.

Judgment will therefore be entered for the plaintiff against the defendants jointly and severally in the amount of $8,000.00 together with prejudgment interest calculated from May 7, 1987. ...

Order accordingly

E. Legislation to Protect Employees

A woman began her employment as a cleaner at the airport for $5 an hour. When her supervisor learned she was pregnant he was very concerned about the effect of the cleaning chemicals on the fetus. He requested that she discuss the situation with her doctor. The employee reported back that the doctor advised that she could continue working. The supervisor himself wrote to the doctor who again responded that the chemicals would not adversely affect the unborn child. A few days later, the supervisor gave the employee a lay-off notice on the grounds that they were cutting staff. The employee complained under *The Saskatchewan Human Rights Code*, alleging that she was discriminated against on the grounds of her sex and pregnancy.

Her complaint was upheld. It was found that she was laid off because of her pregnancy and, although the supervisor's concern was praiseworthy, the firing was discriminatory. She was awarded damages for lost wages, hurt feelings and loss of self-esteem.

Nguyen v. Pacific Building Maintenance Ltd.
Summarized from The Lawyers Weekly
October 25, 1991, p. 29

F. Collective Bargaining

1. Jurisdiction Disputes

In Quebec, The Quebec Federation of Labor and the Teamsters fought over which union would represent the workers of Molson-O'Keefe and Purolator. In these two instances the Teamsters won. In November of 1993 these two "arch-rivals" joined forces.[5]

2. Interests Dispute

Bargaining in Bad Faith

The Canada Labour Relations Board ruled that the owner of the Giant gold mine in Yellowknife had bargained in bad faith leading up to a May, 1992, strike action. The board ordered the company and union to negotiate a settlement within 30 days or face binding arbitration. Four months after the strike began, nine miners died in an explosion; a union member was later charged with nine counts of first degree murder.[6]

Subsequent to the order of the Canada Labour Relations Board, the workers accepted an offer from the owner, Royal Oak Mines. The offer left some contentious issues to be negotiated by representatives from both sides or by a mediator if the two sides cannot agree.[7]

Mr.Devries of Victoria, B.C. had tickets for the Canucks - L.A. Kings game in Vancouver. When the ferries quit running because of an illegal strike called by the B.C. Ferry and Marine Workers Union he missed the game. He sued. He won.[8]

The Supreme Court of Canada upheld two criminal contempt convictions which had imposed a $400,000 fine on the United Nurses Alberta. The nurses had continued to strike despite directives from the Alberta Labour Relations Board forbidding them to do so. Justice McLachlin, for the majority, held that civil contempt for the breach of a court order (the directives were filed and enforced as court orders) became criminal contempt when the nurses defied the court with intent, knowledge or recklessness as to the fact that the disobedience would lower respect for the court's authority.

United Nurses Alberta v. Alberta Attorney General
Summarized from The Lawyers Weekly
May 15, 1992 p. 15

ENDNOTES

1. A more detailed account is given in *Newsweek,* March 9, 1992
2. A more detailed account is given in the *Vancouver Sun,* May 28, 1992, p. A14
3. Adapted from *The Globe and Mail,* October 29, 1992, p. A20
4. *The Lawyers Weekly,* August 30,1991, p. 8
5. *Maclean's,* November 22, 1993, p. 37
6. *Maclean's,* November 22, 1993, p. 17
7. A more detailed account is given in the *Vancouver Sun,* November 18, 1993, p. D2
8. Summarized from *The Lawyers Weekly,* October 29, 1993, p. 12

VII

AGENCY LAW

Questions

If you are acting as an agent, what are your obligations to your principal?
What are your duties as a fiduciary?

Ocean City Realty Ltd. v. A & M Holdings Ltd. et al.

36 D.L.R. (4TH) 94
BRITISH COLUMBIA COURT OF APPEAL
MARCH 5, 1987

I

Wallace J.A.:—The appellant appeals from a decision wherein the trial judge awarded the plaintiff a real estate commission earned in connection with the sale of real property in the City of Victoria.

II

Facts

The plaintiff, Ocean City Realty Ltd. (Ocean City), is a licensed real estate agency. The defendant, A & M Holdings Ltd. (A & M), was the owner of a commercial building in Victoria, British Columbia known as the Weiler Building.

At all material times Mrs. Patricia Forbes was a licensed real estate sales person employed by Ocean City.

In January of 1983, Mr. Holm Halbauer contacted Mrs. Forbes for assistance in locating a commercial building in downtown Victoria which he might be interested in purchasing.

Mrs. Forbes contacted the principals of A & M to inquire as to whether the Weiler Building might be for sale. She also inquired as to the sales commission A & M would be willing to pay.

Following a series of negotiations an interim agreement for the sale of the Weiler Building was concluded between A & M and Mr. Halbauer. It included a commission agreement between A & M and Ocean City whereby Ocean City was to receive 1.75% of the sale price of $5.2 million.

The trial judge found that at some point during the negotiations Mr. Halbauer advised Mrs. Forbes of his intention to proceed no further with the transaction unless Mrs. Forbes agreed to pay him, on completion of the sale, the sum of $46,000, representing approximately one-half of the total prospective commission.

Mrs. Forbes apparently indicated she was prepared to share her commission but declared that she could not agree to such an arrangement without first obtaining the approval of Mr. Fife, nominee of Ocean City.

Mrs. Forbes brought the proposal to Mr. Fife hoping that he would quash it, but he did not. Moreover, because Mr. Halbauer was not satisfied with her written confirmation of the arrangement and required a confirming letter from Ocean City, Mr. Fife advised her it could be provided if she actually owed money to Mr. Halbauer and if it was paid from her portion of the commission and not from Ocean City's. She told Mr. Fife that she did not in fact owe any money to Mr. Halbauer apart from the tentative arrangement she had made with him to share her commission. Mr. Fife none the less gave Mr. Halbauer a letter stating:

> I understand that Mrs. Pat Forbes owes you the sum of $46,000.00. I hereby authorize you to deduct this amount from the commission monies you will be forwarding to us on behalf of A & M Holdings Ltd. on the sale of 921 Government Street.

The transaction contemplated by the interim agreement was not completed. Mr. Halbauer brought an action for specific performance against A & M, which was resolved by a compromise settlement, which resulted in the sale of the Weilller Building to Halbauer on different terms for the price of $5.6 million.

After the compromise settlement it was discovered by the solicitors for A & M that, prior to the conclusion of the agreement, Mrs. Forbes had made an arrangement with Halbauer whereby she agreed to rebate to him the sum of $46,000 from her portion of the commission to be paid to Ocean City. Up to that time A & M were unaware of that agreement.

A & M refused to pay the commission claimed by Ocean City with respect to the transaction. Ocean City brought this action against A & M for the commission.

At the trial Ocean City discontinued its claim against the personal defendant, Mr. Ellis, and abandoned its claim for compensation on a *quantum meruit* basis.

III

Issues

The issues raised by this appeal are of narrow compass:

(1) Is the real estate agent obliged to disclose to its principal the fact that it has agreed to rebate to the purchaser a portion of its real estate commission from the sale?

(2) If it is under such an obligation what effect does such nondisclosure have upon its claim to the real estate commission?

IV

The trial judge in addressing these issues made the following remarks:

> The relationship between a real estate agent and a person retaining him to sell property is a fiduciary and confidential one and the real estate agent's duty to his principal is to be construed strictly. The agent has a duty to obtain the highest price possible for his client and he has a duty to disclose all material facts which might affect the value of the property (*Re Crackle et al. and Deputy Superintendent of Insurance & Real Estate* (1983), 150 D.L.R. (3d) 371, 47 B.C.L.R. 256, 29 R.P.R. 276, *sub nom. Re Crackle and/or Greyfriars Realty Ltd.* (B.C.C.A.)).
>
> In *Canada Permanent Trust Co. v. Christie* (1979), 16 B.C.L.R. 183, Mr. Justice Esson, in the Supreme Court of British Columbia, considered whether an agent had a right to recover a real estate commission from the principal Christie and quoted with approval the following test [at pp. 185-6]:
>
> "The onus is upon the agent to prove that the transaction was entered into after full and fair disclosure of all material circumstances and of everything known to him respecting the subject matter of the contract which could be likely to influence the conduct of his principal. The burden of proof that the transaction was a righteous one rests upon the agent, who is bound to produce clear affirmative proof that the parties were at arm's length, that the principal had the fullest information upon all material facts and that having this information he agreed to adopt what was done."

The trial judge further stated:

> The defendant says that Mrs. Forbes had made an unusual arrangement with the purchaser, Holm Halbauer, to pay over to the purchaser $46,000 of the proceeds of her commission on the sale. The defendant says that this arrangement was a material circumstance and should have been disclosed to the defendant as a matter likely to influence his conduct and that the failure to disclose this arrangement constitutes a breach of fiduciary duty, disentitling the broker to commission.

And further:

> The authorities relied on by the defendant concern situations where the broker gained an

> advantage in the transaction and failed to disclose all material elements of the arrangement to his principal. In the case at bar the plaintiff says that no advantage was being sought by the broker and, indeed, Mrs. Forbes agreed to suffer a very considerable reduction in the anticipated commission in order, on her testimony, to secure the deal for the vendor and to permit the vendor to realize the full asking price for the property, that is, $5.6 million. ...
>
> In the case at bar the legal duty of the agent, if she engaged herself in the subject of her arrangement with the defendant, was to find a buyer for the Weiler Building ready willing and able to pay the sum that the defendant had declared to be the price which the defendant required to be paid, that is $5.6 million. The agent also had an obligation to avoid any conflict of interest with the defendant. In my view, the agreement to pay over to the purchaser a portion of the agent's commission on completion of the sale did not put the plaintiff into conflict with the defendant, as both the defendant and the plaintiff had the same interest to advance, that is to say, to complete the sale at the plaintiff's asking price. Obviously, the defendant had more to gain than did the plaintiff by the completion of the sale on the terms negotiated by the plaintiff.

In my opinion, the trial judge's interpretation of the obligation owed to a principal by its agent is too restrictive. The duty of disclosure is not confined to those instances where the agent has gained an advantage in the transaction or where the information might affect the value of the property, or where a conflict of interest exists. The agent certainly has a duty of full disclosure in such circumstances; they are commonly occurring circumstances which require full disclosure by the agent. However, they are not exhaustive.

The obligation of the agent to make full disclosure extends beyond these three categories and includes "everything known to him respecting the subject-matter of the contract which would be likely to influence the conduct of his principal" (*Canada Permanent Trust Co. v. Christie, supra*) or, as expressed in 1 Hals., 3rd ed., p.191, para. 443, everything which "...would be likely to operate upon the principal's judgment." In such cases the agent's failure to inform the principal would be material nondisclosure. ...

The test is an objective one to be determined by what a reasonable man in the position of the agent would consider, in the circumstances, would be likely to influence the conduct of his principal.

I would emphasize that the agent cannot arbitrarily decide what would likely influence the conduct of his principal and thus avoid the consequences of non-disclosure. If the information pertains to the transaction with respect to which the agent is engaged, any concern or doubt that the agent may have can be readily resolved by disclosure of all the facts to his principal. In the instant case the very withholding from the principal of the information concerning the payments to the purchaser of a portion of the commission could be evidence from which one might properly infer that the agent was aware that such circumstances would be a matter of concern to the principal.

One can readily appreciate that a vendor may wish not to enter into a complex sale arrangement which is subject to a variety of terms, such as vendor financing; a mortgage agreement; or a management agreement with a related company, unless that vendor was confident the purchaser was a person of integrity. ...

In the instant case the trial judge found that the agent justified her non-disclosure of the arrangement to pay the purchaser a percentage of the commission on the ground that she sought no advantage from the arrangement and indeed suffered a considerable reduction in her anticipated commission in order to secure the deal for the vendor and to permit the vendor to realize the full asking price for the property.

One may excuse a somewhat skeptical reaction to this altruistic rationale for non-disclosure of information by Mrs. Forbes. It ignores the fact that, if one accepts the premise that the arrangement was solely for the benefit of the principal, the agent would anticipate that the principal would approve of the agent's beneficence and proceed with the transaction. Accordingly, there would be no reason to withhold the information. ...

In the circumstances of this case, I find that the agent's nondisclosure was motivated by her desire to earn at least a portion of her commission and constituted a breach of her fiduciary duty to her principal and as a consequence she is not entitled to the commission claimed. ...

I would allow the appeal with costs here and below.

Taggart J. A.:—I agree.
Macfarlane J.A.:—I agree.
Taggart J.A.:—The appeal is allowed.

The president of a land development company purported to sign a contract on behalf of his company for the delivery and installation of steel. Unknown to him, at the time he signed the company had been dissolved pursuant to the *Ontario Business Corporations Act* for failure to pay its taxes. The supplier, not paid in full, sued the president himself for breach of contract, and, in the alternative, for breach of warranty of authority.

The court held that the president of the company was liable, not for breach of contract because he was not a party to the contract, but for breach of warranty of authority. By purporting to sign for the company he was warranting that he had the authority to sign on behalf of an existing company.

Unfortunately for the plaintiff, the court concluded that, with regard to the quantum of damages to be awarded, the plaintiff was entitled to receive what it would have received from the company, i.e. what the plaintiff would have received if the defendant's representation were true, that he signed for the company. As the company had no assets, the plaintiff would have gotten nothing from the company and, therefore, could get nothing from the president of the company.

Falvo Steel Co. Ltd. v. Roccari
For a more detailed account see The Lawyers Weekly
May 29, 1987.

VIII

FORMS OF BUSINESS ORGANIZATIONS

A. Partnership

Questions

What is the consequence to you of your partner being incompetent, negligent or dishonest?

What are the terms of the partnership agreement?

What is the consequence of a partner breaching the express or implied terms of that contract?

1. Liability of Partners to Third Parties

Victoria and Grey Trust Company v. Crawford et al.

(1986) 57 O.R. (2D) 484
High Court of Justice
November 12, 1986

Summary of the facts: A partner in a law firm was acting on behalf of an estate which maintained a savings account at Victoria and Grey Trust Company, the plaintiff. The lawyer was given a cheque for $60,025.61 signed by the Executrix of the estate and instructed to transfer the funds from the plaintiff Trust Company to a bank in California. Instead, without the knowledge of his partners, the lawyer destroyed that cheque and created another one on which he made himself the payee and forged the signature of the executrix. He negotiated the cheque at his bank, the Toronto-Dominion Bank in Orillia. The plaintiff trust company, having been told by the estate accountant that the account was being cleared out and knowing that the lawyer was a partner of the defendant firm, honoured the cheque. Later, when the fraud was discovered, the plaintiff trust company (pursuant to the *Bills of Exchange Act*) indemnified (paid back) the Estate because it had paid out on a forged cheque. In this case the trust company is suing the partnership to recover its loss.

Holland J. (orally): — This case involves a claim against partners carrying on the practice of law for the fraud of one of the partners. ...

The plaintiff relies on two sections of the *Partnerships Act*, R.S.O. 1980, c. 370. The defence is that, on the facts of this case, the sections do not apply and that a partnership is not liable for the independent fraud of one of its partners.

Section 11 of the Act reads as follows:

> 11. Where by any wrongful act or omission of a partner acting in the ordinaryof the business of the firm, or with the authority of his co-partners, loss or injury is caused to a person not being a partner of the firm, or any penalty is incurred, the firm is liable therefor to the same extent as the partner so acting or omitting to act.

Section 12 of the Act reads as follows:

> 12. In the following cases, namely,
>
> (a) where one partner, acting within the scope of his apparent authority, receives the money or property of a third person and misapplies it...the firm is liable to make good the loss.

Dealing with s. 11, it is admitted that there was a wrongful act by a partner, that in acting for the estate and in receiving estate funds or property, Mr. Farr was acting in the ordinary course of the business of the firm, and that loss occurred. It is also agreed that the word "person" in the section includes a corporation. It is submitted, however, that the section does not apply because the "person" who sustained the loss — Victoria & Grey Trust Company — was not dealing with the firm.

Sections 11 and 12 of the Act fall under a heading which reads: "Relation of Partners to Persons Dealing with Them". This raises the point to what extent, in considering the meaning of a section, may or should I have reference to this heading.

Section 9 of the *Interpretation Act*, R.S.O. 1980, c 219, reads as follows:

> The marginal notes and headings in the body of an Act and references to former enactments form no part of the Act but shall be deemed to be inserted for convenience of reference only.

The 12th edition of *Maxwell on the Interpretation of Statutes* (1989), at p. 11, has this to say:

> Headings.
>
> The headings prefixed to sections or sets of sections in some modern statues are regarded as preambles to those sections. They cannot control the plain words of the statute, but they may explain ambiguous words, a rule which, whatever the assistance which it may render in construction, cannot stand logically with the exclusion of marginal notes, for headings like marginal notes are — as Avory J. pointed out in *R. v. Hare* —"not voted on or passed by Parliament but are inserted after the Bill has become law."

I can see no ambiguity in the section. There is no indication in the section that the Legislature intended to limit liability of persons who suffer loss to persons dealing with the partnership, and in my opinion there is liability by virtue of s. 11 alone.

I turn now to s. 12(a) of the Act. It is submitted on behalf of the defence that what occurred here was really two transactions. In the first, Mr. Farr received the client's cheque, which was the property of the client. He improperly destroyed this cheque, and it is argued that there was no loss as a result of this act. Mr. Farr then had another cheque prepared and forged the client's signature. It is suggested that this was a separate act and distinct transaction in which he acted on his own, not within the scope of his apparent authority, and that therefore this section does not apply. Reliance is replaced [sic] on the decision of *Hughes v. Twisden* (1886), 55 L.J. Ch. 481, in which a member of a firm of solicitors was negligent in connection with the mortgage in 1875. The court held that the claim arising out of the 1869 transaction was statute-barred, and that the action itself failed because the fraud was not committed in the ordinary course of business. I point out that these two claims dealt with matters that involved separate transactions that were six years apart. One was based on negligence and the other on fraud.

In the present case we are dealing with what I consider to be one transaction — that is, the deposit of the cheque with a firm of solicitors, with the funds to be placed in the partnership account, and it would be improper to break the transaction down into isolated parts; see *Lloyd v. Grace, Smith & Co.*, [1912] A.C. 716, and particularly at p. 739.

For the above reasons there will be judgment for the plaintiff against all defendants for $60,025.61 together with interest at 11% from April 1, 1982, the date upon which the money was replaced in the estate account, together with costs to be assessed.

I have endorsed the record as follows: "Oral Reasons. Judgment for $60,025.61 with interest at 11% from April 1, 1982, together with costs to be assessed."

Thank you, gentlemen.

Judgment for plaintiff.

2. Obligations of Partners to Each Other

Norman Olson v. Antonio Gullo and Gullo Enterprises Limited

Ontario Court of Justice No. 32867/88
July 9, 1992

Boland J.: This action arises out of the purchase and sale of ninety acres of land situate in the Township of Georgina and involves claims for damages for breach of contract, breach of fiduciary duty and payment for unjust enrichment. The counterclaim was not pursued at trial. ...

It is the plaintiff's position that during the month of February, 1988, he and Gullo entered into an oral partnership agreement for the purpose of acquiring, developing and eventually disposing of the 1,000 acres situate on the west side of Woodbine Avenue. Gullo was to contribute his expertise as a real estate speculator and developer, and Olson was to provide his skills in marketing, promotion, public relations and financing. Olson further contends that it was also agreed that he and Gullo would contribute equal amounts of capital as required to purchase the various farms and they would share equally in the profits.

The defendants, on the other hand, flatly deny that there ever was any partnership agreement. They contend that at no time was there any relationship of trust, confidence and dependence created between the parties. It is their position that Gullo was interested in developing an industrial park and devoted a great deal of time attempting to purchase lands within the 1,000 acre tract. His offers were turned down by the farmers and he abandoned the project because of the high price of agricultural land. He decided to purchase the Walshe farm as a long-term investment. Assuming the land assembly went ahead, Olson's sole function was to find investors interested in developing the project and for this service he would receive a finder's fee or commission.

According to the evidence, in March, 1988, Gullo retained real estate agents at Family Trust Corporation. Over the next few months, these agents submitted agreements of purchase and sale in the name of Gullo Enterprises Limited in Trust to a number of farmers owning land within the 1,000 acre parcel. During this period Olson arranged for funds to purchase his share of the various parcels and discussed the project with prospective investors.

The evidence also establishes that during this period the price of farmland in the area increased dramatically and, consequently Gullo led Olson to believe that the project was no longer feasible as it would be virtually impossible to purchase any farms in the 1,000 acre tract because of rising prices. Nevertheless, unknown to Olson, in May of 1988, Gullo Enterprises Limited in Trust, entered into an agreement to purchase a ninety-acre farm, known as the Walshe Property, for approximately $20,000 an acre and, prior to closing, assigned the purchase agreement to Wesrow Estates Inc. at a profit of approximately $2,500,000.

The Walshe farm was part of the 1,000 acres located on the west side of Woodbine Avenue in the Township of Georgina and is shown as parcel 7 on the preliminary study, dated March 1988. In September, 1988, Olson discovered that Gullo had secretly entered into agreements to purchase and sell the Walshe property at a considerable profit. He expressed his disappointment and anger to Gullo and his employment with [Gullo's company] Glacier Clear Marketing Inc. terminated the end of that month. This action was commenced November 4, 1988.

The evidence is overwhelming that in February, 1988, Norman Olson and Antonio Gullo orally agreed that they would be equal partners in purchases of parcels of land in a defined 1,000 acres located on the west side of Woodbine Avenue in the Township of Georgina. It was agreed that the parties would each provide half the moneys required to purchase the various farms and the land would be registered in both their names in due course. It was also agreed that Gullo would negotiate the purchases because of his experience in land assembly and that Olson would find interested investors and prepare promotional material related to the property and the project. Their respective roles were in keeping with their background and expertise.

[The judge reviewed the evidence]. ...

There was a mountain of evidence to support a finding that in February, 1988, Gullo and Olson orally agreed to become equal partners in the purchase of farms within the 1,000 acre tract of land and they anticipated making a great deal of profit. Furthermore, all this evidence supports a finding that the Walshe property was to be purchased and held as partnership lands.

It follows that Gullo and Olson, as partners, were in a fiduciary relationship and each had a duty of the utmost good faith and loyalty to the other and to the partnership. Once the partnership was established, it was not possible for either partner to utilize a partnership opportunity or divert a maturing business opportunity for his exclusive personal gain. Gullo owed a fiduciary duty to disclose all material facts to Olson. The evidence establishes that at no time did Gullo advise Olson of the purchase and sale of the Walshe farm and he never asked Olson to pay his share of the purchase money. He surreptitiously planned to pocket the entire profit of approximately $2,500,000. By secretly purchasing the Walshe property for himself and not for the partnership, Gullo failed to meet the minimum standards the law imposes on a partner and I find this was a serious breach of the fiduciary duty he owed to Olson.

Having found that there was partnership agreement and that Gullo breached that agreement, as well as the fiduciary duty he owed to Olson, one is faced with the difficult issue in this trial which is the appropriate measure of damage to be awarded in these circumstances. Unquestionably Gullo was unjustly enriched as a result of the breach of his fiduciary duty to Olson. At the time the partnership was established, Gullo and Olson had agreed to divide the partnership profits equally. Certainly, Olson is entitled to at least fifty per cent of the profits from the sale of the ninety-acre parcel comprising the Walshe farm. The contentious issue is whether the court should prevent Gullo from retaining any of the proceeds of the sale, including those profits which he was entitled to under the partnership agreement.

Counsel for the defendants argue that should the court find that there was a partnership agreement, Olson is only entitled to his share of the profits in accordance with the terms of that agreement. Counsel for the plaintiff seeks judgment for the entire profit and relies heavily on the decision of our Court of Appeal in *Lavigne v. Robern* (1984) 51 O.R. (2d) 60.

In the case of *Lavigne v. Robern*, a fifty percent shareholder made a secret profit on the sale of all the shares of the company when he was acting as agent for the other shareholders. The Court of Appeal held that a defaulting fiduciary who makes a "secret profit" at the expense of the partnership or the other partners must not be allowed to profit from his own wrongdoing. Consequently, the court held that the defendant's portion of the profit to which he would have been entitled if not for the breach of his duty, was rendered forfeit by his disloyalty. The Court of Appeal attempted to create a disincentive from breaching a fiduciary duty where the defaulting party received a "secret profit". ...

Counsel for the defendants argues that the facts in this case are not similar to those in *Lavigne v. Robern* and the case should be distinguished. He contends that it was Gullo who first discovered the property and realized its potential. Gullo, alone, assumed the risk of this investment and at no time was Olson's money involved. Finally, counsel for the defendants argue that it would be unnecessarily harsh to require Gullo to forfeit those profits which he would have been entitled to under the partnership agreement, and allow the plaintiff double recovery.

I cannot agree with the defendants' position. I have given a great deal of consideration to the evidence heard during the trial and in my view this is not an appropriate disposition of the profit made on the sale of the Walshe property as there would be no penal aspect to the result. Gullo would receive precisely what he would have received if he had acted honestly and shared the proceeds equally with his partner, Olson. The result provides no disincentive. If this were the rule of law, a fiduciary could breach his trust hoping to hide the breach and after a lengthy trial retain his share of the secret profit. In my view, this is the same type of truly repugnant behaviour found in *Lavigne v. Robern* and I am bound by that case.

Gullo compounded his wrongful conduct by attempting to avoid this litigation by obstructing justice and contracting to kill Olson. He pleaded guilty to two charges of attempt [sic] murder and was sentenced to three years in the penitentiary on each charge to be served concurrently. He was punished for this conduct. However, he also threatened witnesses and police officers were required in the courtroom throughout the trial. The court must demonstrate that it will not tolerate this type of behaviour.

The courts have held that the amount of the windfall profit is an immaterial consideration. I agree with the following statement of Mark Vincent Ellis in his article on *Fiduciary Duties in Canada* that:

> An examination of the case law in this Court and in the Courts of other like jurisdictions on the fiduciary duties ... shows the pervasiveness of a strict ethic in this area of the law.

In this case, the appropriate measure of damages is for Gullo to hand over to Olson the entire secret profit. The court is merely removing the millions of dollars secretly pocketed by Gullo and placing them in the pocket of the plaintiff. In my view this is preferable to encouraging fraudulent conduct and weakening our structures of trust.

For the above reasons there will be a declaration that Norman Olson and Antonio Gullo were partners with each entitled to one-half of the profits. The defendants hold fifty per cent of the profits on the purchase and sale of the Walshe farm in trust for the plaintiff.

Damages are awarded on an accounting of profits. After factoring in the initial purchase price, the payment of deposits, payment of balance of agent's fee and legal fees, and assuming that the second mortgage has been paid in full, the award is $2,486,940.

Accordingly, there will be judgment in favour of the plaintiff against both defendants in the sum of $2,486,940. As the money has been paid into court there will be no prejudgment interest. Should counsel wish to speak to me with respect to a further accounting or as to costs, they may do so at their earliest convenience.

[Judgment for the plaintiff]

Mr. Schmidt told his partners that he was taking an early retirement to help his sons on their farms. The partners gave him a very golden handshake. It was learned that while he was negotiating his early retirement he had intended to join a competing firm in the same city and was, in fact, soliciting colleagues to join him. He took sixty-five of the partnership's clients when he did leave. The partnership refused to pay out as per the retirement agreement. Schmidt sued. The B.C. Supreme Court held that the contract was voidable for misrepresentation and that Schmidt had breached his duty as a partner both at common law and under s. 22 of the B.C. *Partnership Act.*

Schmidt v. Peat Marwick Thorne
Summarized from The Lawyers Weekly
September 11, 1992 p. 2;
September 25, 1992 p. 34

Advocates of legal reform in the U.S. have promoted legislation regarding "domestic partnership" which would apply to gays and unmarried straight couples to eliminate injustices and difficulties that arise partly because of the law's failure to recognize gay marriages.[1]

B. The Corporation

Questions

When will the law not allow a person to rely on the prinicipIe that a company is a separate legal entity?

If a person chooses to use the corporate structure for carrying on business, can he or she avoid personal liability?

1. Lifting the Corporate Veil / Liability of Directors

Lockharts Ltd. v. Excalibur Holdings Ltd. et al.

210 A.P.R. 181
Nova Scotia Supreme Court
December 14,1987

Summary of the facts: Mr. Harrison and his wife were the sole shareholders of two companies, Baron Developments Ltd. (Baron), a construction company, and Excalibur Holdings Ltd., (Excalibur), an investment company. Baron bought a piece of property under an Agreement for Sale from Clayton Developments Limited (Clayton) and began construction of a house. The plaintiff Lockharts Ltd. contracted with Baron to supply building materials. When Baron failed to pay its account, Lockharts Ltd. sued Baron and a default judgment was entered in favour of Lockharts Ltd. for $19,513.80 on March 14, 1986. Both Baron and Excalibur had notice of the judgment.

On June 24, 1986 Excalibur bought the land from Clayton and took an assignment from Baron of all Baron's interest in the land under the Agreement for Sale with the result that Excalibur had both legal and equitable interest in the property and Baron, the judgment debtor, no longer owned any property.

Davison, J.: ...

Issues: ...

[T]he plaintiff's submissions to me were:

(1) That the events which took place in June, 1986, constituted a fraudulent scheme designed to defeat the rights of the plaintiff under the judgment. Therefore, it is submitted I should ignore the separate corporate entity of Excalibur and grant an order declaring the judgment "binding upon... the assets and land of the defendant, Excalibur."

(2) That an order should issue declaring the judgment against Baron an encumbrance against the land known as lot 9-44 Grenadier Drive by reason of s. 18 of the *Registry Act*, R.S.N.S. 19967, c. 265, and the equitable interest of Baron in the land pursuant to the agreement of purchase and sale. ...

Lifing the Corporate Veil

Since *Salomon v. Salomon & Co. Ltd.*, [1897] A.C. 22, it has been a clear principle of law that a company is an independent legal entity distinct from its shareholders. In this case the plaintiff asks me to "lift the corporate veil" on the grounds of fraud. The plaintiff says Mr. Harrison used Excalibur to strip the assets of Baron to avoid payment to the plaintiff of the amount of the judgment.

In England there have been signs that the firm principle of *Salomon* has been the subject of some erosion and the most often quoted comments are those of Lord Denning in *Littlewoods Mail Order Stores Ltd. v. McGregor,* [1969] 3 All E.R. 855, at 860:

> I cannot accept this argument. I decline to treat the Fork Company as a separate and independent entity. The doctrine laid down in *Salomon v. Salomon & Co. Ltd.* has to be watched very carefully. It has often been supposed to cast a veil over the personality of a limited company through which the courts cannot see. But that is not true. The courts can and often do draw aside the veil. They can, and often do, pull off the mask. They look to see what really lies behind. ... I think that we should look at the Fork Company and see it as it really is — the wholly-owned subsidiary of the taxpayers. It is the creature, the puppet, of the taxpayers in point of *fact*: and it should be so regarded in point of *law*.

The facts in *Jones v. Lipman* [1962] 1 W.L.R. 832, are similar to the facts before me. The defendant, Lipman, entered an agreement with the plaintiff to sell a parcel of land but before completion under the agreement Lipman transferred the land to a company the sole shareholders of which were Lipman and a clerk at the office of Lipman's solicitor. The court granted an order requiring both defendants to perform the agreement with the plaintiff. Mr. Justice Russell found that the company was a sham or "a mask which he (Lipman) holds before his face in an attempt to avoid recognition by the eye of equity."

In *Merchandise Transport Ltd. v. British Transport Commission,* [1962] 2 Q.B. 173, a transport company which owned vehicles applied for licences in the name of a subsidiary company because it feared it would be unsuccessful if the application was in its own name. The court refused to treat parent and subsidiary companies as independent bodies and decided the issue as if they were one commercial unit. Devlin, L.F., stated at page 202:

> But the fact that two persons are separate in law does not mean that one may not be under the control of the other to such an extent that together they constitute one commercial unit. It may be a case of parent and subsidiary; or it may be a case in which one man, though nominally independent, is in truth the instrument of another; or it may be a case in which a man has simply put his vehicles in the name of his wife.

In Canada, the principle enunciated in *Salomon* is alive and well, but it is also clear that courts will disregard the corporate entity in certain circumstances including situations involving "fraud or improper conduct." Authors of texts on company law are fond of saying that the only consistent principle which has evolved is that in the *Salomon* case (see Gower, *The Principles of Modern Company Law* (3rd Ed.) p. 189). In my respectful opinion the courts have been equally consistent in clearly enunciating an exception to the basic principle by refusing to permit a corporate entity to be used for fraudulent or improper purposes. It is true that there has been inconsistency in the application of this exception but the existence of the exception has been recognized by all levels of Canadian Courts.

In his dissenting judgment in *Jodrey's Estate v. Province of Nova Scotia* (1980), 41 N.S.R. (2d) 181; 76 A.P.R. 181; 32 N.R. 275, Chief Justice Dickson was clearly of the view that the principle of *Salomon* has been rigidly applied in the Canadian Courts but also recognized the exception with these words at page 228 N.W.R., A.P.R.

> Generally speaking in the *absence of fraud or improper conduct* the courts cannot disregard the separate existence of a corporate entity: (emphasis added).

In *Pacific Rim Installations Ltd. v. Tilt-Up Construction Ltd. and Classic Tilt-Up Designs Ltd.,* [1978] 5 B.C.L.R. 231, one Tremblay was the principal shareholder and officer of the two defendant companies. The plaintiff commenced action against both defendants to recover monies due under a subcontract for labour and materials at a construction project. Tremblay represented to the plaintiff that one company was the proper party with which the plaintiff should deal. This company dissipated funds received from the owner to the point where it became a mere shell. The other company refused to pay the plaintiff on the basis that it wasn't party to the contract. The trial judge entered judgment against both defendants and held them jointly and severally liable for the plaintiff's claim and in doing so commented at 235:

> I may say that I have considered some basic company law in this field and some of the leading cases on the so-called 'lifting of the corporate veil' ... I think there is sound reason to do so here, since blindly to ignore that both Tilt-Up and Classic are the alter ego of Mr. Tremblay

> would result in a wholly unconscionable manipulation by this principal to avoid payment of the plaintiff's claim.

Mr. Justice Thompson in *Clarkson Co. Ltd. v. Zhelka et al.*(1967) 64 D.L.R. 457, referred to the conclusions drawn by Mr. Justice Masten in an article on *One Man Companies and Their Controlling Shareholders* (1936), 14 Can. Bar Rev. 663, and expressed approval of the author's conclusions including the following at page 470:

> If a company is formed for the express purpose of doing a wrongful or unlawful act, or, if when formed, those in control expressly direct or [sic] wrongful thing to be done, the individuals as well as the company are responsible to those to whom liability is legally owed.
>
> In such cases, or where the company is the mere agent of a controlling corporator, it may be said that the company is a sham, cloak or alter ego, but otherwise it should not be so termed.

The Saskatchewan Court of Appeal in *Nedco v. Clark et al.* (1973) 43 D.L.R. (3d) 714, referred to *Toronto v. Famous Players Canadian Corp.*, [1936] 2 D.L.R. 129, as an illustration of how the Supreme Court of Canada has recognized "the right to pierce the corporate veil for a specific purpose." After reviewing a number of authorities, Chief Justice Culliton concluded at p. 721:

> ...while the principle laid down in *Salomon v. Salomon & Co. Ltd.*, supra, is and continues to be a fundamental feature of Canadian law, there are instances in which the court can and should lift the corporate veil, but whether it does so depends upon the facts in each particular case. Moreover, the fact that the court does lift the corporate veil for a specific purpose in no way destroys the recognition of the corporation as a independent and autonomous entity for all other purposes.

The recognition of the right by the Supreme Court of Canada is even more apparent since the dicta of Madame Justice Wilson in *Kosmopoulos v. Constitution Insurance Co. of Canada* (1987), 74 N.R. 360: 21 O.A.C. 4; 34 D.L.R. (4th) 208, at 213-214. ...

What can be drawn from the foregoing authorities? In my assessment, the fundamental principle enunciated in the *Salomon* case remains good law in Canada and "one man corporations" should be considered as separate entities from their major shareholder save for certain exceptional cases. A judge should not "lift the veil" simply because he believes it would be in the interest of "fairness" or of "justice." If that was the test the veil in Salomon case would have been lifted. On the other hand the courts have the power indeed the duty, to look behind the corporate structure and to ignore it if it is being used for fraudulent or improper purposes or as a "puppet" to the detriment of a third party.

One of the fundamental purposes of establishing a corporate existence is to limit the liability of the shareholders. In doing so, growth of commerce is encouraged by providing a vehicle by which monies can be invested with the knowledge that losses would be restricted to an amount usually equivalent to the extent of the investment.

The purpose of the corporate entity was not to defraud or mislead others including creditors and shareholders and in my opinion where a company is being used for this purpose the "veil" should be lifted and a remedy made available to the victims of such conduct.

In the case before me the plaintiff supplied materials to Baron when Baron had an equitable interest in the lands on which the building, for which the material was to be used, was to be constructed. After Baron defaulted in payment, the plaintiff secured a judgment which, if the agreement for purchase and sale had been completed, would have attached to Baron's legal interest in the land and dwelling. After the judgment was obtained no effort was made to complete under the purchase and sale agreement and the property was conveyed to Excalibur which, like Baron, is solely owned by the principal, Harrison. The sequence and nature of the documents and events raised a strong *prima facie* inference that the conveyance from Clayton Developments Limited to Excalibur was intended to defeat the rights of the plaintiff. It was incumbent upon the defendants to adduce evidence to rebut that inference. In my opinion, the defendants failed to meet that burden. The plaintiff has convinced me, on the balance of probabilities, having regard to the gravity of the finding (see *Hanes v. Wawanesa Mutual Ins. Co.*, [1963] S.C.R. 154, at 162) that Mr. Harrison made use of Excalibur for a fraudulent and improper purpose.

Mr. Harrison would have the court believe that the reason for having the conveyance in the name of Excalibur was because Excalibur could complete the construction; whereas Baron did not have financial resources to do so. I do not accept this evidence and it is not supported by any other evidence. ...

I was not convinced by the evidence that Baron could not have completed under the agreement of sale. There was no evidence of any attempts by Mr. Harrison to secure funds other than the two conversation he had with Mr. Lisson [the lender]. Even if Baron did not have the ability to secure funds by itself why couldn't Excalibur have guaranteed to loan Baron? This would have achieved the same result and would have permitted the agreement to have been completed as originally contemplated.

If the situation had been such that the agreement of purchase and sale had been completed before the judgment was entered and legal title conveyed from Baron to Excalibur after the entry of the judgment, that conveyance could have been set aside pursuant to the terms of the *Assignments and Preferences Act,* R.S.N.S. 1967, c.16. In effect, that is precisely what occurred in this case, except that title was retained in Clayton Developments Limited until the appropriate time.

In my opinion, the evidence clearly establishes that the corporate entities owned by Mr. Harrison were used as "puppets" to the detriment of the plaintiff and in that respect were used for fraudulent and improper purposes.

My conclusion is that the plaintiff is entitled to declaratory relief and that an order, declaring that the plaintiff's judgment against Baron is binding upon and forms a charge upon the interest of Excalibur on the lands referred to in the deed of conveyance from Clayton Developments Limited to Excalibur dated the 24th day of June 1986 should issue. ...

The plaintiff shall recover from the defendants its costs.

Judgment for plaintiff.

Property owned by Riverside Fisheries Ltd. of Windsor, Ontario was destroyed by fire. When the insurance company refused to compensate the company for its loss on the grounds that the fire was deliberately set, Riverside Fisheries Ltd. sued the insurance company.

The following are the concluding words of Judge Walsh of the Ontario Supreme Court. "There is no doubt whatsoever but that the fire was deliberately set, most probably the work of a professional arsonist. After a most careful and anxious scrutiny of all the facts and circumstances I find that the defendants have satisfied the onus imposed on them.

"Mr. Shulgan [counsel for the plaintiff], in a most novel argument, submitted that even if I should find, as I have, that the plaintiff Irving Goldhar was responsible for the fire, it should not prevent recovery by the corporate plaintiff, Riverside Fisheries Limited on the ground that it is a separate legal entity and its recovery should not be barred by the guilt or wrongdoing of Irving Goldhar, even though he is its president and principal shareholder.

"This submission is based by analogy to the recent decision of the Ontario Court of Appeal in *Higgins v. Orion Insurance Co.*, 50 O.R. (2d) 352, 10 C.C.L.I. 139, [1985] I.L.R. 1-1886, 17 D.L.R. (4th) 90, 8 O.A.C. 259, which held that arson on the part of one partner did not deprive a co-insured innocent partner from recovering from the insurer the loss actually sustained by him.

"A close perusal of the reasons of Robins J.A. in the Higgins case makes it abundantly clear that given the interwoven family business relationships here existent public policy considerations would never qualify Riverside as "an innocent partner" as that term was used in that judgment.

"The plaintiffs' action is therefore dismissed. ..."

Riverside Fisheries Ltd. et al. v. Economical Mutual Insurance Co. et al.
(1986) 19 C.C.L.I. 130
Ontario Supreme Court

Ataya v. *Mutual of Omaha Insurance Co. et al.*

(1988) 34 C.C.L.I. 307
SUPREME COURT OF BRITISH COLUMBIA
APRIL 12, 1988

Spencer J.: — Mrs. Mohiba Ataya went to visit her son in Texas. She was 73 years old and suffered from angina and diabetes. She was apprehensive about the cost of medical care in the U.S. should she fall ill there so she had another son, Rogheb, insure her for excess medical coverage while she would be out of the province. Unfortunately she was taken ill in Texas and died, but not before incurring medical costs agreed at $46,800.13. The insurers, Mutual of Omaha and Constitution Insurance Co., refused to pay because the policy excludes coverage for any illness for which Mrs. Ataya required treatment or hospitalization within 180 days of the effective date of the policy. No issue is now taken with that refusal and the action against those two defendants was dismissed by consent without calling evidence, but as if the case against them had been tried on its merits.

Mrs. Ataya's estate now claims that John Fleming Insurance Agency Ltd. (hereinafter "Fleming Ltd.") and its employee, Mr. Fleming, breached a contract to provide her with unrestricted coverage, or were negligent in failing to provide it to her or breached a warranty of authority to provide such coverage on behalf of the insurers. ...

The case against Fleming Ltd. and Mr. Fleming turns heavily upon whose recollection of what was said some 2 1/2 years ago is to be preferred. ... .

I find as a fact that after he was told of the exclusions in a Four M policy, and its unavailability to Mrs. Ataya, Mr. Ataya stipulated for medical insurance to cover his mother's precise needs, which he described to Mr. Fleming. I find Mr. Fleming was negligent in failing to tell him he did not have that coverage available and in failing to warn him that the Snowbird policy he did sell was subject to a 180-day exclusion. He had a duty to explain that so that Mrs. Ataya would know she had to look elsewhere for the coverage she wanted, or change her plans, or take other steps to avoid the risk. Failure to do so was a want of reasonable care, because it is admitted that Mr. Ataya volunteered the facts, generally, of his mother's age and health and the intended length of her journey. See *Fine's Flowers Ltd. v. General Accident Assurance Co.* (1977), 17 O.R. (2d) 529, 2 B.L.R. 257, [1978] I.L.R. 1-937, 81 DL.R. (3d) 139 at 149 (C.A.), per Wilson J.A. (as she then was) and *Luft v. M.S. Zorkin & Co.*, [1982] 4 W.W.R. 548 at 554 (B.C.Co. Ct.). The fact that the policy, when delivered, contained the exclusion clause to be read cannot assist the defendants. Mrs. Ataya was entitled to rely upon the defendant's absence of warning to her son that the Snowbird policy contained an exclusion clause as a representation that it suited her described needs. Fleming Ltd. is also liable for breach of a contract to sell Mrs. Ataya, as it purported to do, an insurance policy suiting her needs without the 180-day exclusion clause.

The policy contained a term, which was explained to Mr. Ataya and noted by Mr. Fleming on the back of Exhibit 8(6), that required the insured to bear 20 per cent of any loss. Judgment will therefore go against Fleming Insurance Agency Ltd. for 80 per-cent of the agreed medical expenses, which amounts to $37,440.10. If that sum is calculated in U.S. dollars and counsel cannot agree on the proper conversion rate, they may apply.

A claim is also made against Mr. Fleming personally upon the ground that he was the individual within the limited company who committed the negligent act of which the plaintiff complains. The law is now settled that where two parties come into a legal relationship between themselves because of the existence of a contract, the liability of one to the other for some fault committed in the relationship may be governed not only by the terms of the contract but, subject to any exclusion or limitation contained within the contract, by the principles of the tort of negligence. See *Central & Eastern Trust Co. v. Rafuse*, [1986] 2 S.C.R. 147, 75 N.S.R. (2d) 109, 37 C.C.L.T. 117, 42 R.P.R. 161, 34 B.L.R. 187, 186 A.P.R. 109, 69 N.R. 321, [1986} R.R.A. 527 (headnote), 31 D.L.R. (4th) 481, varied [1988] 1 S.C.R. 1206. Liability in negligence springs from a duty of care, and the duty in turn springs from a relationship of proximity however that relationship is established. There have been numerous cases in which employees of limited companies have been found liable in negligence for faults committed by them in carrying out their employer's contractual duty to a plaintiff. A recent example in this province is *London Drugs Ltd. v. Kuehne & Nagel International Ltd.*, [1986] 4 W.W.R. 183, 2 B.C.L.R. (2d) 181 (S.C.).

Mr. Fleming was the employee of John Fleming Insurance Agency Ltd. in this case, but he was also the proprietor of that limited company. Incorporation has, for 300 years in our law, been looked upon as a way of avoiding personal liability. The question argued in this case is whether a proprietor of an incorporated business who commits a negligent act in the course of that company's business with the plaintiff should be in any different position from an ordinary employee. I think he should not. Whether Mr. Fleming or another of the company's employees was the person who dealt with Mr. Ataya, each is brought into the same type of relationship with the plaintiff. Each is put in a position where he or she knew, or ought to have known, that unless reasonable care was taken Mrs. Ataya would be misled to her probable detriment by being sold an unsuitable policy of insurance without any warning. The fact that a customer does business with the proprietor personally rather than with another of the company's employees should make no difference to the result, and the proprietor is as liable as any other employee would be.

An example, involving the directors of a corporation and predating *Central Trust*, supra, is *Nicholls v. Corp. of Richmond (Township of)*, [1983] 4 W.W.R. 169, 43 B.C.L.R. 162, where, on a preliminary point the Court of Appeal affirmed the potential liability of directors for their tortious acts committed in carrying out the corporation's business.

It follows, I think, that the incorporation of a company to carry on business no longer has the effect which businessmen have thought it to have for many years. Where a company's liability is based upon a contract only it , and not its proprietors, can be found liable. But where concurrent liability exists in tort the incorporation of the business does not serve to protect the actual tortfeasor from liability even though he may be a proprietor of the limited company. It is, I think, questionable whether *Sealand of the Pacific Ltd. v. Robert C. McHaffie Ltd.*, [1974] 6 W.W.R. 724, 51 D.L.R. (3d) 702 (B.C.C.A) would be decided in favour of Mr. McHaffie if it were to arise today, after the decision in *Central Trust.*

Judgment will accordingly go against both John Fleming Insurance Agency Ltd. and Mr. Fleming personally. The plaintiff will have court order interest at the rates usually used by district registrars from time to time, and is entitled to its costs also.

Judgment for plaintiff

Regarding the liability of directors:

Note #1: Watch for *Toronto Dominion Bank v. Peat Marwick Thorne, Inc., Trustee of Leigh Instruments Ltd.* In October of 1991 the Ontario Divisional Court refused to dismiss a statement of claim by the TD Bank which includes claims against eight corporate officers and directors personally for negligent misrepresentation and deceit for $40 million. The bank claimed that the directors had a duty to disclose material changes of the company that would affect its obligations to the bank.

***The Lawyers Weekly* November 22, 1991 p. 1, 9.**

Note #2: In *R. v. Bata Industries* two former directors of the company involved with the day-to-day operations, were convicted under environmental protection legislation for *not* taking steps to prevent the release of pollutants by the company. Furthermore, the court order against the convicted company prohibited the company from indemnifying the convicted directors.

***The Lawyers Weekly* May 1, 1992 p. 1, 13**

On appeal the court upheld the order that prohibited the company from indemnifying the directors.

See *The Lawyers Weekly* August 20, 1993 p. 9

2. Duties of a Director

Questions

What are your duties as a director and to whom are they owed?
What is the consequence of being in breach of those duties?

China Software Corp. v. *Leimbigler et al.*

(1989) 27 C.P.R. (3d) 215
Supreme Court of British Columbia
June 15, 1989

Callaghan J.: — The plaintiff claims damages from the defendants, two of its former directors and shareholders, for breach of fiduciary duty in intentionally misleading the plaintiff as to the state and cost of completion of the TM (Tianma) Chinese Text Generator and Word Processor System in order to induce the plaintiff to sell the system to Malaspina College.

The Chinese text generation and word processing system is a system for generating and handling Chinese character text (Hanzi test). The system automatically converts text from the standard romanized form of Chinese (Pinyin) into Hanzi text . ...and permits the user to look up the English equivalent of a Chinese word, as well as the Chinese synonyms of a Chinese word, a useful feature for individuals who work with the Chinese language.

[By 1985 a group consisting of Dr. Leimbigler, a linguist, Mr. Slade, who had expertise in the computer field, Mr. Green a lawyer who could assist in raising venture capital and Kambeitz, who had computer equipment and the willingness to work on the project, formed a company, China Software Corporation, the plaintiff in this case. The development of the software system proceeded on schedule. Regular project review meetings were held. At one such meeting it was agreed that Leimbigler and Kambeitz should go to China and Japan to demonstrate the software system. On their return from the trip, Leimbigler reported to Green that neither Sony or NCR was interested in the system and that it would take another eight to ten months to complete the prototype at a cost of approximately $200,000 to $300,000. The information with regard to timing and cost was contrary to what he had led his partners to believe before the trip.

Later that month, in August of 1985, the company rejected an offer to purchase the system for $100,000 from International Geosystems Corporation. Within a few days Leimbigler advised that Malaspina College was prepared to offer $100,000 cash and urged acceptance. At the meetings in which the offer was discussed, Leimbigler again said the prototype could not be completed for another eight to ten months and would cost an additional $200,000 to $300,000 and that similar systems were being developed. Furthermore, Leimbigler and Kambeitz indicated they would abandon their work on the system if the sale was not completed. Green and Slade reluctantly concluded the company should accept the Malaspina offer.

Unknown to the company, Leimbigler and Kambeitz had surreptitiously negotiated an agreement with Malaspina College under which they would form a limited partnership which would benefit Leimbigler and Kambeitz. When Green learned of the agreement, he demanded the disclosure of its contents to the company. Despite initial statements to mislead the company about the nature of the agreement and reluctance to disclose its contents, meetings were held at which the details of the agreement were disclosed and the parties negotiated an arrangement to resolve the matter. Malaspina rejected the arrangement.

The company later agreed to proceed with the sale without a satisfactory arrangement because it was clear that Leimbigler and Kambeitz would not complete the project. The College insisted that with the sale of the system the company execute a general release of Leimbigler, Kambeitz and Malaspina. The company agreed. Leimbigler and Kambeitz transferred their shares in the company back to the company and gave up their share of the $100,000 of the sale proceeds.

The system was soon sold to three men who sold it to International Geosystems Corporation. Malaspina received $150,000 cash and a promissory note for $150,000. Leimbigler and Kambeitz received $100,000 and 250,000 shares of International Geosystems Corporation valued at $2.00 a share.] ...

Clearly there was a fiduciary relationship. The defendants breached that relationship in order to obtain a more abundant award through the agreement entered into with Malaspina College.

Counsel for the defendants candidly acknowledges that the defendants likely have no defence on the merits since there are no extenuating circumstances sufficient to justify the defendants' positioning themselves as they did to take a corporate opportunity that belonged to China Software Corporation. The defence proceeded on the assumption that the two defendants were guilty of misrepresentation and non-disclosure in order to induce the sale by China Software to Malaspina College, as pleaded. Counsel submits, however, that the plaintiff gave these two defendants a full release and discharge in connection with a claim of breach of trust which was not induced by any fraud or misrepresentation and consequently cannot be set aside. As counsel said, the defendants acknowledged by their actions in giving up their shares in the plaintiff corporation as well as their 48% interest in the $100,000 sale price, that they were in breach of their fiduciary obligations. He argues that just because the fraud was much greater than the plaintiff suspected or was disclosed in the negotiations leading up to the giving of the release, does not justify setting it aside. Counsel for the defendants went on to say that the giving of a general release must release and discharge the releasee from any and all actions up to that time, even though the releasor is unaware of the true extent of any wrongdoing on the part of the party to whom the release is given.

While the argument in many respects at first blush is inviting, it is clear that the plaintiff would not have consummated an agreement with Malaspina College if it had been aware of the ongoing interest of International Geosystems Corporation and Sony, all of which was kept from it by the secretive conduct of the defendants. Malaspina had no interest in keeping to itself the technology acquired but was desirous of marketing the system in order to recoup its $100,000 investment. The defendants' failure to divulge information of the interest of other parties, the representation (which was false) that it would take eight to ten months and $200,000 to $300,000 to complete the prototype, and the refusal of the defendants to work further on the project were the effectual causes of the sale to Malaspina. The plaintiff, because of the intractable position of Malaspina (it refused to purchase unless it and the two defendants Leimbigler and Kambeitz were provided with a final release and discharge), as well as the misrepresentation of the defendants, was left, because of the disparity in their positions, with little choice. To accede to the defendant's' argument would be tantamount to condoning the fraudulent misrepresentations perpetrated by the two defendants. The plaintiff was induced to grant the release as a result of non-disclosure of material information and because of the fraudulent misrepresentations already alluded to.

In dealing with the submission of the defendants that the final release was effective to bar the claim of the plaintiff because the release was not obtained by an fraud or misrepresentation on the part of the defendants, I need only point out that the release and sale were inextricably bound. If the defendants had divulged to the plaintiff that International Geosystems Corporation and Sony had shown great interest in the China Software System and if they had represented the true state of affairs as to the system's cost and completion time, the release would not have been executed, nor would the sale to Malaspina have been proceeded with.

There need not be misrepresentation with respect to the document itself. The releasor may be fully cognizant as to what he is signing but if the defendants, who are in a fiduciary position, have misrepresented the true state of affairs to which the release is directed, breaching their fiduciary duty and thereby inducing the plaintiff to execute the release, the release will be set aside: *Francis v. Dingman* (1983) 2. (4th) 244, 43 O.R. (2d) 641, 23 B.L.R. 234 (C.A.)

The release was obtained as a result of deliberate non-disclosure and fraudulent misrepresentations and, accordingly, is vitiated.

Considering the admissions or concessions made by counsel for the defendants, it hardly seems necessary for me to proceed to discuss the doctrine that company directors stand in a fiduciary relationship to the company they represent, in that they must:

(a) act honestly and in good faith and in the best interests of the company;
(b) disclose the nature and extent of any personal interest they have in a proposed contract, and
(c) disclose any and all conflicts.

These basic principles have been enshrined in ss. 142, 144 and 147 of the Company Act, R.S.B.C. 1979, c. 59.

It is of course a fundamental rule of equity that a person in a fiduciary capacity must not place himself in a position where his duty and personal interest conflict. The rule is clearly enunciated by Lord Herschell in *Bray v. Ford,* [1896] A.C. 44 (H.L.), at p. 51:

> It is an inflexible rule of a Court of Equity that a person in a fiduciary position, such as the respondent's, is not, unless otherwise expressly provided, entitled to make a profit; he is not allowed to put himself in a position where his interest and duty conflict. It does not appear to me that this rule is, as has been said, founded upon principles of morality. I regard it rather as based on the consideration that, human nature being what it is, there is danger, in such circumstances, of the person holding a fiduciary position being swayed by interest rather than by duty, and thus prejudicing those whom he was bound to protect. It has, therefore, been deemed expedient to lay down this positive rule.

The leading Canadian case on fiduciary obligations is *Canadian Aero Service Ltd. v. O'Malley* (12973), 11 C.P.R. (2d) 206, 40 D.L.R. (3d) 371, [1974] S.C.R. 592. At p. 219, Laskin J. (as he then was), in discussing the fiduciary duties of directors, said:

> An examination of the case law in this Court and in the Courts of other like jurisdiction on the fiduciary duties of directors and senior officers shows the pervasiveness of a strict ethic in this area of the law. In my opinion, this ethic disqualifies a director or senior officer from usurping for himself or diverting to another person or company with whom or with which he is associated a maturing business opportunity which his company is actively pursuing; he is also precluded from so acting even after his resignation where the resignation may fairly be said to have been prompted or influenced by a wish to acquire for himself the opportunity sought by the company, or where it was his position with the company rather than a fresh initiative that led him to the opportunity which he later acquired.

After quoting from the judgment of Viscount Sankey and Lord Russell of Killowen in *Regal (Hastings), Ltd. v. Gulliver,* [1942] 1 All E.R. 378 (H.L), at pp. 381 and 389, he went on to say, at p. 220: "The reaping of a profit by a person at a company's expense while a director thereof is, of course, an adequate ground upon which to hold the director accountable." Further, at p. 22 1 :

> What these decisions indicate is an updating of the equitable principle whose roots lie in the general standards that I have already mentioned, namely, loyalty, good faith and avoidance of a conflict of duty and self interest. Strict application against directors and senior management officials is simply recognition of the degree of control which their positions give them in corporate operations, a control which rises above day accountability to owning shareholders and which comes under some scrutiny only at annual general or at special meetings. It is a necessary supplement, in the public interest, of statutory regulation and accountability which themselves are, at one and the same time, an acknowledgment of the importance of the corporation in the life of the community and of the need to compel obedience by it and by its promoters, directors and managers to norms of exemplary behaviour.

The conduct of the two defendants falls far short of the conduct that one would expect of a director and employee and, in effect, was a stratagem concocted and developed in order to appropriate unto themselves a business opportunity which in fairness belonged to the plaintiff.

As a result of this breach there must be a disgorgement of profits. ...

Judgment accordingly.

Leung who organized the sale of Vander Zalm's Fantasy Gardens, was a director of Highpoint International. Other directors were her husband Dean, Jimmy and Edna Leong and Chien and Chung Lin. The Leongs and the Lins and the company itself sued the Leungs, among other things, for breach of their duties as directors. The plaintiffs allege that the defendants misappropriated $180,000 from the company and that $61,000 of that money went to another company controlled by the Leungs.[2]

3. Rights of the Shareholders / Relief from Oppression

Question

Do the statutes that provide for business corporations afford any protection to the shareholders?

Canadian Opera Co. v. Euro-American Motor Cars

(1990) 75 D.L.R. (4th) 765
Ontario Court (General Division)
November 19, 1990

O'Driscoll, J.: The appellant, John Van Essen, appeals under s. 254 of the *Business Corporations Act*, 1982, R.S.O. 1982, c.4. The numbered company has abandoned its appeal.

The numbered corporation, pursuant to an order of Madam Justice Bell, dated May 3, 1989, was found to be a "motor vehicle dealer" under s. 1(f) of the *Motor Vehicle Dealers Act*, R.S.O. 1980, c. 299, and the appellant, John Van Essen, by the same order, was found to be a "salesman" under s. l(h) of the same Act. An appeal was launched from that order, but the material indicates that it was abandoned.

On the material before us, it is undisputed that the respondent paid to the appellants $131,760 and, in return, the Canadian Opera Company was to receive a 1988 red Ferrari. It is also undisputed that the appellants received the money and have not delivered the motor vehicle, nor have they returned the money, save and except $10,000.

It is undisputed that the appellants agreed to repay the money, as set out in the letter of March 10, 1989 (Appeal Book, p. 35). The letter, addressed to the numbered company's trading name, Euro-American Motor Cars, is from counsel for the Canadian Opera Company. It starts out this way: "This letter records our agreement on the terms for your repayment of monies to the Canadian Opera Company: ..."

It sets out the dates, the amounts and the time. Paragraph two states:

> Mr. John Van Essen and 670800 Ontario Inc. both will execute the enclosed Consent to Judgment, and you will deliver the signed Consent to me with your payment on Tuesday, March 14. I will have the Judgment issued immediately but will not file it with the Sheriff so long as the above-listed payments are made in full and on time. If you wish, the Canadian Opera Company will provide a release and satisfaction piece upon final payment being made.

Since the corporation is deemed to be a "motor vehicle dealer" under s. l(f) of the Act because it held itself out as carrying on the business of buying and selling motor vehicles, it is caught by the Motor Vehicle Dealers Regulations, R.R.O. 1980, Reg. 665, as amended by O. Reg. 54/86, s. 5(1), (2).

> 20(1) Where a motor vehicle dealer receives funds in excess of $10,000 towards the purchase of a motor vehicle prior to the delivery of the motor vehicle, the entire amount received shall be deemed to be trust funds.
>
> (4) Where trust funds are paid under subsection (1) whether by way of deposit, down payment or otherwise, on account of an undelivered motor vehicle, the motor vehicle dealer shall retain such funds in trust for the purchaser until,
>
> (a) the motor vehicle is delivered;
>
> (b) the contract is mutually cancelled; or
>
> (c) direction or authority is received from the Registrar concerning disbursements.

On the record before us, it appears that, literally and figuratively, the trust funds have "gone south" to Mr. Van Essen's cohort, Lyle Lathe, in Wilmington, North Carolina. Wherever they went, the appellant has not returned the trust money to the respondent.

Mr. Justice Hollingworth [69 O.R. (2d) 532 (and supplementary reasons at p. 536), 16 A.C.W.S. (3d) 372' held that the funds in question are trust funds within the meaning of the regulations quoted above. He held that the respondent was a "complainant" within the provision of s. 244(b)(iii) of the *Business Corporations Act*, 1982:

> 244. In this Part, ...
>
> (b) "complainant" means,
>
> (iii) any other person who, in the discretion of the court, is a proper person to make an application under this Part.

It was also held that the respondent was a "creditor" in the expanded view of that term: see *G.T. Campbell & Associates Ltd. v. Hugh Carson Co.* (1979), 99 D.L.R. (3d) 529, 24 O.R. (2d) 753, 7 B.L.R. 85 (C.A.), and *First Edmonton Place Ltd. v. 315888 Alberta Ltd.* (1988), 40 B.L.R. 28 at pp. 63-4 and 75-7, 60 Alta. L.R. (2d) 122, 10 A.C.W.S. (3d) 268 (Q.B.)

It is our view that the acts of the corporation were oppressive, were unfairly prejudicial or unfairly disregarded the interest of the respondent creditor (not the appellant corporation).

Section 247 of the Act:

> 247(1) A complainant, the Director and, in the case of an offering corporation, the Commission may apply to the court for an order under this section.
>
> (2) Where, upon an application under subsection (1), the court is satisfied that in respect of a corporation of any of its affiliates,
>
> (a) any act or omission of the corporation or any of its affiliates effects or threatens to effect a result; . ...
>
> (c) the powers of the directors of the corporation or any of its affiliates are, have been or are threatened to be exercised in a manner, that is oppressive or unfairly prejudicial to or that unfairly disregards the interest of any security holder, creditor, director or officer of the corporation, the court may make an order to rectify the matters complained of.
>
> (3) In connection with an application under this section, the court may make any interim or final order it thinks fit including, without limiting the generality of the foregoing, ...
>
> (h) an order varying or setting aside a transaction or contract to which a corporation is a party and compensating the corporation or any other party to the transaction or contract; . ...
>
> (j) an order compensating an aggrieved person;

It was also found by Mr. Justice Hollingworth that this was an appropriate case to pierce the corporate veil because Mr. Van Essen was the president, the sole director and the sole shareholder of the numbered company.

Much argument was directed to us that there should be a trial of an issue to sort out disputed questions of fact. In our view, on this record, there are no material questions of fact in dispute that require a trial and/or the trial of an issue.

In summation, for these reasons, we agree with the result reached by Mr. Justice Hollingworth. [To return the money]. The appeal is, therefore, dismissed.

[Submissions on costs heard.]

I have endorsed the back of the Appeal Book as follows:

For the oral reasons given for the Court by O'Driscoll J., the appeal is dismissed. The costs of this appeal are to be paid by the appellant, Van Essen, to the respondent, on a solicitor-client basis and are set at $5,000 and payable out of the money paid into court as security for costs.

Appeal dismissed.

As a shareholder of Harold E. Ballard Ltd., W. Ballard, son of Harold E. Ballard whose company, by 1972, owned approximately a 70% interest in Maple Leaf Gardens Ltd., sought a remedy under the relief from oppression sections of the *Ontario Business Corporations Act* on the grounds that Harold E. Ballard Ltd. had been conducted by Harold and two directors appointed by him in a manner that was oppressive or unfairly prejudicial or which unfairly disregarded his interests and the interests of his company. He alleged that the company was conducted as if its assets were the property of Harold E. Ballard personally. His applications were granted by Judge Farley in his 172-page decision.

820099 Ontario Inc. v. Harold E. Ballard Ltd.
Summarized from The Lawyers Weekly
March 29, 1991 p. 24

ENDNOTES

1. A more detailed account is given in *Newsweek,* September 14, 1992
2. A more detailed account is given in the *Vancouver Sun,* November 21, 1990, p. B6

IX

NEGOTIABLE INSTRUMENTS

Question

When can the drawer of the cheque say to the holder of the cheque "I don't want to pay you" and succeed in law?

The Bank of Nova Scotia v. The Rock Corporation of Canada Inc.

ONTARIO COURT OF JUSTICE (GENERAL DIVISION)
COURT FILE NO. C5713/91
SEPTEMBER 28, 1992

Hawkins, J.: The defendant The Rock Corporation of Canada Inc. drew a cheque on The Royal Bank of Canada for $5,800.00 payable to the order of Bruno Tessoni. Tessoni took the cheque to his bank (the plaintiff Bank of Nova Scotia) and cashed it without endorsing it in any way. By the time the cheque made its way to the drawee bank, payment had been stopped by the drawer as the cheque was dishonoured.

The plaintiff claims to be a holder in due course of the cheque pursuant to the provisions of s. 165(3) of the Bills of Exchange Act R.S.C. B-4 which provides as follows:

> S. 165(3) Where a cheque is delivered to a bank for deposit to the credit of a person and the bank credits him with the amount of the cheque, the bank acquires all the rights and powers of a holder in due course of the cheque.

As anyone who has ever had a bank account knows, the cashing (as opposed the depositing) of a cheque by the payee results in absolutely no entry whatever to the payee's account. If the cheque is honoured by the drawee bank the payee's bank account is untouched by the transaction. If the cheque is dishonoured the payee's account will be debited with the amount of the cheque and only then will the payee's account bear any trace of the transaction.

Since the cheque in question was *not* endorsed by the payee, the plaintiff, having given value for the cheque by cashing it, acquired such title as the payee had in the cheque. See s. 60(1) of the Act . ... Such title is, of course, subject to the equities between the drawer and the payee.

In order to escape the equities between the drawer and the payee, the plaintiff bank must establish itself as a holder in due course which it can do only if it can fit itself within the provisions of s. 165(3)

On the undisputed facts of this case, the transactions between the payee and his bank have absolutely no resemblance whatever to the requirements of s. 165(3). Tessoni did *not* deliver the cheque to his bank for deposit to the credit of himself or any person. He deliver it to be cashed. The bank did *not* credit him with the amount of the cheque. It paid him in cash.

The purpose of s. 165(3) is discussed in *Bank of Nova Scotia v. Archo Industries Ltd.* (1970) 11 D.L.R. (3d) 593 at 594 (Sask. Q.B.) in which the following passage from *Falconbridge on Banking and Bills of Exchange* 7th ed. (1969) p. 860 is quoted:

> Section 165(3), enacted in 1966, makes it clear that a bank becomes a holder in due course of a cheque received for deposit to a customer's credit and so credited. This subsection was added after an Alberta decision that a cheque endorsed "deposit only to the account of A" and signed "A" was a restrictive endorsement and the bank in which it was deposited was not a holder in due course, *Imperial Bank of Canada v. Hayes and Earl Ltd.* (1962) 35 D.L.R. (2d) 136, 38 W.W.R. 169 (Alta. S.C.). See also 73 Candn. Banker II 34 (1966).

I have absolutely no idea why the protection afforded by s. 165(3) was not extended to the case (as here) of a bank cashing a cheque. Presumably Tessoni could have first deposited the cheque to the credit of his account and then withdrawn the whole sum without the bank losing the protection of s. 165(3), but that is not what happened.

Among the ten cases dealing with s. 165(3) referred to me by Counsel, only one deals with the cashing of a cheque as opposed to its deposit. That one case ...is undistinguishable on its facts but of no assistance because the parties *agreed* that the cashing bank was a holder in due course.

Counsel advised me that the sole issue is whether or not the plaintiff is a holder in due course and that the answer to that question will be determinative of the party's rights. I find that the plaintiff is not a holder in due course. The plaintiff's motion for judgment is dismissed. The defendant's motion for dismissal is granted. The action is dismissed with costs including the costs of these motions.

[*Motion dismissed*]

A British mail order firm received a cheque for 100£ with an order for toys. Although the cheque was not completely filled out, the firm sent the order. The cheque had been forged—by the owner's seven-year-old son.[1]

ENDNOTE

1. Summarized from *The Globe and Mail*, October 28, 1992, p. A28

X

INTELLECTUAL PROPERTY

A. COPYRIGHT

Question

Who owns copyright?

Cselko Associates Inc. and Ernie Cselko v. Zellers Inc. and Display Industries of Canada (Eastern) Ltd.

ONTARIO COURT OF JUSTICE
COURT FILE NO. 33515/88Q
JULY 10, 1992

Hawkins, J: — This is a motion by the defendant Zellers to dismiss the plaintiffs' action. The plaintiff Cselko is a commercial illustrator who carries on his business through the vehicle of the corporate plaintiff of which he is sole proprietor.

Zellers is a retail merchant and the defendant Display Industries of Canada (Eastern) Limited (Display Ltd.) is a commercial art broker.

Zellers developed an advertising and merchandising gimmick which they named "Zeddy Bear." They had some commercial illustrations done of Zeddy with which they were not entirely satisfied. They retained Display Ltd. to find them an illustrator to do some drawings of Zeddy in various activity poses. Display Ltd. engaged Cselko on behalf of Zellers, to do drawings. Zellers had no direct contact with Cselko. Zellers' end of the transaction was handled entirely through Display Ltd. and in particular by the late Mr. James Renwick, Sr.

It was made known to Cselko that the illustration he was commissioned to do were going to be used by Zellers for advertising purposes. No limitation on the use to which Zellers could put the illustrations was ever discussed. The plaintiff billed Display Ltd. by means of invoices which contained no limitations or copyright warnings. He was paid approximately $16,000.00 for his work.

Zellers used the illustrations in connection with usual advertising, packaging and promotional material (e.g. a colouring book) and has even reproduced some of the drawings to be sold in frames.

The plaintiff, after he discovered the extent to which his drawings were being put, registered his copyright in them. He now sues for substantial damages for breach of copyright and injunctive relief.

There is only one issue in this law suit—what limitations on use, if any, are to be implied in the circumstances of this case.

There was, as I have already noted, no limitation discussed. The plaintiff asserts that "advertising" and "packaging" are different and that art sold for use in advertising does not encompass packaging. It is clear from his cross-examination that he did not make this view known to Mr. Renwick.

In his affidavit the plaintiff alleges as follows in paragraph 2(b):

> I negotiate fees for my artwork based on the complexity of the artwork, the extent of the use required by the client and the duration of the use. Payment may be negotiated in the form of a royalty arrangement or straight fees or both. The use of artwork on packaging for products requires a special contractual relationship and special remuneration to the artist, as packaging normally has a long shelf life of many years.

The plaintiff admitted on his cross-examination that in twenty-three years as an artist he has never received royalties on his work.

The plaintiff, in response to this motion has filed an affidavit of David Yaxley who is Art Director of Sears Canada. Mr. Yaxley's affidavit is laudatory, and no doubt rightly so, of the plaintiff's skill and reputation. The thrust of Mr. Yaxley's affidavit is that Sears' practice is to negotiate specific separate fees for each of the various uses to which the artist's work is to be put. He states, in paragraph 4 of his affidavit, that such is "the custom in the advertising industry as far as I am aware." It is clear from his cross-examination that he has no experience whatever in situations where commercial artwork is purchased with no express restrictions placed on its use.

Chris Yaneff has sworn an affidavit filed in support of this motion. It is his evidence that it is the custom of the trade that a commercial artist assigns all rights in the work to his customer and that the custom is so widely known that a written assignment is rarely executed. In other words, it is up to the artist to specifically limit the uses if there are to be limits. Mr. Yaneff's evidence was not shaken on cross-examination.

Danielle Jones a commercial illustrator since 1980, swore an affidavit filed on behalf of the defendant. She testifies that it is standard practice in the industry that all rights are assigned to the client unless the artist expressly limits other use. She was not cross-examined.

Carol Green Long has sworn an affidavit filed by the defendant in support of this motion. She has been involved in marketing commercial artwork since 1983. It is her view that the client is entitled to use the purchased artwork without restriction. She was not cross-examined.

The plaintiff, in his affidavit in opposition to the motion says, in paragraph 8 "the custom of the trade of commercial advertising is to negotiate with the artist the rights for advertising purposes separately from any other rights such as the right to use the work on products ... *I intend to present many expert witnesses at the trial of this action attesting to the aforesaid custom.*" (emphasis mine)

As Bolan J. said in *Vaughan v. Warner Communication Inc.* (1986) 56 O.R. (2d) 242 at p. 247

> ... Rule 20 should not be eviscerated by the practice of deferring actions for trial *at the mere suggestion that future evidence may be made available.* (emphasis mine)

I am satisfied that the plaintiffs' claims do not survive a good hard look on the material presented on this motion.

The Copyright Act Problem

Section 13(4) of the *Copyright Act* R.S.C. Ch. C-42 provides "the owner of the copyright in any work may assign the right ... and may grant any interest in the work by licence but no assignment or grant is valid unless it is in writing ...."

It has been held that a licence to use may be implied by the conduct of the parties and need not be in writing. *Howard Drabble Ltd. v. Hycolith Manufacturing Company* (1928), 44 T.L.R. 264 (Ch.Div.). See also Fox *Copyright* (2nd edition) 298 ff.

Judgment may issue dismissing the plaintiff's claim against both defendants. Since only the defendant Zellers moved Zellers will have its costs of this motion and of the action. There will be no costs to the defendant Display Industries Inc.

[*Plaintiff's claim dismissed*]

Around Christmas one movie seems to dominate the TV selections —*It's a Wonderful Life* with Donna Reed and Jimmy Stewart. The theme is appropriate to the season, but the more important factor affecting its availability is the price — the stations are paying no royalties to the creators because the copyright lapsed.[1]

Question

What can be copyrighted?

Before the amendments to the *Copyright Act* R.S.C. which expressly provide copyright protection for computer software, Apple Computer Inc. et al. sued Mackintosh Computers Ltd. et al. for the manufacture and marketing of its computers, which used programs identical to copyrighted Apple programs. The defendants argued that copyright did not cover programs stored in the hardware in the form of a silicon chip.

In a seventy-five page decision Justice Reed of the Federal Court Trial Division found, without difficulty, that the defendants had copied the programs and ruled that there was a "translation" of Apple's source code when it was encoded onto silicon chips in hexadecimal language understood by the computer.

Summarized from The Lawyers Weekly *May 16, 1986 pp. 1,9*

The Federal Court of Appeal dismissed the appeal.

The Supreme Court of Canada considered the issue as to whether or not a computer program originating in written form which was protected by copyright, continued to have that protection when it was etched onto a silicon chip. It concluded that it was and dismissed the appeal. The unauthorized copying of that program was an infringement of copyright.

Summarized from The Lawyers Weekly
July 6, 1990
Apple Computer Inc. et al. v. Mackintosh Computers Ltd. et al.

Datastate Corp. (a Taiwanese company) was ordered by Taiwan's high court to pay $1 million (US) to compensate Microsoft Corp. for pirating its software and manuals. Datastate Corp. has declared bankruptcy.[2]

Referred to as the "look and feel" case, Lotus sued to stop the sale of a program, VP Planner, developed by a Vancouver company, Stephenson Software Inc., because the program looks and feels like the popular spreadsheet program, Lotus 1-2-3. Lotus sought an injunction to bar Paperback Software International of Berkeley, California from selling the program, compensatory damages of $14 million and punitive damages of $10 million. Lotus based its case not only on copyright infringement, but also on unfair trade practices.[3]

Judge Keeton of the U.S. District Court which first heard the case concluded that the menu command structure of 1-2-3 is an original and nonobvious way of expressing a command structure and is a creative expression deserving copyright protection. It had been settled that a creator could protect underlying source and object code but the court was being faced with questions of the protection of noncode characteristics of software.[4]

Lotus Development Corp. v. Paperback Software and International and Mosaic Software Inc.

Note: *This suit prompted the League for Programming Freedom to picket the Lotus headquarters urging Lotus to 'innovate not litigate.' The group's founder says such law suits stifle innovation, since new programs have borrowed ideas from previous innovations and that users want compatible software. A more detailed account is given in* Newsweek *August 27, 1990*

Apple Computer, in a case which "stunned" the computer industry, sued Microsoft Corp. and Hewlett-Packard Co. for $5.5 billion for illegally copying computer screen symbols used by the company's Macintosh computer. The defendants argued that the symbols were generic and thus not suitable for copyright protection and that the symbols were derived form those used earlier by other companies including Xerox Corp. In April of 1992 a U.S. District Judge ruled that most of the symbols used by Apple were not protected by copyright.[5]

On April 24, a few days after Walker's ruling, Apple asked the judge to reconsider his decision; the motion was granted.[6]

On August 7, 1992 Walker reaffirmed his ruling that most of the symbols are not protected by copyright or that they were allowed by a 1985 agreement between Apple and Microsoft.

Piracy Cases in the Entertainment Field Include:

Won: by Art Buchwald, 63; a suit brought against Paramount Pictures for having lifted his story idea for Eddie Murphy's 1988 blockbuster *Coming to America*, in Los Angeles, Jan. 8. The court awarded the columnist 19 percent of the firm's net profits, but the studio contends that although the movie has already grossed $300 million, it has yet to show a profit.[7]

Awarded: to humorist Art Buchwald, $150,000 in damages by a California court, for his contribution to *Coming to America*; March 16. He and a producer had sought about $6 million from Paramount Pictures.[8]

Tim Anderson sued Sylvester Stallone, MGM-UA Studio and three of its executives for pirating his submitted plot for the script for the film *Rocky IV*. The plaintiff asked for $5 million in general damages and $100 million in punitive damages.[9]

Huey Lewis sued Ray Parker Jr. for the song "Ghostbusters"; the Chiffons (composers of He's So Fine") sued George Harrison for "My Sweet Lord". Harrison lost the case even though the infringement was found to be done unconsciously.[10]

Lee Garrett and Lloyd Chiate sued Stevie Wonder for "I Just Called To Say I Love You".[11]

A U.S. court stopped the sale of rapper Biz Markie's album "I Need a Haircut" because of Markie's unauthorized "sampling" of music from a Gilbert O'Sullivan's song "Alone Again (Naturally)". Sampling, using pieces of old songs to create new music, had not been tested in the court; hereafter, the record companies may insist that every sample used be authorized.[12]

A U.S. Superior Court Judge in Los Angeles ruled that Ms. Cynthia Plaster Caster was entitled to the return of her plaster mouldings of the genitalia of famous male rock stars.[13]

Internal Copying

In 1984 Lotus Development Corporation, without warning, sued Rixon, a company that manufactures modems and other computer products, for $10 million for software piracy. Lotus alleged that Rixon had violated the licensing agreement and copyright laws by making thirteen copies of Lotus 1-2-3 for use in their branch offices. The action was seen as a test case because it was not an action against a company who had made copies to sell for a profit, but against a company who merely made copies for internal use.[14]

This matter was settled out of court for an undisclosed amount of cash plus Rixon's agreement to a permanent injunction. As is the custom in out of court settlements, Rixon did not admit to any wrongdoing.[15]

Infringement of Moral Rights

Question

What rights remain with a creator, even if he has assigned or sold his copyright?

Three days after the death of Peter Sellers, who had starred in films as the blundering Inspector Clouseau, the owners of the copyright of his films approached his wife with their plan to make a movie from the clips of his previous films. She did not want pieces of film to be used "in a film meant to be a tribute to Peter. Peter would have hated it, and we can't let a film like that come out."

The artist, Walt Spitzmiller, was commissioned by L.L.Bean, Inc. to illustrate the cover of its mail-order catalogue with a hunting scene. He painted a rough hunter with his Labrador retriever. The released cover showed a clean-shaven hunter with a "preppified pooch."

Spitzmiller sued the company, *inter alia*, with copyright infringement and breach of contract. He asked for the destruction of the altered copies and damages equal to the total fall catalogue earnings. Spitzmiller's lawyer is quoted as saying "It's a good thing the dog can't sue."[16]

Bryan Adams took court action against David Duke, a right-wing political figure in the U.S., for using "Everything I Do I Do for You" in his political campaigns.

B. Breach of Confidence / Trade Secret

Question

What does the plaintiff have to prove in order to win an action against a defendant on the grounds that the defendant breached a confidence?

Summary of the facts: International Corona Resources Ltd. was drilling exploratory holes on land on which it owned mining rights when it was approached by LAC Minerals Ltd. Discussions followed with a view to a possible partnership or joint venture. Corona revealed the results of its drilling and its interest in purchasing mineral rights of an adjacent property, the Williams property, which looked promising. At one meeting Corona discussed its efforts to secure the property. Three days later, LAC's vice-president for exploration spoke to Mrs. Williams and soon submitted a bid which led to LAC's acquisition of the property to Corona's exclusion. LAC developed a gold mine on the property.

Per La Forest of the Supreme Court of Canada on the issue of breach of confidence [p. 20]: *Breach of confidence*

I can deal quite briefly with the breach of confidence issue. I have already indicated that LAC breached a duty of confidence owed to Corona. The test for whether there has been a breach of confidence is not seriously disputed by the parties. It consists in establishing three elements: that the information conveyed was confidential, that it was communicated in confidence, and that it was misused by the party to whom it was communicated. In *Coco v. A.N. Clark (Engineers) Ltd.*, [1989] R.P.C. 41 (CH.), Megarry J. (as he then was) put it as follows (p. 47):

> In my judgment, three elements are normally required if, apart from contract, a case of breach of confidence is to succeed. First, the information itself, in the words of Lord Greene, M.R. in the *Saltman* case on page 215, must "have the necessary quality of confidence about it." Secondly, that information must have been imparted in circumstances importing an obligation of confidence. Thirdly, there must be an unauthorized use of that information to the detriment of the party communicating it.

This is the test applied by both the trial judge and the Court of Appeal. Neither party contends that it is the wrong test. LAC, however, forcefully argued that the courts below erred in their application of the test. LAC submitted that "the real issue is whether Corona proved that LAC received confidential information from it and [whether] it should have known such information was confidential."

Sopinka J. has set out the findings of the trial judge on these issues, and I do not propose to repeat them. They are all supported by the evidence and adopted by the Court of Appeal. I would not interfere with them. Essentially, the trial judge found that the three elements set forth above were met: (1) Corona had communicated information that was private and had not been published. (2) While there was no mention of confidence with respect to the site visit, there was a mutual understanding between the parties that they were working towards a joint venture and that valuable information was communicated to LAC under circumstances giving rise to an obligation of confidence. (3) LAC made use of the information in obtaining the Williams property and was not authorized by Corona to bid on that property. I agree with my colleague that the information provided by Corona was the springboard that led to the acquisition of the Williams property. I also agree that the trial judge correctly applied the reasonable man test. The trial judge's conclusion that it was obvious to Sheehan, LAC's vice-president for exploration, that the information was being communicated in circumstances giving rise to an obligation of confidence, following as it did directly on a finding of credibility against Sheehan, is unassailable.

In general, then, there is no difference between my colleague and me that LAC committed a breach of confidence in the present case. ...

LAC Minerals Ltd. v. International Corona Resources Ltd.
61 D.L.R. (4th) 14
S.C.C.
August 11, 1989

For another discussion of breach of confidence, see *Ontex Resources Ltd. v. Metalore Resources Ltd.* p. 80

Pierre Marion, former head of the French spy agency, admitted that the French spied on their allies' industries for years. He maintained the spying was essential to keep France abreast of technological advances. Among other projects, the agency schemed to infiltrate IBM and Texas Instruments to recruit employees as agents to pass on trade secrets useful to French companies.[17]

A number of U.S. legislators and business people are pushing to enlist the CIA (Central Intelligence Agency) to aid U.S. corporations. The spy agency would not only search out foreign agents stealing or trying to steal U.S. trade secrets, but would assign undercover agents in firms to see if they are improperly using trade secrets or patents of U.S. firms. Those countries involved in industrial espionage are not only former cold-war adversaries—Russia (formerly through "Department X" of the KGB) and China—but also allies including France, Germany, South Korea, Israel, Japan and "even Canada".[18]

C. Passing Off

Questions

Why is the tort of passing-off significant in protecting a person's intellectual property?

What is its relationship to the law of trade marks?

Institute National des Appellations d'Origine des Vins & Eaux-de-Vie v. Andres Wines Ltd.

40 D.L.R.(4TH) 239
ONTARIO SUPREME COURT
JULY 2, 1987

Dupont J.:

Introduction

The plaintiffs seek injunctive relief restraining the defendants from using the appellation "Champagne" in the manufacture and sale of their products; they also seek damages for loss of sales, diminution of their market, and depreciation of goodwill allegedly resulting from the defendants' use of the appellation "Champagne." ...[T]hey base their claim for injunctive relief upon the common law action of passing off.

The plaintiff, L'Institut National des Appellations d'Origine des Vins et Eaux-de-Vie (I.N.A.O.), is a national organization established by French law; its primary duty is to regulate the areas and conditions of production and sale of wines and spirits bearing controlled appellations of origin. Its co-plaintiffs are companies incorporated under the laws of the Republic of France and carry on business as producers of wine in geographically designated areas located in that part of France described as the Champagne District.

The defendants are companies duly incorporated in Canada who for many years have been producing, advertising and selling sparkling and still wines under various names, some of which incorporate the word "champagne"; in particular, "Canadian Champagne."

The plaintiffs claim the right to sue together on their own behalf as producers of wine in the Champagne District who are engaged in the sale of champagne in Ontario. The common interest they assert is in the goodwill associated with the word "champagne"; they argue that their goodwill has been detrimentally affected by the defendants' alleged improper use of the term.

The defendants strongly take issue with such joint or collective action, submitting that this procedure is without precedent in Canadian jurisprudence and should be rejected.

They also challenge I.N.A.O.'s status as a plaintiff. Although it is not a wine producer, the I.N.A.O. is vested with legal personality and is entitled to be a party to legal proceedings. In fact, one of its functions is to institute legal proceedings for the purpose of protecting the rights of French producers of wines and spirits and of preventing the misuse of appellations of origin nationally and internationally. ...

Canadian case-law

The Ontario Court of Appeal had occasion to deal with the law of passing off, in *Orkin Exterminating Co. Inc. v. Pestco Co. of Canada Ltd. et al.* (1985), 5 C.P.R. (3d) 433, 50 O.R. (2s) 726, 19 D.L.R. (4th) 90. ... [in which it] did consider the general nature of the tort of passing off and clearly stated that, in its view, misrepresentation leading to confusion was a requisite element of the action. Quoting from *Spalding v. Gamage*, Morden J.A. wrote (p. 442 C.P.R., P. 735 O.R., p. 99 D.L.R.: "A fundamental principle upon which the tort of passing off is based is that 'nobody has any right to represent his goods...as the goods... of somebody else'." Later on, he explained (p. 450 C.P.R., p. 744 O.R., p. 108 D.L.R.): "In this kind of case I think that the main consideration should be the likelihood of confusion with consequential injury to the plaintiff."

The Supreme Court of Canada has also approved of the principle that misrepresentation is the underlying basis for an action in passing off. In *Consumers Distributing Co. Ltd. v. Seiko Time Canada Ltd.* (1984), 1 C.P.R. (3d) 1, 10 D.L.R. (4th) 161, 3 C.I.P.R. 223, the respondent, the authorized dealer of Seiko watches for Canada, sued the appellant for passing off on the ground that the appellant, who purchased genuine Seiko watches from an authorized dealer, sold the watches without warranty, point of sale service or instruction booklet. The respondent argued that without these additional features, the watches could not be sold as "Seiko" watches. It had been established by evidence that once the appellant posted a notice declaring that it was not an authorized dealer, that the watches were not purchased from the appellant and were not internationally guaranteed, no instance of public confusion had ever occurred.

The absence of confusion was considered critical by the Supreme Court because of its conception of the basis of the tort (pp. 15-6 C.P.R., p. 175 D.L.R.):

> ...the passing-off rule is founded upon the tort of deceit, and while the original requirement of an intent to deceive died out in the mid-1800's there remains the requirement, at the very least, that confusion in the minds of the public be a likely consequence by reason of the sale...by the defendant of a product not that of the plaintiff's making, under the guise or implication that it was the plaintiff's product or the equivalent.

In its judgment the Supreme Court of Canada quoted and approved of the following passage which defines the nature of passing off (pp. 13-4 C.P.R., p. 173 D.L.R.):

> It consists of the making of some false representation to the public...likely to induce them to believe that the goods...of another are those of the plaintiff...The test laid down in such cases has been whether... the defendant's conduct results in a false representation, which is likely to cause confusion or deception, even though he has no such intention. (Prosser, *The Law of Torts*, 4th ed.)

This test is found, in various formulations, throughout reported cases. There seems no doubt that for both the House of Lords in England and the Supreme Court in Canada, a necessary, constitutive element of the tort of passing of, the very thing which causes damage to the plaintiff's goodwill, is the defendant's misrepresentation of its product which is likely to cause confusion in the public's mind between the defendant's goods and those of the plaintiff. Although the misrepresentation may take a variety of different forms, as indeed it does in each particular case, it must nevertheless exist and be established through admissible evidence by the plaintiff in order for the plaintiff to succeed in an action for passing off. In a sense "passing off" is a synonym for "misrepresentation" or "false description."

Conclusion

A detailed consideration of the evidence brought before the court has led me to conclude that Canadian champagne is a distinct Canadian product not likely to be confused or even compared with French champagne. This conclusion is based on the following evidence: the many years during which the defendant wine producers marketed Canadian champagne in Ontario; the manner in which the defendants' products are labelled, with the word "Canadian" displayed as prominently as the word "champagne," in compliance with government directives, so as to clearly identify the products as Canadian; the way the Canadian product has, for many years, been physically separated from French champagnes in L.C.B.O. stores and listed separately by them as well as by restaurants on their wine lists; the vast body of evidence confirming that Canadian champagne has attained a reputation of its own in Ontario.

The evidence further establishes that the Ontario public concerned with or interested in wines, as purchasers or otherwise, have not been misled and do not confuse the French and the Canadian products. The purchaser who is completely ignorant about wine and wishes to purchase a bottle of champagne for a special occasion will very likely realize the difference between the two products either by the clear labelling of both, or the difference in listing and physical location at the L.C.B.O. stores, or, finally, by the vast price differential between the products.

The evidence indicates quite clearly that the high regard and reputation of French champagne has not been affected by Ontario sales of Canadian champagne and remains well established in this province. This is supported by evidence illustrating the constantly growing sales of French champagne notwithstanding its dramatic price increases, while the price of Canadian champagne, by comparison, has remained basically stable.

I cannot agree with the plaintiffs' submission that the defendants have and continue to engage in conduct designed or likely to deceive the public; they do not misrepresent their Canadian product as one originating from the Champagne District of France or produced by any French champagne houses, nor one which is in any way connected or associated with French champagne. The marketing, advertising, labelling and general reputation of Canadian champagne, and the evidence as a whole in this regard, has satisfied the court that deception and confusion are not likely to occur in Ontario.

The evidence in support of the parties' submissions, as well as the exhibits illustrating and clarifying them, has been copious. While I have not dealt with each in this judgment, I have considered them all in order to draw justifiable inferences of fact to permit the court to arrive at a decision.

This court has concluded, for the reasons detailed throughout this judgment, that the plaintiffs have not established the defendants' misrepresentation and have therefore failed to prove all the elements which constitute the tort of passing off.

The Plaintiff's claim is dismissed

Note: The appeal from this decision was dismissed by the Ontario Court of Appeal on January 18, 1990. The reasons for judgment began: "Mr. Justice Dupont delivered very full and careful reasons for judgment. ...He dealt with all of the issues arising at trial and anticipated all of those arising in this appeal. We are in complete agreement with his conclusions." 30 C.P.R. (3d) 279

Walt Disney Productions successfully enjoined the West Edmonton Mall from using the name "Fantasyland" for its indoor amusement park.[19]

Walt Disney Productions v. Triple Five Corp.

D. Trade Mark

Questions

What constitutes infringement of one's trade mark?

What must the court consider before it grants an injunction prohibiting the use of a trade mark?

697234 Ontario Inc. carrying on business as The Loose Moose Tap & Grill v. The Spruce Goose Brewing Co.

(1991) C.P.R. (3d) 449
Federal Court, Trial Division
November 7, 1991

Jerome A.C.J.—This application for an interlocutory injunction came on for hearing at Toronto, Ontario, on October 7, 1991. The plaintiff owns the trade mark THE LOOSE MOOSE TAP & GRILL and seeks to restrain the defendant, pending trial, from commencing operations of a restaurant also in Toronto under the name The Spruce Goose. At the conclusion of argument, for reasons given orally from the bench, I dismissed the application and indicated that these brief written reasons would follow.

The plaintiff has operated continuously since March of 1989, a restaurant in downtown Toronto known as The Loose Moose. I accepted submissions that through the expenditure of effort and money it has had a successful operation and has established substantial goodwill. In late August of this year, the plaintiff became aware that the defendant intended to operate a restaurant called The Spruce Goose Brewing Co. Ltd.

at 130 Eglinton Avenue East. It is the plaintiff's concern that the public will inevitably refer to the defendant's restaurant simply as the Spruce Goose and through an advertising campaign in the publication *Now Magazine*, it will propose to offer the same service and atmosphere to the same clientele, causing confusion with the plaintiff's registered trade mark and resulting damage.

My reasons for the dismissal of the application are that I find all relevant issues, the facts, the law and the discretionary considerations involved in injunctive relief to be uncertain at best.

Facts

The plaintiff argues that the defendant's use of the words "spruce goose" is the focal point of this dispute and that I should find them to be so similar to the trade mark or trade name Loose Moose as to enjoin them. It is the plaintiff's contention that any connection between the defendant's intended trade name and the well-known aircraft built by Howard Hughes is incidental, the purpose and in any event the effect being to create confusion with the plaintiff's trade name and trade mark.

The defendant's documentary evidence contains photographs of the signage on the restaurant's exterior and interior decor. The exterior sign has a depiction of the Howard Hughes aircraft. The theme is carried through to the interior decor which includes murals depicting Howard Hughes, the Spruce Goose aircraft and the head and neck of the Canadian goose. Clearly, therefore, the principal factual allegations are vigorously disputed.

The law

I have in mind my earlier decision in *Horn Abbot Ltd. v. Thurston Hayes Development Ltd.* (1985), 4 C.P.R. (3d) 376 (F.C.T.D.), and that of former Chief Justice Thurlow in *Mr. Submarine Ltd. v. Amandista Investments Ltd.* (1987), 19 C.P.R. (3d) 3, [1988] 3 F.C. 91, 16 C.I.P.R. 282 (C.A.). These are cases where the duplication of a substantial part of the trade mark led to interlocutory injunctions to restrain copying of high profile and highly successful trade marks. In the present case, the plaintiff asks me to do the same with respect to words that may sound the same, but are in fact different. Not only are they different, but they have a distinctive connotation in the connection with Howard Hughes and the famous aircraft. As a matter of law, therefore, the plaintiff's right to the relief sought is far from clear.

Discretion

The plaintiff's business has enjoyed success for over two years. The defendant's business at the time of this hearing was yet to open. If I am wrong in my conclusion and confusion is established at trial, it seems unlikely that in the interim the defendant's restaurant would inflict severe damage on the plaintiff. I also expect that what harm will occur will be capable of calculations and monetary compensation. The defendant, on the other hand, has completed all negotiations with advertisers, staff and landlord to open soon. If I were to wrongly enjoin them from opening, I would consider the injury to them to be more severe and more difficult to redress with monetary compensation. The difference is not great, but what difference there is favours the defendant.

For these reasons, on October 7, 1991, I declined the application and directed counsel to prepare the appropriate order which I signed and filed on October 17, 1991.

Application dismissed.

Franklyn Novak, a commercial artist and anti-nuclear activist in Omaha, Nebraska designed a shirt which read "When the world's in ashes, we'll have you covered. Mutuant of Omaha." The insurer, Mutual of Omaha whose logo was parodied sued for trademark infringement. The lawyer representing Novak argued it was a freedom of speech case as the shirts gave a political statement, viz. there is no insurance against a nuclear holocaust.[20]

Procter & Gamble sued James and Linda Newton who wrote and distributed pamphlets claiming that the company's 100- year-old trademark depicting the moon and stars was a satanic symbol. The pamphlets claim the company's customers are supporting the Church of Satan. The defendants are distributors of Amway, a commercial competitor.[21]

(The action was framed in tort, for injurious falsehood.)

George Lucas asked the court for damages and an order barring the Coalition for the Strategic Defence Initiative from using the term "Star Wars" in its TV commercial supporting the Reagan Administration's proposed defence system. Lucas objected to the unauthorized use in a political advertisement of the registered trademark "Star Wars" associated with his movie trilogy and with a multitude of toys and products.[22]

In 1981 the Beatles' company Apple Corps Limited gave the California Computer company, Apple Computer Inc. the right to use the Apple name and logo similar to its own as long as it did not sell machines "intended for synthesizing music." By 1989 Apple computers were used to compose and play music. Apple Corps Limited asked the court to order them to call the musical computers something else or pay a substantial licensing fee.[23]

Miss Universe Inc. had its appeal dismissed by the Federal Court Trial Division. The company appealed the decision of the Registrar of trade-marks who allowed the registration of the trade mark "Miss Nude Universe." Among his reasons for dismissing the appeal, Judge Strayer said "while the two trade-marks have two words in common, my first impression when looking at the two is that the word "Nude" in the middle of the Applicant's trade-mark is of an arresting significance which would convey to all but the most indifferent reader a profound difference between the two contests. Therefore the Applicant's trade-mark is distinctive."

Miss Universe, Inc. [Opponent/Appellant] v. Dale Bohna [Applicant/ Respondent]
Court No. T-976-91
Federal Court of Canada, Trial Division
July 3, 1992

Hogg Wyld Ltd. and Oink, Inc. of New Mexico, manufacturers of jeans to fit large women, were unsuccessfully sued by Jordache Enterprises for using a mark that included the name "Lardashe."[24]

Mattel Inc. the manufacturers of Barbie and Ken dolls successfully sued Michael and Saundra Cherwenka for trademark infringement. The Cherwenkas performed as nude dancers under the names of Malibu Barbie and Malibu Ken. In a consent decree the couple agreed to quit using references to the Ken and Barbie dolls and Ms. Cherwenda also agreed to stop wearing the type of chiffon dresses associated with the Barbie doll.[25]

E. Patent

In 1985 Polaroid won its case (begun in 1976) against Eastman Kodak Co. for infringing on its patent on instant photography. In 1990 the court assessed the damages at $909.4 million.[26]

Mr. Moore suffered from leukemia which resulted in an enlarged spleen. The spleen was removed and without his knowledge his doctor at the University of California Los Angeles Medical Centre used some of the tissue to create a laboratory cell line which he patented. The cells could be used to make drugs capable of controlling the count of white blood cells, which would be useful for the treatment of leukemia and AIDS. Mr. Moore sued for battery, fraud, unjust enrichment and conversion.

The California Supreme Court held that he should have been informed of the doctor's research interests but he did not have a property right in the cell line. The Court of Appeal, in a 2-1 decision, held that Moore did have a property right to his spleen. The issue as to whether or not human tissue is considered tangible personal property was appealed to the U.S. Supreme Court.[27]

F. Industrial Design

Mirabai Art Glass of Ontario asked the court for an interlocutory injunction against Paradise Designs of Vancouver to stop it from selling designer toilet plungers, a popular Christmas present. The request was refused.

G. Remedies

Anton Piller Order

Lawyers representing the Software Publishers Association (SPA), Lotus Development Corp., Microsoft, Activision, Ashton-Tate, Broderbund, Infocom and Lifetree, obtained a court order which allowed them to seize evidence from the offices of a Vancouver firm, Software Information Services, a software rental agency. The plaintiffs claimed that the firm, which rented popular software to potential purchasers, was renting illegal copies of copyrighted software. The executive director of SPA reported that during the raid materials were thrown from an office window to a person below waiting on a motorcycle; all were recovered. The Copyright Infringement Fund of the SPA paid the legal bill.[28]

Lotus, Microsoft and WordPerfect, members of The Canadian Alliance Against Software Theft (CAAST), launched an Anton Piller raid against Vancouver Island Business College Inc. to seize unlicensed software.[29]

Injunction/ Contempt of Court

In its Statement of Claim, Apple Computer alleged that the defendants were importing, assembling and selling computers that contained programs for which Apple owned the copyright. It also alleged that the defendants used a computer case and symbols that would confuse the public. Apple was awarded an interlocutory injunction. The defendants continued to import and assemble the Apple clones. Apple then returned to court for a contempt of court ruling.

The court found the defendants were in contempt of court, and fined Minitronics of Canada, O.S. Micro Systems and Comtex Micro System $1000, $10,000 and $20,000 respectively. The court further fined Lam of Minitronics $1,000, Lam, Lieu and Wu of Micro Systems and Comtex, $5,000 each and ruled that they would be sent to jail unless they paid the fines, apologized to the court, conducted themselves properly for a year and posted a $100,000 performance bond. Lam of Minitronics had to pay Apple's legal costs up to the morning on which he entered a guilty plea; the other defendants had to pay costs of $60,000.[30]

Endnotes

1. Summarized from *The Globe and Mail,* July 1, 1993, p. A9
2. Summarized from *The Globe and Mail,* June 21, 1993, p. B2
3. Summarized from *The Province,* January 16, 1987
4. Summarized from *BYTE,* September 1990, p. 19
5. A more detailed account is given in the *Vancouver Sun,* April 16, 1992, p. D11
6. A more detailed account is given in the *Vancouver Sun,* August 8, 1992, p. B11
7. From *Newsweek,* January 22, 1990. © 1990, Newsweek, Inc. All rights reserved. Reprinted by permission.
8. From *Newsweek,* March 30, 1992. © 1992, Newsweek, Inc. All rights reserved. Reprinted by permission.
9. Summarized from *The Globe and Mail,* November 5, 1986
10. *The Lawyers Weekly,* July 28, 1989
11. Summarized from *The Globe and Mail,* November 5, 1986
12. A more detailed account is given in *Newsweek,* January 6, 1992, p. 55
13. Summarized from *The Globe and Mail,* April 28, 1993, p. A7
14. A more detailed account is given in *Infoworld,* March 5, 1984, p. 6
15. A more detailed account is given in *Datamation,* May 1, 1984
16. A more detailed account is given in *Newsweek,* March 16, 1987, p. 53
17. A more detailed account is given in *Newsweek,* September 23, 1991, p. 40
18. A more detailed account is given in *Time,* February 1993, p. 46
19. *The Lawyers Weekly,* July 24, 1992, p. 3
20. *Ontario Lawyers Weekly,* March 8, 1985

21. Summarized from *The Lawyers Weekly*
22. A more detailed account is given in the *Vancouver Sun,* November 13, 1985
23. A more detailed account is given in *Newsweek,* March 6, 1989
24. *The Lawyers Weekly,* Jeffrey Miller, December 16, 1988
25. *The Lawyers Weekly,* July 13, 1990
26. Summarized from *The Globe and Mail,* October 13, 1990, p. B5
27. Summarized from *The Globe and Mail,* November 10, 1992
28. A more detailed account is given in *Datamation*
29. A more detailed account is given in the *Vancouver Sun,* December 10, 1993, p. E1, 2
30. A more detailed account is given in the *Vancouver Sun,* March 19, 1988, p. 1, D12

XI

LAW OF REAL ESTATE

A. Legal Interests in Land

Question

When a person buys property, what is included, what is one getting?

The Minister of Finance of Manitoba , pursuant to the Manitoba *Retail Sales Tax*, submitted a tax bill of $1,375,387 to Air Canada in respect of aircraft, aircraft engines and parts consumed and services, meals and liquor consumed in and over the Province of Manitoba. One of the arguments by Air Canada in its appeal from the assessment of the Minister of Finance was that the Province of Manitoba did not have the power to tax aircraft in the airspace over the Province. Justice Morse considering this issue wrote:

> The respondent in the present case relied on the hoary maxim: *Cujus est solum ejus est usque ad coelum and ad inferos* ("Whoever owns the soil owns all that lies above it to the sky and to the centre of the earth"). However, in my view, there has never been in England or Canada any interpretation of this maxim requiring me to hold that the owner of the land does, in fact, own or have the right to possession of the airspace above his land to the sky. I adopt the following statement made by Mr. Richardson in the article to which I have referred (at p. 134):
>
> > 1. It has not been necessary for an English court to give literal effect to the maxim *cujus est solum, ejus est usque ad coelum*, and no court has done so...
>
> In my view, the effect of the maxim goes no further than to protect the owner or occupier of land in his enjoyment of the land and to prevent anyone else from acquiring any title or exclusive right to the space above the land which would limit the landowner or occupier in making whatever proper use he can on his land. And in Fleming, *The Law of Torts*, 4th ed. (1971), the following is stated (at pp. 43-4):

> The extent of ownership and possession of superincumbent air-space has become a topic of considerable controversy since the advent of air navigation. Much play has been made of the maxim *cujus est solum ejus est usque ad coelum*, but the 'fanciful phrase' of dubious ancestry has never been accepted in its literal meaning of conferring unlimited rights into the infinity of space over land. The cases in which it has been invoked establish no wider proposition than that the air above the surface is subject to dominion in so far as the use of space is necessary for the proper enjoyment of the surface.

The appeal was allowed.

Re Air Canada and the Queen in Right of Manitoba
77 D.L.R. (3d) 68
Manitoba Queen's Bench
February 18, 1977

The further appeal by the Province of Manitoba to the Manitoba Court of Appeal was allowed in part, but on the issue of ownership of the airspace the Court of Appeal agreed with the Queen's Bench. About the maxim, argued even in the Court of Appeal, Justice Monnin said:

> The Latin phrase, much more picturesque than the English, speaks of 'up to heaven and down to hell'. ... The maxim cannot go further than direct the owner or occupier of land in his enjoyment of the land and also to prevent anyone else from acquiring any title or exclusive right to the space above such land so as to limit a person to whatever proper use he can make of his land. Further than that it cannot go. Academic writers and modern jurisprudence reject its literal application. So must I in this age of jet aircrafts, satellites, supersonic Concordes, orbital travel and visits to the moon. The sooner the maxim is laid to rest, the better it will be.

Re the Queen in Right of Manitoba and Air Canada
86 D.L.R. (3d) 631
Manitoba Court of Appeal
January 19 and February 16, 1978

B. Tenancy in Common and Joint Tenancy

Questions

If a person decides to co-own property with another, should he or she buy as joint tenants or as tenants in common?

What is the significance of the difference?

Caluori v. Caluori

ONTARIO COURT OF JUSTICE
COURT FILE NO. 59859/92
JULY 16, 1992

Rutherford, J.: The applicant, a dependant within the meaning of s. 57 of the *Succession Law Reform Act* R.S.O. 1990, Chapter S. 26, seeks relief by way of proper support from the estate of her late husband, pursuant to s. 58 of the Act.

It is clear from the evidence that this 72 year old widow is not destitute. Her monthly income from all sources will be between $1,200 and $1,700 a month depending on how this application is determined. The real issue concerns the house in which she and her husband lived since 1964. It was their matrimonial home for all those years and the house in which the applicant insisted on maintaining and caring for her late husband during his declining years. He was not well in his last 6 years and required close care and attention in his final year or two. The applicant expresses a strong, emotional attachment to the home saying she wants to die there, as did her husband.

The marriage was the second for each of them. It lasted almost 20 years and the Caluoris were close. They shared the burdens and benefits of life equally. Their financial contribution to their overall situation was roughly equal.

When the Caluoris purchased the house in question at 1284 Lambeth Walk in the City of Nepean, they took title to it as joint tenants, having discussed the mutual objective they had at that time of having the house left to the survivor of the two. Sometime later, without disclosing it to his wife, the late Mr. Caluori obviously changed his mind about that mutual objective and conveyed his interest in the home to himself in a deed to uses, thus creating a tenancy in common. Then, in a will created at about the same time, he left his entire estate to the children of his first marriage, making no provision for the applicant. The respondent as executor of the will, seeks an order by way of counter application to sell the house and divide the proceeds between the estate and the applicant. The house is worth about $130,000 and if sold, the applicant would receive approximately $60,000 for her own use. This would be her sole asset, apart from savings of about $15,000 and pension and old age security income of about $1,200 per month.

In assessing the applicant's claim that she has not been adequately provided for, I have evaluated the evidence against the criteria set out in s.62 of the *Succession Law Reform Act*. In particular, I have considered the 19 year, close, caring relationship between the applicant and her late husband; the length of time they lived in the house in question; the applicant's expectation which was reciprocal as far as she knew, that the house was jointly owned and she and her late husband each intended the survivor to have it; the relatively equal sharing and contributing the applicant and her late husband had and made to their financial circumstances; and of course, the contextual circumstances including the applicant's assets, means and other legal recourse for support together with the estate of the applicant's late husband and his testamentary wishes.

I am guided by the views expressed in such cases as *Re Davies v. Davies* (1980) 27 O.R. 98 and *Re Dentinger* [1981] 128 D.L.R. (3d) 613, holding that "proper support" as contemplated by s. 58 of the *Succession Law Reform Act* includes more than necessities of life and may extend to non-essentials and even luxuries. The difference between "adequate support" and "adequate proper support" involves consideration of the life-style of the parties. such that the support is fitting or appropriate to the circumstances.

In *Re Mannion* (1984) 45 O.R. (3d) 339, Dubin J.A. (now Chief Justice of Ontario) said at page 342 concerning s. 58:

> The new statute being remedial, it should be given a broad and liberal interpretation...

When I balance the evidence as applied to the criteria in s.62 and apply the s. 58 formula of "adequate provision for the proper support of the applicant," I am driven to the conclusion that her proper support must include being able to live in the house at 1284 Lambeth Walk for as long as she wishes. It is the matrimonial home, her home for the last 18 years and one, in a neighborhood, to which she attaches a strong emotional tie. The applicant shuns apartment life as "living in a tomb" and in my view, is entitled, by the legislation, to stay where she is.

I appreciate that the half-interest in the house is the only asset in the estate, apart from a few items of personal property of relatively small economic value, but the beneficiaries under the will are the next generation and all good things come to those who wait, especially each in their proper turn.

Accordingly, under the authority of subsection 58(1) of the *Succession Law Reform Act,* it is the order of the Court that the respondent as executor and trustee of the Will of Eugene Caluori hold the interest of the estate in the house at 1284 Lambeth Walk, more particularly described in the Deed of Land registered as instrument no. 671288 in the Registry Office for the Registry Division of Ottawa on May 30, 1975, in trust for the benefit of the applicant and for her use as long as she wishes to live in that house. Upon her death or upon her no longer residing in the house, the estate's interest therein shall be disposed of as directed in the will. While the applicant resides in the house, she will be responsible for maintaining it and will bear all the expenses necessary therefor.

Because there are no other liquid assets in the estate, I make no order as to costs in this application. The counter-application for sale of the estate's interest in the house is dismissed and no costs are awarded in relation to it either.

Dated at Ottawa, this 16th day of July, 1992.

C. Mortgages

Question

What is the relationship between the mortgagee and the mortgagor?

Bayshore Trust Company v. Assam

Ontario Court of Justice
No. 75510/90
April 9, 1992

MacDonald, J: At the opening of trial in this matter, I was advised by counsel for the parties that there was consent to judgment on the claims advanced by Bayshore Trust Company against the defendant Philip Assam. Accordingly, I have endorsed the record for judgment to go in the form provided to me on the consent of counsel. There remains to be determined the issues arising from the counterclaim advanced by the defendant, Mr. Assam.

The relevant background is the following:

Philip Assam is the owner of a residential property municipally known as 2117 Lawrence Avenue West. Mr. Assam obtained from Bayshore Trust Company, a first mortgage which was registered on title on April 7th, 1989 for a period of one year in the principal amount of $210,000. Monthly payments were $2,540.00. Interest was at the rate of 14% per annum. By agreement between the plaintiff and the defendant, this mortgage was renewed on April 25th, 1990 for one year with an interest rate of 14.5%. Default occurred in or about February, 1991 and continued at the time of proceedings before me.

In April, 1991, the defendant Bayshore advised Mr. Assam in writing that they would not consider further renewal of the mortgage due to poor prepayment history.

Mr. Assam has consented to judgment in the amount of $241,667.06. He has also agreed to deliver possession of the land and premises in question to the plaintiff.

The amended counterclaim is against Bayshore Trust Company and one Robert Christopher, jointly and severally. Robert Christopher was then the Chief Executive Officer of Bayshore Trust Company, although at the time of trial, he was no longer associated with the company. Mr. Assam's claim is for $50,000 in general damages together with special damages in an undefined amount. Mr. Assam alleges that the plaintiffs caused him to suffer economic loss by reason of granting him the mortgage. Mr. Assam states that the monthly obligations for service of the mortgage were so high as to make it impossible for him to meet these obligations. Mr. Assam was employed at the time of the application for mortgage in a position that had income of $28,000 a year on a gross basis. He indicated to Bayshore Trust Company that he would have additional income by reason of certain undefined tenancies which he proposed to have on the premises in question. His intentions were to rent out rooms in the premises, but there was never a precise estimate given of the rental income which he anticipated. The monthly mortgage obligation was in fact significantly more than Mr. Assam's monthly income on a net basis, and he alleges that Bayshore, with this information in hand, ought not to have granted him the mortgage in question. It was also known to Bayshore Trust that a second and third mortgage were being postponed by the placement of the first mortgage with Bayshore on the property in question. The second and third mortgages were privately held. Mr. Assam also suggested that he was induced into the transaction by Bayshore and its agents.

The transaction respecting the mortgage had disastrous results for Mr. Assam. Clearly it was not possible for him to meet his monthly obligations, and although he tried very hard to do so, he soon fell into default on a regular basis. Bayshore was prepared at certain times during the early stages of the default to accommodate Mr. Assam to some degree, and in fact, on one occasion entered into an arrangement with him whereby he could make the payments one month late.

Mr. Assam alleges that the activities of Bayshore induced him into a situation of financial disaster and it is on this basis that his counterclaim is based. Mr. Christopher gave evidence. He was very familiar with all aspects of the transaction as it related to Mr. Assam. Mr. Christopher struck me as a straightforward witness who tried to accommodate Mr. Assam as much as possible. Mr. Christopher advised me that Bayshore Trust is what is known as an "equity lender;" that is to say that Bayshore Trust assesses a prospective borrower on the basis of the equity of the property in question. Bayshore loans up to 70% of the value of the property, and in Mr. Assam's case, the loans extended to Mr. Assam by Bayshore never exceeded 70% of the value of the property in question. Mr. Christopher indicated to me that the application form does make enquiries about the level of one's income, but the only consideration in respect of the decision to extend funds is based on the equity in the property. I asked Mr. Mandel and Mr. Christopher for a copy of the application made by Mr. Assam. This document was not available to me.

The issue is whether or not Bayshore Trust, an equity lender, owes a fiduciary duty of care to the borrower, Mr. Assam? If Bayshore Trust is found to have a fiduciary duty of care, then the court would have to address the question of damages that may arise from any breach of this duty.

It is well settled that as a general rule, a mortgagee is not in a fiduciary relationship with the mortgagor. In the absence of evidence of special circumstances upon which to base a fiduciary duty, the relationship between the parties is purely one of a lender and a borrower or debtor and creditor.

The Supreme Court of Canada considered the test to be applied to determine whether a fiduciary relationship had arisen in *Lac Minerals Ltd. v. International Corona Resources Ltd.*, [1989] 2 S.C.R. 574. Mr. Justice Sopinka was of the opinion a fiduciary obligation is one that arises out of a fiduciary relationship. He concluded that there was no precise test, but that certain characteristics were so frequently found in relationships which had been found to be fiduciary, that they served as a guide. He quoted with approval the enumeration of those characteristics by Madam Justice Wilson in *Frame v. Smith*, [1978] 2 S.C.R. 99 at pp. 135 and 136. They are as follows:

1) The fiduciary has scope for the exercise of some discretion or power.

2) The fiduciary can unilaterally exercise that power or discretion so as to affect the beneficiary's legal or practical interests.

3) The beneficiary is peculiarly vulnerable to or at the mercy of the fiduciary holding the discretion or power.

Mr. Justice Sopinka pointed out that a fiduciary relationship could exist even though not all of the above characteristics were present. However, he stated that the third, that of dependency or vulnerability, was indispensable.

In *Northland Bank v. 230720 Alberta Ltd.* [1990] A.J. No. 838, the defendant debtors sought to establish a fiduciary relationship between themselves and the plaintiff creditor. The defendants argued that the plaintiff breached its fiduciary duties by making the loan to the defendants to invest in a project which it knew or ought to have known was a sound [sic] investment with knowledge that the defendants did not have the capacity or earning power to repay the loan. The Alberta Court of Queen's Bench held that it was a straightforward case of a lender-borrower with no "special circumstances" to create a fiduciary relationship of any kind. The court stated as follows:

> It is not a defense for a borrower to say that the lender knew or should have known that he did

not have the ability to repay the loan so the lender should not have made it.

The wisdom of a lender in giving a loan is not a defense to why the loan should not be repaid. Poor business decisions belong in a court of business, not a court of law.

Houlden J.A. in *Hayward v. Bank of Nova Scotia et al.* (1985), 51 O.R. (2d) 193 (C.A.) reviewed the law with respect to when a fiduciary relationship comes into existence in a relationship between a bank and its customer, and considered *Lloyds Bank Ltd. v. Bundy*, [1974] 3 All E.R. 757 and the more recent case of the House of Lord's of *National Westminster v. Morgan*, [1985] 1 All E.R. 821. *Litwin Construction (1973) Ltd. v. Pan, Nicholson and Nicholson* (1988), 29 B.C.L.R. (2d) 88 C.A.) discusses the "exceptional cases" where the law imposes a fiduciary obligation in a commercial relationship.

The facts in this case do not fit into this line of authorities. The three characteristics to establish a fiduciary relationship are not disclosed in the evidence before me. I do not find that Mr. Assam was vulnerable or dependent upon Bayshore Trust. He was an educated person who understood the extent of the obligation he was undertaking. He had legal counsel. The relationship between him and Bayshore was that of a lender and a borrower. There was a lot of contact between Mr. Assam and Bayshore Trust and its agents, particularly over his inability to make monthly payments, but I cannot find that Bayshore had any duty of a fiduciary nature to Mr. Assam. It is not appropriate to transform the relationship of a lender and a borrower into a fiduciary relationship. I cannot find that Bayshore exercised a dominating influence over Mr. Assam and there is nothing in the evidence that would bring me to the conclusion that Bayshore went beyond a normal business relationship so as to place itself in the position of a fiduciary. The counterclaim against both defendants is, therefore, dismissed.

In the judgment on the main action which I referred to earlier, costs were reserved both in the main action and the counterclaim. If arrangements cannot be made between the parties with respect to costs, I may be spoken to.

To complete a real estate transaction, a borrower, through a series of transactions, ended up obligated to pay a total of $2,113,660 plus monthly interest on a mortgage debt of $1,556,8300. The borrower defaulted on the loan. The lender began foreclosure proceedings. The borrower argued that the rate of interest was contrary to s. 347(2) of the *Criminal Code* which prohibits a rate of interest that exceeds 60%. The judge, in a chambers hearing, held for the borrower.

The B.C. Court of Appeal dismissed the appeal by the lender and concluded that in this case the effective rate of interest was 148.2 9%.

Kebet Holdings Ltd. v. 351173 B.C. Ltd
Summarized from The Lawyers Weekly
January 29, 1993 p. 27

XII

ENVIRONMENTAL LAW AND THE REGULATION OF BUSINESS

Question

If the court orders a person or company to stop polluting a water system or stop blocking the roads, what can be done if they don't obey the court order?

A. CONTEMPT OF COURT

Regina v. Jetco Manufacturing Ltd. et al.

C.E.L.R. (N.S.) 243
ONTARIO SUPREME COURT
MAY 21, 1986.

Montgomery J. (orally):—The Municipality of Metropolitan Toronto brought contempt proceedings against Jetco Manufacturing Limited ("Jetco"), and its president, Keith Alexander, for alleged contempt of an order of a Justice of the Peace pursuant to s. 326 of the *Municipal Act,* R.S.O. 1980, c. 302, dated April 30, 1985.

Jetco operates an electroplating plant in Weston, Ontario, and has operated it since August 8, 1974. Jetco has been convicted of 69 violations of the anti-water pollution by-laws of the Municipality of Metropolitan Toronto, specifically By-law 148-83 and its predecessor, By-law 2520, with respect to discharging waste water containing chemical substances in excess of permissible limits. Jetco has been fined $97,950.

On April 30, 1985, Justice of the Peace White made an order referring to Jetco convictions on January 18, 1985, for discharge of waste water containing excess amounts of nickel and chromium into sanitary sewers prohibiting Jetco pursuant to s. 326 of the

Municipal Act from continuation or repetition of the offences. Since that order, there have been five separate incidents of breaches of the by-law between May 27 and October 28, 1985, resulting in 14 separate convictions of Jetco and fines imposed of $28,000.

Tests conducted on March 11, 1986, indicate that Jetco waste water continued to violate By-law 148-83.

Jetco has failed to install pollution control abatement equipment which successfully ensures that plant operation will comply with the court order and By-law 148-83.

According to expert evidence, the conduct of Jetco discharging excess nickel, cadmium and cyanide into the water system has the tendency and effect to:

(i) interfere with, impair, upset or completely retard sewage treatment plants and processes;

(ii) enhance the toxicity of other chemicals in the system;

(iii) interfere with and poison biological systems in Lake Ontario;

(iv) cause contamination of surface and ground water in the area of landfill sites where sludge containing cyanide is applied;

(v) cause air pollution when sludge containing cyanide is incinerated;

(vi) corrode sewers requiring their costly replacement.

The issue raised by the respondents is whether the respondents had notice of the order of the Justice of the Peace.

Jetco saw fit to absent itself from Court when facing summonses. It was not, therefore, made immediately aware of the prohibition order of the Justice of the Peace, but that was because it saw fit to absent itself from the criminal trials. I am satisfied, however, beyond a reasonable doubt that Jetco and Alexander had knowledge of the prohibition order of April 30, 1985. The attitude of Alexander is exemplified in his cross-examination when he said: "I treated the fines as licencing fees for doing business."

The bald statement in his affidavit that he was not aware of the order is not credible in light of the evasive nature of his answers under cross-examination. …

The criminal standard of proof is applicable to these proceedings. I have considered the totality of the evidence before me and I have applied the strict criminal test. I have no difficulty on the evidence in finding that Alexander acted knowingly and in contravention of the order of the Court, as did Jetco. I find the conduct of Jetco and of Alexander to be a contempt of the order of the Justice of the Peace, and as such, they are both guilty of criminal contempt.

It was never suggested that the Court lacked the jurisdiction to impose a finding of contempt. That power is inherent in a superior Court. Mr. Justice O'Leary commented in *Can. Metal Co. v. CBC* (No. 2) (1974), 4 O.R. (2d) 585, 19 C.C.C. (2d) 218, 48 D.L.R. (3d) 641 (Ont. H.C.), affirmed (1975), 11 O.R. (2d) 167, 29 C.C.C. (2d) 325, 65 D.L.R. (3d) 231 (Ont. C.A.), on matters of contempt and stated in clear language [at 4 O.R. 613] that: "To allow Court orders to be disobeyed would be to tread the road toward anarchy."

That is clearly what has happened here. The remaining question for my determination is, therefore, the question of sentence. The sole consideration in determining sentence is one of deterrence. …

If Courts fail to enforce their orders and allow the continuation of the attitude displayed by Mr. Alexander of treating fines for pollution as a cost of doing business, there can be no deterrence to the evils of pollution. One hundred thousand dollars in fines have had no effect so far. I therefore assess a fine for contempt against Jetco in the sum of $200,000.

I now turn to the conduct of the president, the directing mind of the corporation, Mr. Alexander. I consider the conduct of anyone who permits excessive amounts of contaminants, including arsenic, to enter our water supply, to be grossly offensive. Such conduct must be deterred, specifically and generally. I therefore sentence Keith Alexander to 1 year in jail. On May 12, the respondent's solicitor wrote to the Municipality of Metropolitan Toronto and said:

> It is obvious that Jetco will not undertake a major works program while contemplating the simultaneous closure of the factory. As a result, any works project will be adjourned by the company until litigation has been adjudicated or otherwise disposed of.

That means that pollution will continue until the respondents decide to amend their operation. It flies in the face of any attempt to purge contempt. I therefore sentence Keith Alexander to a further 1 month in jail for every single day that he delays his decision to undertake a major works program to comply with the by-law and the order of this Court up to a maximum of a further 15 months. That, of course, would result in a penitentiary sentence.

The message is clear to these and all other polluters—clean up or close up. In the absence of the accused Alexander, I direct the sheriff of the County of York to apprehend Mr. Alexander on his return and take him into custody so that he may commence serving his sentence.

Costs to the applicants on a solicitor-and-client basis forthwith after assessment.

Application granted.

Court of Appeal
57 O.R. (2d) 776 at p. 780

...In my respectful view the trial judge erred in convicting the appellants. I think he erred in law in finding that the appellants or either of them had notice of the prohibition order on the basis of the affidavit evidence and hearsay evidence before him. ...

From the moment of the filing of the appellant Alexander's affidavit, the matter was no longer one in which, as the applicant alleged, none of the facts were in dispute. When there are controverted facts relating to matters essential to a decision as to whether a party is in contempt of court, those facts cannot be found by an assessment of the credibility of deponents who have not been seen or heard by the trier of fact, as was done in this case. The judge here quite simply was in no position to make the factual determination upon which his contempt order was predicated. On the disputed state of the evidence before him he could not properly conclude that the municipality had established beyond a reasonable doubt that the appellants were aware of the prohibition order of the justice of the peace. In the circumstances of this case, a trial of the issue raised by the application ought to have been ordered.

It follows that the order finding the appellants guilty of contempt of court cannot stand and their convictions and sentences must be set aside.

In the result, I would allow the appeal and set aside the order appealed from. The municipality should be at liberty to take such further or other proceedings in this matter as it may be advised. I would make no order as to costs.

Appeal allowed.

Background Facts:
When the government of British Columbia made a decision to allow some logging in Clayoquot Sound on Vancouver Island, protesters began a blockade. Those who ignored a court order against disrupting the logging were arrested in the "largest mass arrest in B.C. history" for contempt of court.[1]

By November 11, 1993 more than 800 protesters had been arrested.[2]

The following are excerpts from Justice Bouck's decision reprinted by the *Times-Colonist* of Victoria, B.C.

Before fixing the actual sentences, something must be said about the legal concept of contempt of court. ...[D]emocracy allows a society to govern itself by the rule of law and not by the rule of the individual...Some Canadians take democracy for granted. It is easy to forget that democracies have failed. It can happen to us unless we as a people co-exist by the rule of law. If we do not, Canada could collapse into a form of tyrannical rule. Our country will ultimately deteriorate if people feel they are entitled to abuse the rights of others when they are unable to convince the majority of the rightness of their cause. ...[T]he right to peacefully protest brings with it the responsibility of avoiding interfering with the rights of others. ...

Preserving the dignity of the court is only a minor part of contempt proceedings. The fundamental issue is much deeper. Underneath it all, contempt proceedings are taken primarily to preserve the rule of law. Without the rule of law democracy will collapse. Individuals will then decide which laws they will obey and which ones they won't. Government by the rule of law will disappear. People will then be controlled by the rule of the individual. The strongest mob will rule over the weak. Anarchy will prevail.

Most of you have indicated that you prefer to follow the law of God. No doubt encouraged by submissions of your counsel, who ought to have known better, some of you have invited me to apply the law of God. This court does not apply the law of God, irrespective of whose interpretation of that law is offered for consideration. This court applies the law as it is determined to be by the legislators of this country and by the decisions of this court, which have accumulated now for 700 years. …

The rule of law exists in this society only because the overwhelming majority of citizens, irrespective of their different views on religion, morality, or science, agree to be bound by the law. That agreement, which cannot be found recorded in a conventional sense, has survived the deepest and most profound conflicts of religion, morality and science. In that sense it might be thought that its strength is overwhelming and its future secure. But that is not the case at all, for the continued existence of that agreement is threatened by its own inherent fragility. That fragility was described by former Chief Justice Farris of this court in the celebrated case of *Canadian Transport Co. Ltd. v. Alsbury* (1952), 6 W.W.R. (N.S.) 473 (B.C.S.C.), to which counsel have referred, I quote from p. 478:

> Once our laws are flouted and orders of our courts treated with contempt the whole fabric of our freedom is destroyed. We can then only revert to conditions of the dark ages when the only law recognized was that of might. One law broken and the breach thereof ignored, is but an invitation to ignore further laws and this, if continued, can only result in the breakdown of the freedom under the law which we so greatly prize. …

[In response to the contention that the actions of the protesters followed the path of Ghandi, Martin Luther King and the suffragettes, Judge Bouck said:] But here, the elected representative of the people of this province made the law allowing MacMillan Bloedel Ltd. to log the timber in Clayoquot Sound. It was not decreed. … Except for the out-of-province defendants, the others have the right to vote. They were simply unable to persuade the elected representatives of the people to adopt their point of view. Unlike Mr. Gandhi, Mr. King and the suffragettes, they could attempt to change the law through their vote and the votes of others whom they could persuade. Unlike Mr. Gandhi, Mr. King and the suffragettes, they infringed a legal right: the right of MacMillan Bloedel Ltd. to cut timber in Clayoquot Sound. Their behavior in no way follows the noble ideals of Mr. Gandhi, Mr. King or the suffragette movement. …

I turn now to fix the sentence for each of the defendants found guilt of contempt of the court orders made 20 July 1992 and 16 July 1993. It is not a pleasant duty. I take no joy in the task. …

Despite repeated comments by various judges concerning the necessity of working within the democratic system, and despite relatively modest sentences, disobedience of court orders continues. Many people do not seem to get the message. …

The only way the law can deal with continuous breaches of court orders is to increase the penalty in the hope it will dissuade others from committing the same kinds of acts.

The sentences I am about to impose should reflect a degree of penalty for their unlawful behaviour. Mostly, it should serve as a deterrent to others who contemplate undermining the rule of law.

[The sentences imposed ranged from fines of $1,000 to $3,000 and jail terms from 45 to 60 days]

MacMillan Bloedel Limited v. Simpson
Times-Colonist
October 15, 1993 p. A5

B. Administrative Law

Prerogative Writs and Declarations

Sue Rodriguez is afflicted with Amyotrophic Lateral Sclerosis (known as Lou Gehrig's Disease) which causes a person to lose control of muscle functions. Death is ultimately caused by the inability to swallow and breathe because of the failure of the requisite muscles. The disease, however, does not affect the mind.

Unwilling to endure such a death, Ms. Rodriguez would like to end her life when it became unbearable, but is physically unable to do it without assistance. Because s. 241 of the *Criminal Code* makes it a crime to assist anyone in committing suicide, she has commenced a court action in which she asked for a declaration that s. 241 of the *Criminal Code* violates her rights under s. 7 of the *Charter* which reads:

> Everyone has the right to life, liberty and security of the person and the right not to be deprived thereof except in accordance with the principles of fundamental justice.

Her application was dismissed by the B.C. Supreme Court.

She appealed to the B.C. Court of Appeal. The three justices who heard the appeal agreed that s. 241 of the *Criminal Code* did violate her rights under s. 7 of the Charter; nevertheless, the appeal was dismissed. Justice Hollinrake held that the violation was not contrary to the principles of fundamental justice; Justice Proudfoot held that the declaration sought would establish a bad precedent in that it would exempt unnamed persons from future criminal liability. Justice McEachern, dissenting, interpreted s. 7 of the *Charter* as ensuring individual control and held that s. 241 of the *Criminal Code* denied her rights, and those rights were not deprived in accordance with the principles of fundamental justice. He would not have struck down s. 241, but instead would have allowed a doctor-assisted suicide, for Ms. Rodriguez only, if she would follow certain prescribed rules.

The Lawyers Weekly
March 26, 1993 p. 1, 22;
April 9, 1993 p. 16

Ms. Rodriguez appealed to the Supreme Court of Canada which heard argument on May 20, 1993 in a nationally televised session.

Summarized from The Globe and Mail
May 21, 1993, p. A1

The reserved judgment, released in October, held against her. By a 5-to-4 vote, the court rejected her argument that the ban on assisted suicide should be struck down. The majority felt, *inter alia,* that society had not reached a consensus on the issue of assisted suicides and that allowing assisted suicides could lead to abuse affecting the more vulnerable members of society.

Rodgriguez v. British Columbia (Attorney General)
Maclean's
October 11, 1993, p. 27

On February 12, 1994, Sue Rodriguez died. It was determined that it was an assisted suicide. The response has ranged from cries to prosecute, to the full extent of the law, the person who assisted her to calls for a bill to be presented to Parliament to legalize assisted suicide.

Government Regulations

A committee of the Toronto City Council rejected Wayne Gretzky's proposal to rename part of Peter Street Blue Jays Way and to renumber the address of his restaurant to 99, his uniform number. A vote of the full council is expected on November 22.[3]

The Toronto city council approved his request to rename the street Blue Jays Way.[4]

Endnotes

1. Summarized from *Maclean's,* August 23, 1993, p. 13 and October 25, 1993, p. 11
2. *The Globe and Mail,* November 11, 1993, p. A6
3. Summarized from *Maclean's,* November 15, 1993, p. 4
4. *Maclean's,* December 27, 1993, p. 11